Food lovers' GUIDE to PERTH

**Julie Mews
Lisa Hummel-Robson**

ABOUT THE AUTHORS

Julie Mews worked in British television production as a script supervisor and film continuity girl for 20 years before founding her own London-based catering and event organising company, Babette's Feast, in 1991. She is now living in the Chittering Valley with her retired journalist husband, Nelson Mews.

Lisa Hummel-Robson is a Leith's, London-trained cook with more than 10 years food experience in Europe and Australia. She was head cook at Babette's Feast in London before returning to Perth to work as a cook, specialist food advisor and cooking teacher at such establishments as Van's, The Grocer and Matters of Taste Cooking School. Lisa lives in Cottesloe with her husband Fraser and their three children, Hunter, India and Scarlett.

CONTENTS

Perth Locality Guide	6	Food Stores and Grocers	182
How to use this book	7	Food-to-go	232
Introduction	8	Gourmet Cafés and Breakfast	243
Asian Food	10	Greengrocers	267
Books for Cooks	26	Ice Cream and Gelati	283
Bread	29	Kitchenware	291
Butchers	45	Markets	306
Cake Decorating Supplies and Services	90	Organic and Health Food	318
Cakes and Patisserie	93	Tea and Coffee	330
Caterers	117	Wine Stores and Courses	343
Chocolates and Confectionery	128	Useful Information	345
Cooking Schools	132	Meat Standards Australia	346
Delicatessens and Cheese Shops	139	Seasonal Food Charts	347
Eclectic Shops	150	Acknowledgements	350
Fishmongers	154	Business Name Index	351
Florists	177	Locality Index	359

PERTH LOCALITY GUIDE

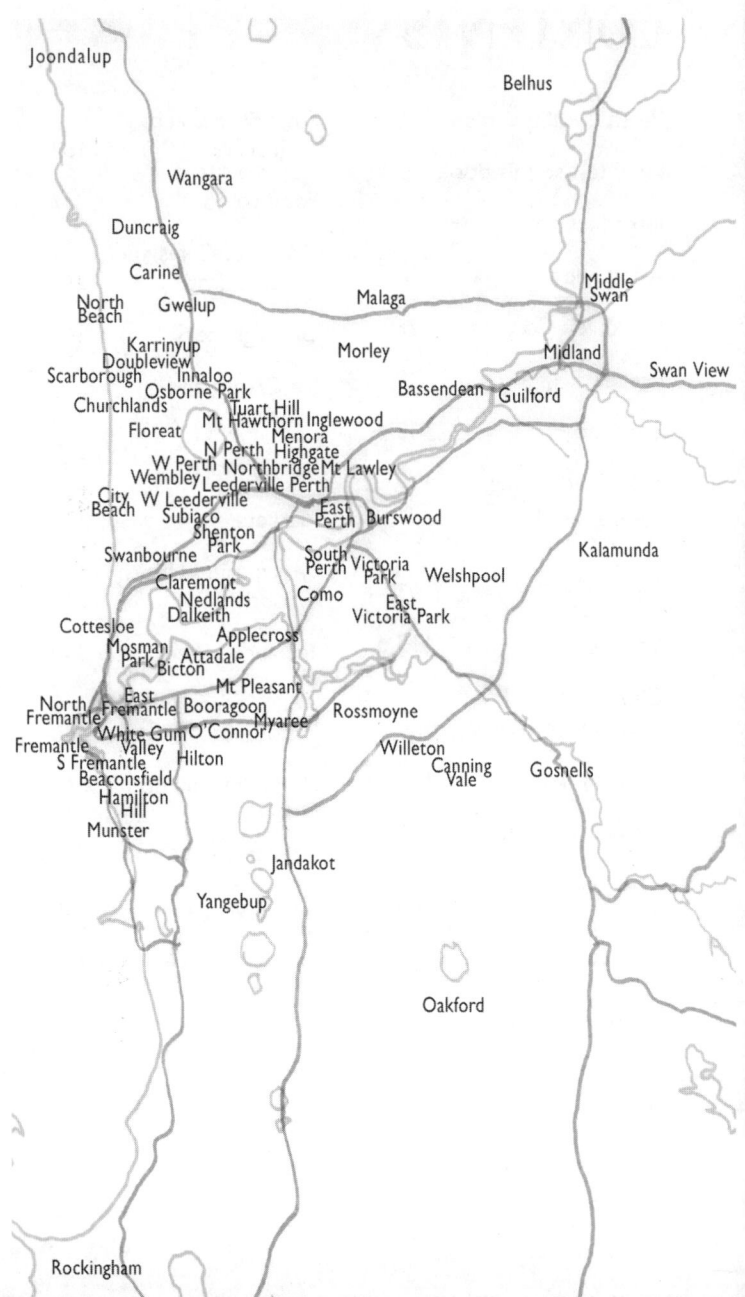

HOW TO USE THIS BOOK

The Food Lovers' Guide to Perth is organised in categories, listed in alphabetical order.

Within these categories, shops are listed by name, alphabetically.

At the top of each business entry is the full name, address, phone number, contact details, opening hours and parking details.

Most shops take EFTPOS and major credit cards like Visa and Master Card so we have only indicated if a business takes *CASH ONLY*.

At the end of the book there are two indexes.

The first is the Business Name Index: here businesses are listed alphabetically by name, followed by the category (chapter) where the entry appears and the page number. For example:

Carl Torre and Sons: *Butchers*, 50

The second index is the Locality Index. Every suburb that is mentioned in the book is listed, in alphabetical order. Under each suburb, the business name entries in that suburb are listed alphabetically, which category the business is in and the page number of the entry. For example:

APPLECROSS
　　Reid's Meats and Delicatessen: *Butchers*, 79
　　Sensations en Ardross: *Gourmet Cafés and Breakfast*, 261
　　Sugar Cube: *Cakes and Patisserie*, 113

The Locality Guide opposite shows the suburbs mentioned in the book and their proximity to one another. The Locality Index and this map are designed to be used together.

INTRODUCTION

Eating is one of life's great pleasures, and the better the food, the greater the pleasure. Good food is fun, it's delicious, and it makes us happy. What could be nicer than finding something new and inviting friends and family around to share a celebratory meal. So, if you're going to eat lemon tart, make it the tartiest tart with the sweetest, crispest pastry; if it's asparagus, make it the youngest, greenest and freshest; and a croissant? Make it the most buttery and flaky in town.

The essence of good food is good ingredients – the better the ingredients the less the cook has to do, allowing the food's characteristic flavours to speak for themselves. And the best way to do this is to buy seasonally and locally – which will be the freshest. In the case of fruit and vegetables, good food means fresh food whereas with meat, good husbandry, humane slaughter and skilful butchery are what produce quality. Fresh fish smells of the sea and has bright, black eyes and, if you buy frozen fish, make sure it's snap frozen at sea and buy it frozen, not thawed.

A bonus in buying seasonal is not just that it is usually cheaper, but it contains nutrients that suit the body's needs for that time of year – summer fruits are full of juice and help maintain body fluid levels and winter vegetables are full of carbohydrates, which the body burns to produce heat. Even though certain fresh produce is not available all year round, you can look forward to the changing seasons and all the produce a new season brings, such as strawberries and asparagus in spring, and hearty vegetables for warming winter soups.

In this busy, modern world most people find the convenience of the supermarket hard to resist. However, we think it is more interesting and satisfying to search out the specialist shops who source their produce personally, often from individual growers or farmers, who know the provenance of everything they sell and are happy to talk to you about what's best today.

So we decided to write *The Food Lovers' Guide to Perth* – the book that we wanted to have in our handbags. We began by sending out more than 200 questionnaires to food-loving friends and acquaintances, asking them to share their food secrets and shopping preferences. We had an overwhelming response and these recommendations formed the basis for our research.

Using these valuable personal recommendations and our own local knowledge, we tasted our way around Perth and talked to the owners of all the food shops we have included. We discovered a treasure-trove of fascinating and interesting people. Everyone we talked to was passionate and committed. They gave us much of their time and many valuable insights into their lives and businesses and we cannot thank them enough.

We have chosen what we consider to be the best food stores in Perth together with a selection of food-associated businesses. The purpose of this guide is to help you find these wonderful shops and to introduce you to some of the finest retailers that we have in WA.

ASIAN FOOD

The biggest concentration of Asian shops in Perth is in what is slowly but surely becoming Chinatown: William Street north of Northbridge and the streets running off it between James and Brisbane.

If you haven't shopped for food in this area before, you're in for a real treat. You'll find a whole new world of fascinating food, sights and smells, exotic and unfamiliar products. Once you get to know this world even a little, you will probably sort out your own favourites among the many supermarkets, tea shops, butchers, fish shops, grocery emporia and dim sum restaurants.

There are lots of places to choose from and sometimes it's difficult to work out which are really the best. What we've decided to do is recommend just one or two in each category, to give you a hint of the excitement to be found. It's by no means a comprehensive list of the best ones – more of a tasting, and a place to start.

We suggest, if you have the time, that you just go exploring: wander in and out of the various shops, getting a feel for each and seeing what they have on offer, rather than buying at the first one you come across.

And when you've finished your shopping, why not go for yum cha? A Cantonese term, 'yum cha' literally means 'drinking tea' and refers to the custom of gathering with family and friends, often at weekends and always during the daytime, to eat small servings of different food – dim sum – while sipping Chinese tea.

CHINATOWN, NORTHBRIDGE

ATLANTIC SEAFOODS
Shop 3, William Street Shopping Centre
375–379 William St
9328 2168

Monday–Saturday 9.00–5.00
Closed Sundays and public holidays

A very good range of live, fresh and frozen fish and seafood, including live blue swimmer crabs, cooked mudcrabs and live barramundi.

CAFÉ MOZART
Shop 1, 339 William St
9227 7066

Monday–Friday 9.00–5.30
Saturday 9.00–5.00, Sunday 10.00–4.00

If you need to rest and have a coffee and a cake, this is the place to come.

Catering for mixed tastes, they make and sell beautiful Western and Asian cakes, pastries, pies and Chinese buns – BBQ pork, red bean, spring onion and curry chicken. The proprietors are Sheng and Jenny Shen, both of whom came to Australia from Shanghai nearly 25 years ago. He's an engineer turned pastry chef; Jenny, who is very friendly and helpful, manages the shop.

CENTURION SEAFOOD
415 William St
9328 2813

Monday–Saturday 9.30–5.30
Sunday 10.00–2.30

This is the place for exotic, fine seafood: abalone (fresh, frozen, tinned or dried), shark fins, conch meat, pearl meat, scallops, fish maw, sea cucumber, snow frog jelly or bird's nest.

DAT THANH BUTCHER
Shop 2
364 William St
9227 6538

Monday–Friday 8.00–5.30
Saturday 8.00–2.30 Closed Sundays and public holidays
This place is always busy. Beef, lamb, chicken and lots of different cuts of fresh pork.

DRAGON SEAFOOD CHINESE RESTAURANT
108A James St
9227 8882

Dim sum: 7 days 10.30–3.00
BYO wine only

Come here for yum cha. There are many different varieties of dim sum available: steamed, pan-fried, deep-fried and rice flour rolls. Find a table as far inside the restaurant as you can – you're nearer the kitchen then – order your Chinese tea and just wait for the staff to bring a variety of piping hot, freshly cooked dim sum to your table. If you don't want one particular offering, don't worry, because the next will be coming along in a couple of minutes. The tea is important: it helps digestion and is a good counterbalance to the richness of some of the dim sum.

DRAGON TEA HOUSE
Shop 3, 369 William St
9228 3305

Monday-Wednesday 10.30-5.30 Closed Thursdays
Friday-Sunday 10.30-10.30

This very beautiful and elegant tea house in traditional style, specialising exclusively in tea from China, was opened in early 2007 by owner Sandy Ng. She stocks many different kinds of exotic teas, including flower teas, and some teawares and accessories for display or use. You can drink tea here or buy tea to take home. Tea tastings are available on an impromptu basis but if there is a crowd of you wanting to taste, phone ahead and speak to Jun Liew, the helpful manager, and let her know you are coming. And remember, it's only Chinese tea here.

EMMA'S SEAFOOD YONG TOFU
319 William St
9228 8899

365 days 9.00-7.00

Many of the products here are pre-prepared for you to use in steam pots or as entrees: fish balls, Thai fish cakes, prawn cakes and frozen fish. Owner Sally Ng also sells many different varieties of Asian snacks.

Also @:

EMMA'S SEAFOOD AND DIM SUM RESTAURANT
886 Albany Hwy
East Victoria Park WA 6101
9470 2238

Monday-Friday 11.00-2.30
Saturday-Sunday 10.30-3.00 for yum cha

GOOD FORTUNE ROAST DUCK HOUSE

344 William St
9228 3293

Wednesday-Monday 10.00-10.00
Closed Tuesdays

At the front of this restaurant, you can buy whole, cooked herbal chickens and pork (both BBQ and roast belly), but it's their whole, cooked roast duck which is the speciality here. They will chop them for you into whatever size portions you like, but we recommend that you take them home whole and serve them for the easiest ever Sunday lunch. There's a ginger sauce to go with chicken; BBQ sauce for the pork and plum sauce for the roast duck. You can make stock from the carcass, which is a good base for Tom Yum soup.

ICEY ICE

297 William St
9328 8058

Monday-Friday 12.00-11.00
Saturday-Sunday 11.00-11.00

This is a terrific discovery. Shaved, flavoured milk ice is what they sell. It's the Taiwanese version of gelato but as light as a feather and with the kind of melt-in-the-mouth quality of fairyfloss. There's the Original Milk Ice, Coffee, Mango, Strawberry, Yogurt, Peanut and Green Tea Ice. All come with standard toppings, or you can choose from their fourteen different Mix & Match extra toppings. Just the thing to finish off a yum cha brunch. Bright, light and modern and full of young people.

KONGS TRADING
425 William St
9328 2943

Monday-Saturday 9.00-6.00
Sunday 10.00-4.00

This was one of the first Asian shops in Perth and is still one of the biggest. They offer a huge range of groceries: Malaysian, Singaporean, Korean, Thai, Indonesian, Filipino, Chinese and some Japanese. Locally made fresh noodles – Hokkien, Shanghai and Japanese – arrive three times a week; fresh greengroceries arrive on Wednesdays and Thursdays. There's good quality kitchen equipment, and the imported china – both plain white and coloured – is some of the best we've seen.

Also @:

784a Albany Hwy
East Victoria Park WA 6101
9362 2817

Monday-Friday 8.30-5.30, Thursday 8.30-8.30
Saturday 8.30-5.00, Closed Sundays

LUCKY IMPORT AND EXPORT
112 Brisbane St
9328 9262

7 days 8.30-6.30

This huge emporium carries a very comprehensive range of Asian food, both fresh and dry. There are two whole aisles of different types of noodles, and freezer cabinets full of frozen dim sum, fish and squid. Also some fresh fruit and vegetables.

The owner is usually on the premises and is very friendly, and happy to answer your questions.

MELA INDIAN SWEETS & EATS
428 William St
9227 7367

Monday–5.30–10.00
Tuesday–Sunday 11.30–10.00

A large Indian café-style restaurant which has a counter selling a lovely range of Indian sweets to go. They are all freshly made on the premises.

NEW LIFE BAKERY
410b William St
9328 2002

Monday–Saturday 9.00–5.30
Sunday 10.00–4.00

A small family business, owned and run by a family of chefs: the Aus. They try to cater for all tastes here, so there are up to 40 different kinds of Chinese and Hong Kong buns sitting alongside French-style patisserie and cakes. Their Wife Cake, flaky pastry filled with sweet coconut, is a house speciality.

PRIME PRODUCTS
414 William St
9228 4221

Tuesday-Saturday 9.00-6.00 Closed Mondays
Sunday 10.00-6.00

This shop is the place to go if you want to cook Indian, Pakistani or Sri Lankan dishes. There's not much they don't have: huge wire racks of dried pulses, grains, flour, rice and spices of every kind. They also have an extensive range of large cooking pots. As this is primarily a wholesale shop, many of the items are available in bulk.

Also @:

493 Albany Hwy
Victoria Park WA 6100
9361 6686

Unit 1, 69-73 Hector St
Osborne Park WA 6017
9446 8002

Tuesday-Saturday 9.00-6.00
Sunday 10.00-6.00 Closed Mondays and public holidays

THE RED TEAPOT
413 William St
9228 1981

Monday-Saturday 11.30-3.00 for lunch, 5.30-10.00 for dinner
CASH only
BYO

Although this book is not a restaurant guide, if you need something to eat after a long day's shopping in Chinatown, this is the place to go. Always freshly cooked, their deep-fried squid tentacles with chilli and garlic are the most delicious appetiser. Fabulous food served in a completely unpretentious way. We love it here and think it's one of Perth's best-kept secrets. Dine in or takeaway.

THE ROASTING DUCK

Shop 8, William St Shopping Centre
9228 9883

7 days 9.30-9.30

Excellent cooked whole ducks and pork to go. We bought a piece of cooked pork belly with crackling and a piece of Char Siu (BBQ) lean pork and served them together with steamed rice. Not on the CSIRO diet … but yummy. They will chop and cut your purchases for you in whatever way you like.

TRAN'S EMPORIUM

358 Newcastle St
9228 3099

7 days 8.30-6.00
Closed major public holidays

There's a huge range of products at Tran's Emporium, a family-run business catering for both wholesale and retail customers. Restaurants buy oil and rice in bulk; locally made fresh noodles arrive twice a week; fresh fruit and green Asian vegetables arrive daily. They specialise in Asian grocery products but there are some Western products too (cereals, pasta, etc), so it's a good, all-round shop. Tran's Emporium has a large kitchenware range. The same family has the smaller grocery shop, Ton Sian, on the corner of Palmerston and Myrtle.

VHT PERTH
412 William St
9328 6255

Monday-Friday 9.00-6.30
Saturday 8.00-6.30 Sunday and public holidays 9.00-6.00
(364 days a year)

This is a big, modern, busy Asian supermarket, specialising in Chinese products and catering especially for the Chinese palate. There's a smallish selection of fresh vegetables but it's all local produce, coming directly from the growers. You'll find fresh noodles and tofu alongside a vast range of frozen food.

WALSON FOODS
Shop 1, 375 William St
9227 1883

Monday-Friday 8.00-6.00
Saturday-Sunday 8.00-5.00

The speciality here is tofu – homemade on the premises. Mr Lin and his staff make up to nine different types of tofu every day. There are lots of other Asian groceries on sale too, both wholesale and retail, frozen and dry, but it's the homemade tofu that is their unique selling point.

WANDERING WOK TOURS

Pauline Lynch
132 Rosewood Ave
Woodlands WA 6018
9204 1001
0417 091 343

www.wanderingwok.com.au

There's a terrific half-day walking tour of this area, created and led by Pauline Lynch, who runs Wandering Wok Tours. Pauline loves Asian food, culture and travel. In 2001, recognising a need to open up the Chinatown area of Northbridge to the non-Asian local population, she began her 2-hour walks of the area.

Her tours are an education in Asian products, where to shop, what to buy and how to cook. They are unique, informative and great fun. Tours take place on Saturday mornings or by special arrangement.

WING HONG BUTCHER

402-406 William St
9227 6379

Monday-Friday 8.30-5.00
Saturday 8.30-2.30 Closed Sundays

This is the biggest Asian butcher in Chinatown: the shop is the public showcase for a much larger wholesale business in Canning Vale which supplies most of Perth's hospitals, prisons, schools and a large proportion of Asian restaurants. There is a high turnover here, and Nathan Tate, son of owner Raymond Tse, says they pride themselves on the freshness of their product. They offer a huge range – pork, beef, chicken, ducks and some lamb – all WA produce and much of it cut specially for the Asian market. Their pork buyer, Cosimo Tassone, buys all the pork direct from the growers, some as far south as Albany.

ASIAN FOOD IN OTHER LOCALITIES

DAILY SUPERMARKET
527 Beaufort St
Highgate WA 6000
9328 9570

Monday-Saturday 8.00-7.00
Sunday 8.00-6.00 Closed public holidays, Chinese New Year

In the Highgate and Mt Lawley part of Beaufort Street, a new trendy shop or café seems to spring up every week, and for every new one, an old one closes. Amidst all this churning activity, it's reassuring to see that there are some constants, some old faithfuls. The Daily Supermarket, a busy, thriving business, owned and run by Ming and Kim Tran for over 12 years, is regarded as an institution by the locals and is much loved.

There are lots of fresh fruit and vegetables and the fridges are full of spanking fresh Asian greens, Chinese broccoli, bok choy, beansprouts and fresh herbs – fabulous mint, basil, coriander, curry leaf and coriander – plus soft and hard tofu, fresh noodles, Kala Jamin Indian sweets and kimchi pickles.

Every day, Ming's sister Yen makes the wonderfully fresh Vietnamese rice paper rolls for which they are famous, and there's always a Chinese bun or two in the warming cabinet to have as a snack.

The freezers are full of frozen fish, prawns, curry puffs, dim sum and samosas and a large selection of frozen vegetables.

It's hard to believe that such a small shop can carry such a large variety of dried grocery goods: there's a huge stock of Japanese products, Indian and oriental herbs, spices, sauces, and a vast range of Indian sweets.

Ming said to us: 'You have to stock *everything* – and we do.'

Don't miss coming here.

FREMANTLE MINI MART

Shop 5, Westgate Mall
Cantonment St
Fremantle WA 6160
9430 5839

CASH only
Ticket parking in Cantonment St

Run by the Lim family for the last 20 years, this wonderful shop sells the most amazing variety of groceries, dried fruit, noodles and mushrooms, many different kinds of tea and rice, sacks of coffee beans, tubs and sacks of wholefoods (including lentils, borlotti, kidney, black-eyed and lima beans), maize (kernels and ground), mealie meal (they have some African customers), rice flour, polenta, chickpeas and nuts as well as fresh Chinese and Asian greens and a selection of fresh fruit and vegetables. They stock products from China, India, Pakistan, Malaysia, Vietnam, Japan, Indonesia, Thailand and Spain.

Eileen Tay, one of the daughters, told us that their green vegetables and fresh fruit come from local farmers in Wanneroo. We saw green pawpaw for Thai pawpaw salad, bitter melon (good for high blood pressure or diabetics), wonderful-looking watercress and kang kong, a long, sharp-leaved green with hollow stems, which is good in stirfries. The beansprouts, delivered in small quantities three times a week, are the freshest we've found.

There's a whole section of exotic sweets, lots of different sauces, dried leaves (curry, banana, lime), every imaginable spice, and in the right-hand corner, a huge selection of cooking pots, rice steamers, bamboo steamers and rice bowls.

By the checkout counter there's a little cabinet containing hot steamed buns and glutinous rice wrapped in banana leaf.

Eileen told us: 'You have to learn how to cook to use all the stuff in our shop.' It's certainly the place to go for some unusual ingredients.

KONG'S ORIENTAL SUPERMART

Shop 9, Broadway Fair Shopping Centre
88 Broadway
Nedlands WA 6009
9386 1939

Monday–Saturday 9.00–6.00
Sunday 10.00–2.00
Parking in shopping centre car park

Kong's has a cave-like feel, and is jam-packed with Asian food of every imaginable kind. Whether it's Chinese, Japanese, Malaysian, Indonesian, Indian, you'll find most things here.

There's a small greengrocery section, with good quality local vegetables, many from Wanneroo, including small, narrow Asian eggplant, baby okra, bok choy, chillies and fresh ginger.

There are several cabinets of frozen fish, prawns, a good selection of frozen dim sum and dumplings, and fresh and frozen tofu.

Many different kinds of rice come in big, medium and little bags. There are also nuts, dried mushrooms and fruit, poppadoms, pancakes and spices from India and Pakistan, and Chinese sweets in tins and packets. There are lots of sauces, oils and vinegars for cooking, including soy, fish, chilli and mirin (rice wine).

The section of Asian cooking equipment includes Chinese bowls and chopsticks, cleavers and cooking pots, steamers and strainers, whisks and woks, rice cookers and ramekins, and teapots of every shape and size.

'When they miss home, they come here,' says John Kong of his customers, many of whom are students at nearby UWA.

Also @:

Unit 2, 21 Wanneroo Rd (cnr Robert St)
Joondana WA 6060
9242 4855

NIPPON FOOD SUPPLIES

Shop 26, Crossways Shopping Centre
180 Rokeby Rd
Subiaco WA 6008
9380 6783

Monday–Saturday 10.00–6.00
Sunday 11.00–5.00
Off-street parking

When he took over this Japanese food store in early 2007, Koji Maruura expected his customers to be predominantly Japanese, or Asian at least, but he has found more and more Australians experimenting with Japanese cooking and coming to his shop for supplies and advice.

Nearly all the food in the shop is imported from Japan. Some essential items, though, simply can't be imported because of quarantine requirements. The advice Koji and his staff give on how to adapt a Japanese recipe to Australian produce is important.

'We have to explain clearly so that Japanese food culture can grow here,' he says. Koji spent several years in the food industry in New Zealand before coming to Australia, so his English is good. The shop is not big, but it stocks a comprehensive range of products.

YEE SENG ORIENTAL SUPERMARKET

36 Hulme Court
Megaplex Business Centre
Myaree WA 6154
9330 9096

7 days 9.00–7.00
Closed Christmas Day, Boxing Day, New Year's Day,
Chinese New Year
Ample parking in front of store: Megaplex Centre is off the Leach Highway on the left-hand side travelling east, after the Suburu Showroom and before the Mobil garage.

Yee Seng Oriental Supermarket is a brilliant place to shop for all your Asian culinary needs. It's a large, well-kept and spacious area with a huge variety of lines. Every conceivable kind of rice, noodle, chilli sauce, curry paste, spice, cooking oil, soy and pickle can be found here.

The fresh produce is delivered every second day direct from the growers: we saw kang kong, spinach, kai choy, kai lan, jeruk, pak choy, big and small choy sum, chive shoots, long beans, garlic shoots and white radish, to name but a few.

The fridges and freezers are well stocked with hard, soft and Malay tofu, dim sum, dumplings, samosas, spring rolls, crab claws, prawn balls and steamed bananas.

There's a kitchen equipment corner selling bamboo steamers, crockery, woks and rice cookers.

The Wong family, who went into business together more than 50 years ago in Brunei, provide a service which is both friendly and knowledgeable, so there is no difficulty finding what you want in their massive range of goods.

BOOKS FOR COOKS

If, like us, an afternoon browsing through cookbooks is your idea of heaven, here are some bookshops you can visit – they will satisfy any cookbook addiction. Most of these are small, independent shops that offer a range of cookbooks, from the latest celebrity chef to more specific titles, including food styles, regions, ingredients and techniques, and will happily seek out unusual requests or hard-to-find titles. Some even have cafés attached, which always makes shopping that little bit more pleasurable.

AMANO COOKING SCHOOL AND KITCHENWARE SPECIALIST
12 Station St
Cottesloe WA 6011
9384 0378
www.amano.com.au

Monday-Friday 9.30-5.30 Saturday 9.30-4.00

BOFFINS BOOKSHOP
806 Hay St
Perth WA 6000
9321 5755
www.boffinsbookshop.com.au

Monday-Thursday 9.00-5.30 Friday 9.00-9.00
Saturday 9.00-5.00 Sunday 12.00-5.00

BOOKCAFFE
137 Claremont Cres
Swanbourne WA 6010
9385 0553

www.bookcaffe.com.au
7 days 8.30-6.00

CUT IT OUT
413 Murray St
Perth WA 6000
9321 9539
www.cutitout.com.au

Monday-Friday 9.00-5.30 Saturday 9.00-3.00

DYMOCKS
705-707 Hay St Mall
Perth WA 6000
9321 3969
www.dymocks.com.au

There are nine other independently owned stores in the metropolitan area: Booragoon, Cannington, Claremont, Fremantle, Joondalup, Karrinyup, Midland, Morley and Subiaco.

EPICURIOUS
Shop 8, Subiaco Village
531 Hay St
Subiaco WA 6008
9380 4799
www.epicurious.com.au

Monday-Saturday 9.00-5.00

MILLPOINT CAFFE BOOKSHOP
254 Mill Point Rd
South Perth WA 6151
9367 4567
www.millpointbookshop.com

7 days 8.30-5.30

NEW EDITION BOOKSHOP
82 High St
Fremantle WA 6160
9335 2383

7 days 9.00am-10.30pm

THE LANE BOOKSHOP
Old Theatre Lane
52c Bayview Tce
Claremont WA 6010
9384 4423
www.lanebook.com.au

Monday-Wednesday, Friday 9.00-5.30 Thursday 9.00-9.00
Saturday 9.00-5.00 Sunday 11.00-5.00

WINE LIAISONS
48 George St
East Fremantle WA 6158
6424 9400
www.wineliaisons.com.au

Monday 9.30-5.00 Tuesday-Thursday 9.30-7.00
Friday-Saturday 9.30-8.00 Closed Sundays

BREAD

Once upon a time about the only thing you could get in your neighbourhood that was more exciting than a sandwich loaf was a submarine-shaped poppyseed, and a horseshoe roll was the only thing more interesting than a vegemite sandwich. However, with the influence of European immigrants and their traditional baking skills and passion, our best bakers rediscovered the art of baking bread in the traditional, hands-on, labour-intensive, time-consuming way.

Researching this book we've seen what hard, hot work it is to bake a batch of perfect ciabatta in a stone-soled oven and we've eaten the delicious result – in fact, we could hardly stop. The bread to be found in the mostly small, specialist bakeries listed here is as good as any in Europe and sometimes better.

ABHI'S BREAD

270 South Tce
South Fremantle WA 6162
9430 4373

Tuesday–Friday 7.00–5.00
Saturday 7.00–3.00 Sunday 7.00–12 noon Closed Mondays
CASH only
Parking in South Terrace outside and opposite the shop

'A small crazy bakery specialising in organic and sourdough' is how Heinz Muller, proprietor and head baker, describes Abhi's.

They sell 30 or 40 different breads and about half as many pastries, but it is their organic and sourdough breads – and particularly the three or four different wheat-free sourdough breads, made daily – that set them apart.

Swiss-born and trained, Heinz makes biodynamic and organic loaves using organic flour from Millers Foods in Byford, and uses up to ten other different flours and fifteen different grains and seeds every day. A full range of yeasted, lighter white and wholemeal breads, sandwich loaves and rolls is also available alongside an impressive number of continental and speciality breads.

Many of the sweet and savoury tarts, pies and pastries, rolls, brioche, muffins, cakes, cookies and slices available are organic; almond croissants, chocolate croissants and escargots are the most popular pastries, and we thought the lemon tart was exceptionally good. We tried a seasonal fresh fig tart that was very rich and delicious. Their gluten-free orange cake is popular.

Heinz used to bake on the premises – a drawcard in itself – but has now moved the breadmaking and baking down the road to O'Connor, where four bakers and three pastrycooks work through the night: 40 per cent of the output goes to some of the better local shops, Fremantle Market and cafés, and 60 per cent goes to Abhi's in time for the doors opening at 7.00, when the regulars are already waiting.

His customers are particularly important to Heinz, not just because they buy his wares, but because he's always looking for new kinds of loaves to bake and they give him a benchmark: 'It is really important to see what the customer wants and respond. You can't just produce something and say: "That's as good as it gets." You have to develop,' he says. The afternoon we spoke to Heinz he had experimented with a new wholemeal sourdough with linseed the night before and was very pleased with the result.

Like most fresh food, bread is seasonal. In the colder months, the sesame sunflower sourdough and fruit and nut loaf are the most popular loaves. In summer, lighter breads, panini, yeasted white and wholemeal are the order of the day.

If you want to choose from the full selection, come as early in the day as you can: the stock is much depleted by the afternoon, and when it's gone, they close.

If you're coming from afar on a special journey, phone before you set off.

They will take special orders.

In June 2007, when Annie Benjamin retired after nearly 30 years running Annie's Bread Shop in Fremantle Markets, Abhi's bought it, to loud cheers of approval from all concerned – *and* all lovers of good bread.

ANNIE'S BREAD SHOP

Stall 88/97, Fremantle Markets
Cnr Henderson St and South Tce
Fremantle WA 6160

Friday 9.00-9.00
Saturday 9.00-5.00; Sunday 10.00-5.00;
Monday public holidays 10.00-5.00 Closed Good Friday
CASH only
Parking in surrounding car parks: Henderson St, Parry St

Annie's Bread Shop has been in the Market for nearly 30 years, and what a great institution it has been. In June 2007, Annie Benjamin retired and sold her business to Heinz Muller, proprietor and head baker of Abhi's Bread.

In the immediate future, it is Abhi's intention to continue to operate Annie's Bread Shop the same way it has been operated in the past – that is, stocking a wide variety of bread, sourced from many bakeries. Many of the staff are staying on, so familiar faces will be there to greet regular customers.

You'll find bread from New Norcia Bakery, Vastese, Barrett's and Abhi's here: a wonderful variety of all kinds of bread in all shapes and sizes to suit all tastes. Delicious organic bread, sourdoughs, wheat and rye breads, gluten-free, organic European breads, organic essene bread and Kosher bagels can all be found at Annie's.

Each week they also receive a consignment of the wood-fired biodynamic Yallingup bread from the bakery in Margaret River: this is one of the very few places in the Perth area where you can buy this bread.

Rolls, cakes and pastries from local sources, plus meat, chicken, vegetable and spinach pies are on sale too.

BARRETT'S BREAD

19A Broadway
Nedlands WA 6009
9389 6404

Monday-Friday 6.30-5.30
Saturday 6.30-4.30 Sunday 6.30-3.00
CASH only
Some short-term parking on Broadway

Greg Sommer, a chef with a leaning towards pastrycooking, took over this business 5 years ago from its highly regarded founder, Andrew Barrett. Since then Barrett's has continued to produce good, interesting bread – their pain de campagne and ciabatta are bestsellers – and excellent patisseries, including tarts, cakes and croissants.

Greg's head baker, Ben Mercer, leads a team of five, working through the night in Barrett's new (and larger) premises in Welshpool, making hand-moulded bread. It is available at many Perth shops, including Claremont Fresh, The Pearl of Highgate, Herdsman Fresh or here in Nedlands.

Greg himself and his team of pastrychefs concentrate on the patisserie: croissants, tarts, pastries and cakes, much of which is sold wholesale.

BAYVIEW BAKERY

4 Bayview Tce
Claremont WA 6010
9385 2646

Monday-Friday 7.30-5.30
Saturday 7.30-4.30 Closed Sundays
CASH only
Parking in station car park

Joseph Jacob has been quietly baking away at the top of Bayview Terrace for the last 7 years. Originally from Romania, where he trained with his Master Baker father, he specialises in handmade sourdough breads, German rye bread, vollkorn 100 per cent rye and fruit breads. He also makes focaccia, ciabatta and other lighter European-style bread.

Pastries, escargots, cheesecakes, sandwiches, meat pies, cakes, lemon tarts and wonderful pretzels – everything is made by Joseph on the premises.

Joseph loves making cakes to order. 'Nothing gives me more pleasure than making something special. When it comes out of the oven you get so much satisfaction … you get sentimental.'

Very much a one-man band, Joseph doesn't automatically make every kind of bread every day – so if there is something specific you want, ring and place an order.

'If you put love and passion into what you do, you will succeed.'
We hope he does.

FRESH 'N CRUSTY

Shop 18, Carine Glades Shopping Centre
473 Beach Rd
Duncraig WA 6023
9246 1167

Shopping Centre hours 8.00–8.00, 364 days a year
Closed Christmas Day
CASH only
Car park

Damien Duffield might not have a bakery ... but what he *does* have is the freedom to buy from anyone and anywhere. He sources the very best breads and sells them in his shop, which is right in the centre of the Carine Glades Shopping Centre. You'll see customers standing four deep at the weekends to buy his bread (note the long opening hours, 7 days a week).

'No bakery does *everything* perfectly, so I buy from each only what they do best. I use everyone who I think is good.' This policy means each type of bread tastes different because each is made from different doughs from different sources. So you'll find New Norcia sourdough alongside Lawley's Cape seed, alongside Barrett's, Temptations, Batard and a few secret sources which Damien, quite rightly, didn't want to give away. He stocks 32 types of bread roll from four suppliers and there's a wonderful selection of cakes, biscuits, lattice fruit pies, custard tarts and slices too.

This was one of the first places to stock New Norcia Bakeries' long-awaited ciabatta. Damien told us about its imminent arrival when we first met him and we went back and were treated to a few gratis loaves. We're very, very stringent in our judgement of ciabatta ... and this was wonderful.

When discussing the price of handmade, beautiful bread, Damien said to us: 'Never forget, the taste of quality lingers.'

If you haven't already found Carine Glades, Fresh 'n Crusty is a good reason to seek it out.

IL PANINO BAKERY

Shop 6, Beaconsfield Plaza
115 Lefroy Rd
Hilton WA 6163
9331 5010

Monday–Saturday 6.30–5.30
Sunday and public holidays 7.00–2.00
CASH only
Ample parking

Nick Agustino is a very traditional Italian baker who unashamedly makes his bread the old-fashioned way: slowly and carefully.

Pagnotta, Calabrese, Siciliano, pane de casa, Tuscan, Filoni, rustico – they're all here, but it is his ciabatta, both plain and olive, which is his biggest seller. Golden brown and very crusty on the outside with a soft white aerated centre, it takes 24 hours to make. He uses flat wooden shovels called peels to slide the bread onto the stone floor (the sole) of his big double oven, which can handle 60 loaves at a time.

'I could make bread in an hour,' Nick says, 'but it wouldn't taste as good. You can't rush good bread: you need patience and understanding.'

Nick underwent his formal training as a baker in his native Calabria, but also learned from Nonna, his grandmother, whose old recipes he still uses.

There are half a dozen tables outside the bakery on a shaded brick patio. Il Panino bakes for Princi's at Romano next door, and for many hotels, restaurants and cafés as well as his retail clients.

Unbaked dough is also available, and special orders are taken.

LAWLEY'S BAKERY AND CAFÉ

562 Beaufort St
Mt Lawley WA 6050
9328 6866

7 days 6.30–5.30 Closed Christmas Day and Boxing Day
Parking – good luck

This was Bagels on Beaufort until 2003, when Sarah and Trefor Thomas bought it from David Katziv, renamed it Lawley's and reinvented it as a bakery and a good, unpretentious gourmet café.

Everything used to be made on the premises in the bakery behind the shop, and the cakes, tarts and petits fours are still made here, by the French pastry chef Christian Wirtz and his team of eight. But this year the breadmaking moved to Lawley's new factory in Osborne Park – where there is a small retail outlet and a café. It is still under the guidance of David Katziv, head baker, and his wife Elizabeth, who is the Operations Manager.

Lawley's fourteen Daily Breads (including their Cape seed loaf), the hand-moulded sourdoughs (most, but not all, are yeast-free: ask), five different, very tasty flatbreads, ciabatta, dense pagnotta, baguettes and flutes are all popular. Some organic and gluten-free breads are available, but only at the weekends. We particularly like their Cape seed loaf – it's special.

Lawley's roast their own blend of coffee on the premises and you can drink it here or take home a bag of roasted beans.

This is still a good destination for breakfast or a light lunch. Try one of their renowned boiled bagels with smoked salmon schmear (cream cheese) or snack on a delicious tart or cake. The petits four Lemon Delight is delightful, and if it's sinful, well, it is only two bites.

Also @:

Unit 20 Powell St, Osborne Park WA 6017
9444 8886
Monday–Friday 7.00–3.00

Fremantle Markets (see page 310)
Subiaco Station Street Markets (see page 314)

LITTLE HOME BAKERY

455 William St
Northbridge WA 6003
9227 5200

Tuesday-Friday 8.00-4.00
Saturday 8.00-12.00 Closed Sundays and public holidays
CASH only
Limited parking in front of shop

Tucked away at the top of William Street, among the food emporia of Chinatown, is the tiny shopfront of Little Home Bakery. Master Baker Glenn Marder and his pastrycook wife Carmen Bertram emigrated from southern Germany in 2005 in order to 'do something different,' but wound up doing something not so different: running a German-style bakery and baking the same kinds of breads, such as German rye and vollkorn, that they produced back home – but in a gleaming new German MIWE electric oven – and selling it to German and European shops including Elmar's Smallgoods (see page 58) and Hela Continental Smallgoods (see page 65).

Although most of their bread is sold wholesale, they welcome customers to the retail counter at the front of the small bakery. All the bread is made from sourdough with a little added yeast and it is all very authentically German. They have already won two First Prizes at the Perth Royal Show for their German rye.

NEW NORCIA BAKERIES
163 Scarborough Beach Rd
Mt Hawthorn WA 6016
9443 4114

7 days 7.30–6.00
Car park at rear of shop in Anvil Lane

The New Norcia Bakeries team – partners Kingsley Sullivan and Mark Young together with their production manager and head baker Alain Fourrier – are perfectionists. It took them 6 months of constant experimenting to get their new ciabatta just right before they added it to the bread range in May 2007. Serious food lovers say it is the real deal, and we agree.

Breadmaking is a passion for Kingsley. He took it up in an amateur way, making bread at home in Melbourne, as a therapeutic exercise when he worked in the high-stress world of marketing. In 1992, after a career change, a move to WA, and while he and his wife Chrissie were running The Gourmet Grocer, he met Dom Christopher Power, one of the monks at the Benedictine Monastery at New Norcia, who showed him the monastery's old wood-fired bread oven. He was instantly smitten – and the rest is history.

For the first 3 years, the bread was made at New Norcia; then the baking moved to Mt Hawthorn. They still use the New Norcia oven, but these days only to make the famous nutcake and almond biscotti. The magnificent wood-fired oven below the café in Mt Hawthorn has recently been refurbished. One of the master bakers now uses it to bake hand-crafted traditional loaves for the café upstairs and the Subiaco shop. If you ask nicely you may be allowed to watch.

The rest of the New Norcia bread – between 12,000 and 15,000 loaves a week, available at 80 retail shops in Perth – is baked in German thermocoil ovens at their new state-of-the-art bakery in Malaga. These new ovens replicate the effect of a wood-fired oven, even achieving the same rich crust, by circulating very hot oil beneath the oven sole. The technology may be new, but the ingredients – only flour, salt, and water – have not changed, and nor, they say, has their artisan integrity.

New Norcia still uses the same sourdough culture Kingsley made on 29 December 1990. It has been fed every day for 17 years. They now make twelve different kinds of sourdough: San Franciscan-style; French; Casalinga; wholemeal; seven grain; olive; light and dark rye; 100 per cent organic; raisin and walnut; fig and fennel; and fruit bread sourdough. Each of these beautiful breads has a distinctive flavour – the brown paper bags used for the bread list some comments on each style of bread and its use.

New Norcia also have a range of yeasted breads: French baguette, pain de campagne, Parisian, zucchini bread, multigrain fruit bread, olive, rosemary and sun-dried tomato bread and, of course, the ciabatta.

If there was a world championship for breadmaking, New Norcia would probably enter, and we reckon they'd be in with a chance: their standards are very high. 'We benchmark ourselves against the best ciabatta in Italy and the world, not Sydney or Melbourne,' says Kingsley. When we visited, partner Mark Young had just come back from Paris where he'd been – guess what? – looking at bakeries.

There is a team of sixteen bakers, all trained by Alain Fourrier. The business has a huge commitment to training; Kingsley spends a lot of time in schools encouraging young people to consider a career in baking. 'Anyone can become a good baker if they apply themselves,' he says. He still gets great satisfaction from his profession. 'I love it. I still get huge joy when people stop me in the street and tell me how much they like our bread.'

Also @:

225 Bagot Rd
Subiaco WA 6008
9381 4811

TEMPTATIONS BAKEHOUSE AND PATISSERIE

Boatshed Fresh Food
40 Jarrad St
Cottesloe WA 6011
9383 4011

7 days 6.30-8.00
Closed Christmas Day
Parking in the Boatshed car park

This was Hans Sanders' first shop; he was here at the start, when the Boatshed opened in October 1989 and, though he has since expanded his operations to include three other shops, he still considers this to be his flagship store.

Hans trained as a baker in his native Germany, under a very tough, but fair and passionate teacher; he spent the next 20 years travelling and gaining experience in international hotels in Europe and Asia before settling in Australia. He still makes his German rye signature loaf, just the way he was taught, using sourdough leavened with a little yeast to lighten it. All his bread is slowly matured and slowly baked, without preservatives and additives. Much of his bread is yeast-free and organic.

When we met him for a coffee in Napoleon Street, Hans told us excitedly about how he had just spent much of the previous night, lightly dusted with flour, finally perfecting his brioche, which is now in the shops. Brioche is not always easy to get in Perth and Hans's is very rich; to 7kg of flour he adds about 80 eggs and 4kg of butter. Don't try this at home. You can buy the brioche as loaves or buns, or wrapped around a German sausage and baked.

Hans has a team of six bakers and four pastrycooks at his central bakery in Jandakot, and his two grown-up children, Sarah and Sebastian, now work with him in the business. As well as traditional-style bread, Temptations produce a large range of cakes, tarts and biscuits, and celebrations cakes to order.

Also @:

Mindarie Quay Shopping Centre
Anchorage Drive
Mindarie Quay WA 6030
0448 251 802

Rossmoyne Village
5/55 Central Rd
Rossmoyne WA 6148
9259 4433

Tony Ale & Co.
84 Hammond Rd
Jandakot WA 6164
9414 1756

UNITED BAKERY

35 Adrian St
Welshpool WA 6106
9361 9945

Monday–Saturday 10.00–7.00
Sunday 10.00–1.30
Parking by shop

They do not bake on Friday or Saturday

Tucked away on an industrial estate in Welshpool, United Bakery, a large wholesale bakery, who make Lebanese bread, pizza bases, wraps and pitta bread, usually bake in the afternoons, except on Friday and Saturday. Many of their regular customers often arrive just as the bread is coming out of the oven, so that they can take some of it away hot. They bake in the afternoons, so that the bread is still fresh for the markets the following day.

Next to the huge wholesale bakery there is a small retail shop – run by general manager Elias Kopti – which operates mainly for the convenience of the bakery clients, but where retail customers can buy bread as well as specialist Middle Eastern groceries and delicacies that can be hard to find elsewhere. We saw Halah burgers, Lebanese pastries, halva, baklava, Jordanian spice mixes, olives, frozen vegetables imported from Egypt, nuts, spices and seeds, including four different kinds of melon seed.

'No one finds this place by accident. It's a head-in spot for customers,' says director Jim Hishmeh. 'Most people hear about us by word of mouth.'

The following shops also sell good bread:

Chez Jean-Claude Patisserie (see page 95)
Choux (see page 97)
François (see page 102)
No. 44 King Street (see page 258)
Prinz of Vienna (see page 107)
The Kosher Food Centre (see page 225)
The Pearl of Highgate (see page 115)

BUTCHERS

Perth has many excellent independent butchers and food lovers need to make sure that they survive. In this book we have chosen butchers because they know the provenance of the meat they sell. Many have told us they go personally to the market or even to the farm and buy on the hoof or from the grower. The most humane methods of slaughter are those that result in the highest quality. Butchers told us again and again that stressed animals do not produce good meat. Once humanely killed, freshness is not so important – properly hung meat is better, beef in particular. It should be aged by being hung for up to three weeks. Recently some Perth butchers are maintaining that hanging meat for a shorter period and then ageing it in vacuum-packaging, or cryovac, gives an even better result.

Some of them still operate in the traditional, old-style but, in response to customer demand, many are now 'adding value' to their produce by pre-preparing cuts of meat and marinating for the time-poor shopper.

A big threat to the survival of independent butchers comes from customers voting with their feet for lower-priced meat. Cheap meat comes at a terrible price. To keep the price down, birds and animals have to be reared in unnatural conditions (hens in cages too small to flap their wings; pigs that can never snuffle in the soft dirt; calves in stalls too small to turn around) and fed on unnatural foods, too horrible to describe in a family publication, and then dosed with chemicals to ward off the diseases which would otherwise sweep through their ranks. Even so, outbreaks of endemic salmonella, foot and mouth in the UK and BSE in the UK and continental Europe, warn us we could be hovering on the edge of disaster.

Find the butchers in this book that suit you best, patronise their shop and ask them about their meat.

BARLEYFIELD MEATS

Shop 2a, Midland Junction Markets
380 Great Eastern Hwy
Midland WA 6056
9374 0744
www.barleyfield.com.au

Monday-Friday 7.00-6.00
Saturday 7.00-5.00 Sunday 9.30-5.00
Off-street parking in car park

This shop opened 4 years ago as the retail outlet for the prize-winning Barleyfield Beef, which is bred and reared by Arthur Dewar, his wife, Jane Bellinge, and daughter, Laura, on the historic family properties north of Gingin.

The premium quality yearling beef is free from antibiotics, hormonal growth promotants and chemical treatments, and genetically modified substances. After slaughtering, the beef is hung for 7–10 days. Lamb from Katanning, excellent free-range pork and chickens from Bindoon are also available.

The meat is consistently of a high standard – it's not certified organic, but they are committed to ethical meat production.

This is not a big shop. Jane says: 'We depend on quality and consistency rather than turnover.' Surprisingly, Jane was a vegetarian before she started producing her own meat.

Home deliveries on orders over $300.00 are free within the metropolitan area. They deliver bulk packs throughout WA by freezer courier. You can place special orders through the shop or the website.

Also @:

212 Main St
Osborne Park WA
9349 3533

Monday-Saturday 8.00-7.00
Sunday 9.00-4.00

BOATSHED QUALITY MEATS
42 Jarrad St
Cottesloe WA 6011
9385 3185

www.boatshedmeats.com.au
7 days 6.30-8.00
Closed Christmas Day
Parking at the Boatshed car park

In February 2006, Boatshed Quality Meats moved out of their small corner of the main shop into their own space. From their new, much enlarged premises, set off to the right of the main shop, they now offer a huge variety of carefully sourced meat, poultry and game, much of it organic.

Owners Peter and Penny Griffiths say their aim is to sell 'fresh, healthy, free-range and organic meats with excellent service and advice'. About half their meat has been pre-prepared for easy cooking but there is, apparently, still a big demand in Cottesloe for plain meat that is taken home, prepared, then cooked in the traditional way – so their biggest seller is still steak.

The organic, free-range pork comes from the Butler family's farm, Gimlet Ridge, in the northeast wheatbelt: it's so popular that they sell all that Butlers can produce. They also source organic lamb from this farm, as well as from the well-regarded Amelia Park farm near Busselton; organic beef is Red Angus or Red Angus cross from the Cook family at Dandaragan; free-range organic chickens and ducks come from Bendele farm, which has its own certified organic abattoir and kitchen, and Inglewood Creek; other free-range chickens are from Mahogany Creek and Mt Barker.

Boatshed Quality Meats was the first butcher in WA registered as ACO (Australian Certified Organic) – this is the biggest and most widely accepted of the several organic certifying authorities.

All the meat looked delicious and was well presented in brightly lit glass-fronted cabinets, behind which the smartly uniformed staff were working in full view of the customers. Our eye was caught by Dandaragan organic beef Wellingtons, fillet mignons and a standing rib roast, the Gimlet Ridge rolled loin of organic pork, free-range chicken mini rolls filled with fresh bocconcini and semi sun-dried tomatoes, rolled and wrapped in pancetta, and a big array of homemade sausages, including pork chipolatas and boerewors.

When Jamie Oliver was doing his cooking demonstrations in Perth all the meat he used came from here. Peter and Penny are still big fans of Jamie and much influenced by his healthy food philosophy.

BRIGHTON MEAT SUPPLY

111 Brighton Rd
Scarborough WA 6019
9341 1865

Monday-Friday 7.30-6.00
Saturday 7.30-2.00 Closed Sundays and public holidays
Parking outside the shop

Phil Rollings has run this small, modern, recently refurbished butcher's shop for 20 years, although this family business has been in existence for 37 years. It's a bright, clean, absolutely no fuss sort of place, but it comes well recommended by locals and the competitively priced meat is of a high standard.

There's beef from the southwest, free-range eggs from Busselton, and Mt Barker free-range chicken. There's also some value-added produce, including marinated chicken and lamb shanks – all simply displayed, and all made on the premises, including the sausages.

CARL TORRE AND SONS

41–43 Lake St
Northbridge WA 6003
9328 8317

Monday–Friday 6.00–5.30
Saturday 4.00am–1.00pm
Closed Sundays, Christmas Day, Boxing Day, Good Friday
Small car park at rear: for customer use only when in shop

We very rarely walk into a shop and say, 'Wow!', but that's what we did the first time we went into Carl Torre's exceptional shop. This is the apogee of the traditional continental butcher's shop, and about as good as it gets. It is not big, and the beautiful produce seems to fill it, shouting 'Quality!' at you wherever you look.

The glass-fronted counters are full of prime cuts and joints of meat, mostly relatively unadorned. These are quite large: you select the one you prefer – perhaps one will have more marbling of fat than its neighbour – and Carl, son David or one of the skilled butchers will cut off the amount you want to buy. 'Nothing is pre-cut. It is all cut to your own requirements; we are not pushing anything on to you,' says Carl.

In several spacious coolrooms at the back of the shop hang whole beef carcasses, all personally selected by Carl while still on the hoof and marked with his sign of approval. Carl personally goes every Sunday to Gingin to do this. 'I love my work, particularly the buying and the relationships I've built up with growers over a long period.' All the meat is fresh, nothing is frozen, and it is virtually all from WA. 'We do everything ourselves. Very few butchers break everything on the premises these days, but we do.'

The Torre family, beginning with Carl's grandfather, his uncles and then his father, have been butchers in Perth since the 1920s, and in the province of Messina, Sicily before that. There's nothing Carl doesn't know about good meat, from the best varieties of animals (English cross-breeds for lamb), the right age for each (all beef is less than 1 year old, veal 4 weeks minimum) to the best time for each. 'Meat is seasonal. We can only go with the climate and the area we have. We start buying up north and move south as the summer goes on.'

The emphasis here is on traditional butchery: 'We sell meat you have to prepare yourself. That's what families are about – the kitchen is the centre of family life.'

But there is some pre-prepared produce, too, such as chicken or veal schnitzel, stuffed and crumbed whole Portobello mushrooms and Italian meatballs. There are trays of homemade sausages (we particularly like the pork Cumberland ones, plump and herbily aromatic), a cabinet of Mt Barker free-range chicken, some homemade pies and another counter of packaged smallgoods, a few cheeses and dairy products, including Bannister Downs milk.

Below the counters are wicker baskets of beautifully fresh seasonal vegetables, and on top are crusty Italian campagna loaves, bottles of olive oil and condiments. They sell a few other items, including rice, dried pasta imported from Italy, muesli from Food By Emily, and even a few fresh flowers. You could certainly buy everything you need for a complete meal.

Though the Torres' shop is traditional, it is not at all old-fashioned; in fact it has quite a modern feel about it. If you shop here, you are buying from a family with a lifetime of experience and expert knowledge, who know the provenance of everything they sell, who work to the very highest standards and offer wonderful, personal service. Their passion for what they do is evident the moment you set foot in the shop.

CLAYTONS QUALITY MEATS

271 Mill Point Rd
South Perth WA 6151
9367 1110

Monday–Friday 7.00–5.45
Saturday 7.00–12.30 Closed Sundays and public holidays
Plenty of off-street parking next to the shop

Trevor Clayton's great-grandfather opened this shop in 1931 and four generations of the Clayton family have run it ever since, modernising from time to time, but always maintaining the time-honoured feeling of a traditional butcher's shop. In 76 years they have built tremendous customer loyalty: 'The customers decide everything,' says Trevor, 'even our opening hours.' It's true. Last year he asked them if they wanted him to open on Christmas Eve, which happened to fall on a Sunday. 'No, don't bother,' they said. 'We can do our shopping the day before: it will make us be organised.' Trevor is very knowledgeable about meat – 'it's in the blood' – and is happy to advise on the right product for recipes.

He is a member of The Red Meat Networking Club, a group of WA independent butchers who go on fact-finding trips together to look at the eastern states and exchange information: 'One on one against the supermarkets, we will never win, but if we join forces, we will.'

Claytons' meat is from WA where possible – Harvey beef, Amelia Park lamb, Mt Barker chicken, Linley Valley pork – and they sell some fresh fish (king snapper, salmon) from WA Seafoods. Some of the meat is pre-prepared (butterfly lamb leg with rosemary and garlic, sirloin steak with honey and mustard, peppered Scotch fillet) but if you like to do the work yourself, he will sell you anything, cut to order. All their meat is of the very best quality, properly hung, prepared and beautifully presented. You can also buy some of their meat, packaged, at Scutti – a taste of Europe, in Angelo Street (see page 219).

CONTINENTAL MEAT SUPPLY

Shop 2/3, 54 Rockingham Rd
Hamilton Hill WA 6163
9336 3402

Monday to Friday 7.00-6.00
Saturday 7.00-1.00 Closed Sundays
Off-street parking in front of shop

Continental Meat Supply make some exceptional pies. The pastry is thin, crisp (even on the bottom) and flaky. The steak, hand-diced on the premises, comes in big chunks in, but not swamped by, a rich gravy; the kidney is in just the right proportion. The chicken in the chicken pie was also in big, identifiable chunks with no anonymous mince or gristle. Other pies included Indian butter chicken, lamb, kangaroo and chilli steak.

The meat is first class as well, bought on the hoof from the southwest of WA, with an eye to the right proportion between fat and lean, and then hung in the big coolrooms attached to the shop. Many cuts are pre-prepared, some in marinades of the owners' own invention and made on the premises. Chickens are free-range. Vito's handmade sausages are one of the shop's specialities. They will supply the meat for your barbecue and, should you wish it, come and cook it for you. There are usually one or two bargains advertised on blackboards outside.

We bought four beef ribs, which were well trimmed of fat, and which Vito obligingly cut into smallish pieces, then made a classic beef bourguignon, but with the meat still on the bone. Cooked for several hours to a rich, gelatinous softness, our dinner guests said it was the best they'd ever had.

CREATIVE MEATS

Herdsman Fresh Essentials
9 Flynn St
Churchlands WA 6018
9284 9884

7 days 8.00–8.00
Parking in Herdsman Fresh car park

The L-shaped glass-fronted counters of Creative Meats open directly onto the Herdsman Fresh shop floor, but this is a separate business, owned and run for the last 10 years by Nathan Holmes and Shane Fuchsbichler.

'We're pretty heavily into WA meat here,' Nathan told us. 'People are very quality conscious, and they shop for quality – so the quality *has* to be consistent.'

About half the meat is fresh, simply trimmed and unadorned, and the rest is value-added by way of marinades, pre-preparation, pastry wrapping or kebabbing. The fillet mignons looked enticing; there were also New Orleans-style porterhouses, souvlakia lamb roasts, ham, cheese, asparagus and chicken parcels, and tandoori chicken.

All the lamb is from Amelia Park; the chickens are free-range from Mt Barker; all the beef is WA. They also had farmed rabbits, frozen quail, duck and venison.

'We have a large variety of meat on show every day. Because of our location, we sell a large volume. For customers in a hurry, we have a counter of packaged meat which they can just come and grab and pay for at the checkout.'

In the summer months, they sell a huge amount of barbecue meat and sausages – they make all their own sausages on site – but with the beginning of winter his customers are moving into casseroles and warming, slow-cooked dishes.

The staff at this very busy shop are friendly and helpful. Creative Meats also has a knife-sharpening service.

CRIMEA QUALITY MEATS

Cnr Morley Drive and Crimea St
Morley WA 6062
9276 6087

Monday-Friday 8.30-6.00
Saturday 8.00-1.00 Closed Sundays
Off-street parking in front of shop

Joe Di Fulvio spans the whole gamut of contemporary butchering: he will cook a single lamb shank for you, very nicely, in the big oven in the room behind his shop or sell you an entire rump of beef, raw. It was the whole rump that we first encountered at a friend's barbecue. Our friend praised it highly (and we thought it was pretty good, too), and then when we were asking friends about butchers for this book the name of Crimea kept cropping up ... again and again. When we went to see Joe, we discovered that he is also pretty much acknowledged as a sausage supremo around Perth, having won both national and state awards for his traditional BBQ sausages.

We have a soft spot for a good sausage. As AP Herbert wrote:

> *When love is dead*
> *Ambition fled*
> *And pleasure, Lad, and Pash*
> *You'll still enjoy*
> *A sausage, boy*
> *A sausage, boy, and mash.*

And our discoveries went on from there. Joe buys whole animals, usually locally, on the hoof when he can, mostly free-range, some organic, and breaks them out on the premises. You can buy your meat cut to order or he'll prepare it for you. As well as being a fine butcher, Joe is a cook. He will just as happily turn those same cuts and joints into delicious and imaginative roasts, such as White Rocks Veal stuffed with Chicken; Beef, Lamb or Chicken 'Al Forno'; or Pork Loin with Apricots and Macadamia Nuts. You can take these home and put them straight in the oven or he will cook them for you. His wife, Anna, is the custodian of the family recipe for lasagna and also for Bolognese sauce, and these dishes of hers are available in trays for the oven or containers for microwaving. At Christmas they offer their own special ham, duck and turkey dishes.

The Di Fulvios have been running their small family business here for 30 years now and say that it is only by offering customers high quality meat – Linley Valley pork, Amelia Park lamb, Dandaragan beef, White Rocks Veal and Mt Barker chicken – and this level of service that they have been able to compete with the deadly advance of the supermarket chains.

Joe and Anna say they are just trying to be good, honest, local suppliers – and we think that's exactly what they are. Where would we be without them?

DUBROVNIK BUTCHERS
204 Railway Parade
Meltham WA 6053
9272 1453
www.dubrovnikbutchers.com.au

Monday–Friday 8.00–5.00
Saturday 8.00–12.00 Closed Sundays and public holidays
15 minutes free parking in front of shop

Paul Marinovic Snr migrated here from Dubrovnik as a teenager in the early 1960s and soon came under the influence of two master butchers, one originally from Austria, and the other from Germany, who together had a huge influence on his life. As a result, nearly half a century later he is running his continental-style butcher's shop – specialising mainly in handmade and smoked smallgoods – with one of his sons, Paul Jnr, in a way that would be recognisable at once to any middle-aged middle European.

Many of Paul's customers are what used to be called New Australians, and 90 per cent of them are regulars. Trying to find one style that suits them all, however, has proved impossible: 'We have to have a big range because Australia has a very mixed culture and very mixed taste buds.'

So the smallgoods they make here in this great little shop by the railway bridge at Meltham follow recipes in the style of those from Germany, Holland, Austria, Poland, England and Spain; all authentic and all delicious. We tried English Cumberland sausages – they tasted wonderful, dense and full of pork, and a vast improvement on some of the ones we've tasted in England in the last decade.

Smoked chorizos are becoming popular all year round and, particularly at Christmas, there's a big demand for their traditional leg ham, which is smoked over pine or karri sawdust: no extensions and *nothing* artificial going on with their ham. Beautiful.

Also @:
Shop 12, 168 Wanneroo Rd
Madeley WA 6065
9409 5894

ELMAR'S SMALLGOODS

493 Beaufort St
Highgate WA 6003
9328 4050

Monday 10.30-5.00 Tuesday 8.30-5.00 Wednesday-Thursday 8.30-5.30
Saturday 8.30-12.00 Closed Sundays
Some parking in front of shop and side streets

The German-style bratwursts, wieners and smoked meats in this very atmospheric shop are absolutely authentic and pure. There are no artificial colourings, flavourings or preservatives used, and nothing is bulked out with carbohydrate extenders, and all produce is gluten-free. Everything is made just the way it would be back in Dusseldorf; even the beechwood chips for the smoker are imported from German forests.

Elmar and Anette Dieren first came here on holiday in 1980, soon after Elmar had qualified as a master butcher in Germany. They went back to Germany and opened a shop but were always homesick for Australia, so they returned to Perth and opened this shop in 1987: 'Our philosophy was to bring quality produce to Perth. At that time, no one was gluten-free; people used artificial colourings, flavourings, preservatives and added extenders and extra fat and we just wanted to introduce traditional German methods and recipes,' Anette told us.

Elmar is still hands-on every day in the factory behind the shop, assisted by two qualified butchers. As well as their own handmade smallgoods – about 160 different types and flavours of bratwurst, cooked, smoked and dried sausages, hams, bacon and many kinds of smoked meats as well as meat, fish and potato salads – Elmar's also sells imported European cheeses, and tinned and packaged groceries. Bread from Little Home Bakery is available here.

There is a big demand for vacuum-packed produce for customers travelling overseas, particularly to southeast Asia.

Elmar's products can be found at The Gourmet Deli in Midland, Fig Jam in Mount Hawthorn and a very few other fine food stores.

Also @:

Shop 1 North Lake Shopping Centre
North Lake Rd
Myaree WA 6154
9330 2304

Monday-Wednesday 9.00-5.00 Thursday-Friday 8.00-5.30
Saturday 8.00-2.00 Closed Sundays

ELMAR'S IN THE VALLEY
8731 West Swan Rd
Henley Brook WA 6055
9296 6254

Wednesday-Sunday 10.00-10.00

FINESSE BUTCHERY (City Beach)

Shop 11, The Boulevard Shopping Centre
31 Gayton Rd
City Beach WA 6015
9385 9761

Monday–Friday 7.00–6.00
Saturday 7.00–2.00 Closed Sundays, and from Christmas Eve for 10 days
Ample parking around shopping centre

At Finesse Butchery the aim is to do as much work for the customers as possible, so that they have only to put the meat into the oven, cook it and take it out again. 'We want to put the emphasis on really good quality and really good service,' says proprietor Simon Lawes, 'and we do as much as possible for our customer.' So almost all of his meat has been pre-prepared, very often in a most enticing way, and the service is of the old-fashioned, high quality kind.

The cushion of (boned) shoulder of lamb with honey, mint and rosemary stuffing – which customers are advised to cook for more than two hours at 140°C, 'snip the three bits of string and serve' – would grace any dinner table, as would the beautiful pork tenderloin, trimmed right down to just the eye with the soon-to-be crackling stripped of its fat, slashed and wrapped around the loin. Simon's wife and partner, Simone, is a dab hand with pastry, so many of the pre-prepared dishes are 'in pastry'.

It's quality all the way here ... Amelia Park lamb, Spencer Brook Farms' organic pork, Butterfield beef (always aged for at least 2 weeks), Mt Barker chickens, organic eggs from Keysbrook, six kinds of sausages and some wonderful-looking ham on the bone. It is all chemical-free, hormone-free, free-range, hung and homemade on the premises. Everything is simply and elegantly displayed on white china dishes.

Simon very much encourages his customers to ask questions and deliberately doesn't provide much information in print: cooking instructions are handwritten directly onto the wrapping paper.

Demand is growing rapidly and this, coupled with his desire to expand into cooked food-to-go, means that by the time you read this, he may have added a full-time chef to his 5-man team. Watch this space.

FINESSE BUTCHERY (Dalkeith)

Shop 7, 81 Waratah Ave
Dalkeith WA 6009
9386 2535

Monday–Friday 6.00–6.00
Saturday 6.00–2.00 Closed Sundays
Parking in car park by shop

This beautiful small shop was Simon Lawes' first, but after a couple of years here, in a desperate quest for more space, he's now acquired a second, at City Beach in the Boulevard Shopping Centre (see entry above).

The produce and range of goods, style of presentation and high standard of service are identical in both establishments … 'As long as you don't mind waiting, we'll do whatever you want.'

Staff move between the two shops: Simon comes to Dalkeith each Friday and Saturday, when Ben Smith, his Dalkeith manager, goes to City Beach.

FRANK'S GOURMET MEATS
17 Wray Ave
Fremantle WA 6160
9335 2536

**Monday–Friday 7.00 to 6.00
Saturday 7.00 to 4.00 Closed Sundays
Ticket parking on Wray Ave**

Frank Carbone has had a butcher's shop in Wray Ave for two decades, and his reputation for service and general friendly neighbourliness is unrivalled in Fremantle. Everyone goes to Frank's; 90 per cent of his customers, who include many local cafés and restaurants, are regulars.

He sources his pork, organic lamb and beef from pasture-reared stock in Bunbury. Frank hangs his beef (aged about 18 months) and lamb (1 year old) for about 10 days. 'The longer you hang it the more tender it becomes,' he says.

Free-range chicken, eggs and farmed rabbits come from Baldivis, as do his Christmas ducks and turkeys, quail and spatchcocks. Frank makes his own sausages – 28 different kinds, of chicken, beef, Italian, lamb, pork. He also stocks a fair range of exotic meats, including crocodile, ostrich, venison, buffalo and haggis.

Beef is his biggest seller around Christmas time; veal and goat are in season and excellent around Easter; and spring lamb is a favourite around September. Frank estimates that 50 per cent of what he sells is cut to order and 50 per cent has value added.

Frank carries a large stock of many different varieties of meat and meat products. He's been using most of his suppliers for 20 years and the produce is all local or from WA (except the crocodile meat and some ducks from NSW). If you can't think what to buy for supper, this is the place to go and ask what's best today – you'll be guided helpfully and skilfully in the right direction.

GREAT NORTHERN MEAT SUPPLY

46 Great Northern Hwy
Middle Swan WA 6056
9274 1689

Monday-Friday 6.00-5.30
Saturday 6.00-1.00 Closed Sundays
Off-street parking

We can attest, personally and enthusiastically, to the quality of the meat here, and the locals swear by it, but you'd never guess how good it is by just driving past. Great Northern Meat Supply is in a nondescript, stand-alone, small white brick building in a pot-holed car park, almost opposite the Swan District Hospital, with only a blackboard propped up by the side of the road to alert you to what lies within.

Bill McCreery and his son Will are old school: they run a completely unpretentious, small family business. They buy their meat locally and hang it carefully. Not much fresh meat is on display. When you decide what to have – and it is well worth asking Bill, Will or Alex, one of their faithful staff, for their opinion – they will take a carcass from the coolroom and cut for you what you want. We watched Alex take a large shoulder of pork and swiftly and expertly bone out the Scotch fillet for a customer. It is about the only place we've been where, when you ask for a leg of lamb, they bring out the whole carcass and jokingly ask you: 'Left or right leg?' Will says meat keeps much fresher if left on the carcass until it is needed, so he doesn't pre-cut it: 'Besides, everyone's different: some like their steak thick, others like it thin. We cut it to order for you.'

They make all their own produce, including ham on the bone, black pudding, brawn, salami and cured sausages of many kinds, as well as smoked meats, including delicious smoked sides of bacon. There are three smokehouses on the site. They don't go in much for pre-prepared meals or value-added products, though they will prepare any meat the way you want it. They Cryovac meat for many of their regular customers who live in the country.

HADLEY'S

Shop 3, Burrendah Shopping Centre
61 Apsley Rd
Willetton WA 6155
9457 1667

Monday-Friday 7.00-7.00
Saturday 7.00-6.00 Sunday 7.00-5.00
Closed Christmas Day, Boxing Day, New Year's Day, Good Friday, Easter Sunday

Previously, Neil Nesbitt worked for Peters' in St Quentin's Ave, Claremont, and his display at his present shop shows much of the same attention to detail. The cabinet of produce, about half of which had some value-added, is one of the most appetising we have seen.

'My aim is consistency with high quality produce, good service and getting the little things right,' he says. All his meat is MSA approved: beef and lamb from Dardanup and Harvey, free-range chickens from Mt Barker, and Watsonia pork. His beef is aged in Cryovac, which Neil believes is superior to hanging because the meat loses less moisture. Could Cryovac be the new hanging?

Neil has a resident chef and a cook on site, making marinades, pre-prepared dishes and hot meals to go. Everything is handmade on the premises. Between 4.00 and 7.00 on weekdays, this place is buzzing with food-to-go activity: there's always a roast of the day, a dish of the day, lamb curry and lamb shanks, meat pie and gravy, potato bake, vegetables au gratin and much more. At the weekends, the food-to-go service is much smaller.

He attributes much of his success to his loyal staff. 'I'm only as good as my staff. I really focus on them. They are really important to me,' he says. He and his right-hand man, Mark Bailey, are training two apprentices.

HELA CONTINENTAL SMALLGOODS
290 South St (Junction with Carrington St)
Hilton WA 6163
9337 4193

Monday 9.00-4.00 Tuesday-Wednesday 8.00-5.00
Thursday-Friday 8.00-5.30
Saturday 8.00-12.00 Closed Sundays
Off street parking by the shop: up a steep ramp off South St

Wonderful smoky, meaty smells greet you in this little shop with its cabinets full of rosy-flecked paprikawurst, plump bockwurst, smooth liverwurst, glistening black pudding, slim Vienna sausage, sulze (a brawn-like sausage, full of cubes of meat in aspic), homely fleischkase (the meatloaf every South German housewife makes from her granny's recipe), pale weisswurst (white veal), smoked beef, kassler (smoked pork chops) and double-smoked sausages; the shelves are full of mixes for dumpling, spaetzle (egg noodles), jars of rollmop herrings, sauerkraut, beetroot and dill pickles.

All the smallgoods are made by Helmut Fehrenbach, a master butcher trained in the Black Forest in Germany, in the small, two-oven kitchen behind the shop. His wife, Anita, runs front of house with quiet efficiency. This *is* a very German shop. We could hear many of the customers speaking German, and all the products are German – there are no Italian salamis tucked in among the wurst – but you don't have to speak German to buy here. Anita will guide you carefully and perhaps introduce you to something you haven't tried before.

Helmut told us that as well as his German, Swiss, Austrian and Polish regulars, he and Anita now welcome many Asian customers.

Hela's carries only WA-sourced pork and beef – no lamb or poultry. The pork loin with crackling we bought was delicious. Everything in this small friendly shop appears to be of the highest quality: Helmut, confident in knowing he is the master of his trade, simply says: 'I stick to what I know; making the product the way I learned it.' *Gemütlich* would be the word to describe Hela's.

J. & A. MARCHESANI
Shop 6, 308 South St
Hilton WA 6163
9331 8686

Monday–Friday 8.00–5.00
Saturday 8.00–1.00 Closed Sundays and public holidays
Off-street parking at rear via Victor St

John Marchesani is a traditional, no-frills butcher of vast experience who has never deviated from the high standards he learned as a 15-year-old apprentice at the feet of the Torre and Princi families more than 35 years ago.

He still buys his animals on the hoof at the Midland Markets, and insists they are to be well cared for – he makes sure they are rested for 24 hours before travelling to the abattoir at Australind and rested again overnight before they are slaughtered. 'Stressed animals do not produce good meat,' he says, regretting the trend to move abattoirs away from saleyards.

John sells quality meat, expertly butchered – Paul, his right-hand man, has been with him for nearly 20 years – and though he does offer a few pre-prepared, value-added, marinated dishes, that is not what most of his regular, dedicated customers come here for. They come, by the way, from all walks of life – he understands people who have to watch their budgets – and some travel considerable distances.

The huge wooden chopping blocks, the butchers working in the back of the shop and the glimpse of carcasses hanging above them, will remind you of the butchers' shops your mother patronised. But don't think John is an old-fashioned butcher in a backwater. He has won many awards, particularly for his BBQ sausages (and has revealed some of the secrets of the art of the Aussie BBQ sausage – selected meat, natural skins – to butchers in the US).

Free-range Liberty chicken from Baldivis, farmed rabbit, pork fillet and veal cutlets all looked tempting.

JEREMY'S EXCLUSIVE BUTCHERY

131 Claremont Tce
Swanbourne WA 6010
9384 6108

Monday–Friday 7.00–7.00
Saturday 7.00–5.00 Closed Sundays and public holidays
Angle off-street parking opposite and outside shop

From the moment you walk through the door into these modern, sparkling premises, it's quality all the way – in the welcome, the goods and the service.

A wide choice of premium quality WA produce is on offer: Dandaragan and Harvey beef; Spencer Brook pork; Amelia Park lamb; White Rocks veal; Baldivis free-range eggs. Jeremy buys his beef and lamb carcasses and hangs them for 2–3 weeks: 'The only way to have tender meat is to age it.'

All the meat preparation is done on the premises by Jeremy and his team. About 80 per cent of the produce is value-added and ready to go. 'We've just responded to customer demand,' says Jeremy. 'Many of our customers have busy lifestyles, and during the week, they tend to want something they can just take home and put in the oven.' He finds, though, that at weekends, the husbands who want to cook come in and he cuts to order for them.

They make many of their marinades and stuffings themselves, and will prepare a stuffing to your own requirements. There are butterflied, marinated boned legs of lamb (6 different ways!), rolled joints of beef and pork, stuffed free-range chickens, mature capretto (goat) in season, pickled silverside, all ready to take home, cook and eat.

Sausages are made on the premises: pork, beef, BBQ, Italian, Mt Barker free-range chicken. There is a freezer full of game meat: quail, oxtail, spatchcock, ducks from Mahogany Creek and venison.

Jeremy now also sells fresh fish fillets, which come daily from Sealanes.

MARCO'S FUSSY MEATS

86 Hammond Rd
Yangebup WA 6164
9417 3878

7 days 8.00–6.00
Closed Good Friday, Christmas Day and New Year's Day
Ample parking

Alongside the famous Tony Ale & Co. and within the same huge hangar-style building is a butcher's shop run by the young and keen Chris Faulds, in partnership with Marco Panizza of Marco's Fussy Meats in Applecross.

The shop has a modern feel, with much of the produce being value-added: chicken and prawn filos; lamb shank pie; beef swirls; lamb lagonda; Victoria Bitter swags (Victoria Bitter beef stew in pastry); and much more.

Forty per cent of their sales are of Mt Barker free-range chicken, so there's chicken in every shape and form. Chris has recently started to stock Margaret River wagyu beef. They make all their own sausages, including English Cumberland, and all their own pies.

A catering service is available for parties and barbecues.

MEAT DIRECT

Shop 13 (under The Royal George Tavern), 147 Canning Hwy
East Fremantle 6158
9319 8300
sales@meatdirect.com.au
www.meatdirect.com.au

Monday–Friday 9.00–5.00
Saturday 8.00–1.00 Closed Sundays
Ample parking at rear: turn into Council Place, then left into car park

Meat Direct is a new idea and the first foray into retail from a long-established WA meat exporter. Where the general trend in WA retail butchers is to add value to the meat by pre-preparing it for cooking, Meat Direct instead sell fairly large (800g to 4.5kg) vacuum-packed cuts of export-quality WA-grown yearling beef and lamb to which little has been done. You save by buying untrimmed meat in bulk and cutting it up yourself at home. The meat, which may be aged up to 3 weeks when you buy it, carries on ageing and tenderizing in the vacuum packaging and will keep for at least a month in a domestic fridge. Many cuts require trimming, but this is reflected in the price.

Whole Scotch fillets and porterhouse come in 2–3kg packs; eye fillet a little smaller. Whole rumps of beef weigh in at about 4.5kg, and legs of lamb are boned. French-cut racks of lamb are sold cap on, so if you like your lamb lean, you may find yourself cutting 150g off a 900g rack, but again, this is reflected in the price.

They also stock a good range of high quality Margaret River sauces, vinegars, vinaigrettes, chutneys and relishes.

This is a no-frills operation, but run by people with vast experience in the meat trade. If you have not bought meat in this way before, the helpful staff, Brad McGuinness and Michele Mason, are happy to advise you.

MEAT LOVERS' PARADISE

102 Wanneroo Rd
Tuart Hill WA 6060
9349 6205

Monday-Friday 7.00-6.00 Saturday 7.00-1.00
Closed Sundays and public holidays
Parking across the road

Nothing is bought in here except the carcasses themselves. From that point on everything is done on the premises by Angelo D'Orazio or one of his butchers or chefs. His wife, Milva, has many of her grandmother's old family recipes which she experiments with for some of the prepared or marinated dishes. 'Yes, I'm the guinea pig,' says Angelo, looking none the worse for the experience. If a new dish passes the Angelo test, it is introduced into the shop.

Angelo trained as a butcher with Milva's father and has owned this shop for 15 years. 'We try to keep up the traditional way of doing things as handed down in the family,' Angelo told us. So most of what you see in the shop has been prepared in this way and is ready for the oven: Italian crumbed schitznel, the roulades, curries and joints of pork, veal, ham or poultry, plain or filled with sweet or savoury stuffings.

All the fresh meat is broken out, cut up and jointed on the premises. Some is sourced from individual family farms – the pork is reared for them by Robert and Helen Forrester of Merredin and Ron and Kerry Burra, who farm near Southern Cross. Beef is from Harvey; chickens from Inghams.

There's a small display of organic meats, and some cheeses and frozen pasta. They make their own antipasto, salamis and pies and specialise in pure pork Italian-style sausages.

They make hampers to order and there is a special Christmas menu. Order online by email at info@meatloversparadise.com or by phone, and collect from the shop. Orders of over $150.00 can be delivered free to your door.

MONDO DI CARNE
824 Beaufort St
Inglewood WA 6052
9371 6350
www.mondo.net.au

Monday-Friday 8.00-6.00
Saturday 7.00-2.00 Closed Sundays
Parking outside shop on Beaufort St and in Sixth Ave

White Rocks Veal is Mondo's signature meat. Nearly 20 years ago Vince Garreffa made an arrangement with the Partridge family of White Rocks Farm, 160km south of Perth, to produce veal calves, fed on full-fat milk, without hormones or antibiotics, in corrals open to the sun and breeze. The calves grow more slowly than those in countries where they are virtually force-fed, but the meat is of much higher quality and doesn't shrink during cooking. Under the agreement, if a calf falls sick and has to be treated with antibiotics, it is removed from the herd and sold in a different market.

The great care taken with breeding, rearing, feeding and raising contributes to the high quality but so does slaughtering. The calves, aged 5–7 months, are taken to an abattoir only half an hour away from White Rocks Farm and slaughtered within an hour of arriving to minimise the stress of being in an abattoir. Stressed animals do not produce good meat, as many butchers have told us. 'Treat animals with respect; it affects the quality,' Vince says.

Vince is very opposed to additives such as hormones, antibiotics and chemicals, and some of his meat is organic – all properly labelled in its own cabinets, whether fresh and frozen. But by no means all of it is organic, and for a good reason: there isn't enough to go around. 'I started working with a couple of small organic farmers 15 years ago and have helped them grow: all our organic chicken is sold frozen and all other chicken is free-range, but there just isn't enough organic meat in WA for me to go wholly organic.' However, many farmers in WA have gone free-range and chemical-free. So Vince's preference is, as far as possible, for this naturally raised meat: 'We are trying to go down the path of all our food done naturally, the way we would do it for our families. We hope to be able to say "100 per cent natural" when we can.'

Vince was one of the first butchers in Perth to add value to his meat, and it happened almost by accident. When his wife Anne was pregnant with their son Michael in 1979, Vince would start to prepare their evening meal between tasks in the shop. A customer would see him making, say, meatballs, and ask: 'What's that you're making? Can I buy some?' 'So,' says Vince, 'I would sell it. Anne often accused me of selling our dinner.'

There are now a lot of value-added dishes: beef Swiss roulade, satay kebabs, chicken Florentine, veal and chicken meatballs, lamb saltimbocca, sweetheart lamb, pork pastry delight, veal béchamel, beef surprise wolf and beef Wellington.

There's also a team of experienced cooks under Executive Chef Denise Holusa making food-to-go, including pea and ham soup, chickpea and leek soup, Moroccan lamb shanks beef and lamb curries, gnocchi with anchovy, chilli and zucchini sauce, homemade steak pies and pasties (made with a preservative-free pastry) and pasta, lasagna and shepherd's pie. Home catering services are also available.

In the last year, this well-known and much-loved shop has trebled in size, adding a hot food-to-go counter: pick up your beef dinner on the way home.

'The best customers are the ones who ask a lot of questions. They embarrass you into being honest,' says Vince. He'll tell you the name of the farmer he got your standing rib roast from if you ask: he probably knows the name of the animal it came from. Mondo's motto is: 'For the professional, the passionate and the hungry.' He told us he has realised many of the dreams he had as a young man, but he does have one unfulfilled one: to sell a piece of White Rocks veal to the Vatican for the Pope to eat. Don't be surprised if he succeeds – then the motto could become: 'For the professional, the passionate, the hungry *and* the Pope.'

PETER'S BUTCHERS
Shop 6, 20 St Quentin Ave
Claremont WA 6010
9383 3637

Monday-Saturday 7.00-6.00
Closed Sundays and public holidays
Some parking in St Quentin Ave

Peter Bryson was among the very first Perth butchers to add value to his meat by pre-preparing it for the oven. 'Fifteen years ago, butchers were trying to compete with each other on price ... No more. Now it's on how much they can do for their customers in the way of value-added service.' Peter has continued to lead the field in oven-readiness, and now by far the largest percentage of his sales are of food – not only meat, by the way, because he also sells vacuum-packed vegies and even handmade apple pie – that has either been cooked ready to go or is so trimmed, marinated, wrapped in pastry, stuffed or skewered that the customer needs spend no more than a few minutes on it before cooking.

Everything in the shop is butchered, made or cooked on the premises, and all is of the highest quality. Peter's is much more than a butchery; it is an exceptionally good food shop by any standard.

Peter has always believed that all the meat he uses has to be of the very highest quality before he does anything to it: 'If it's no good, we send it back.' Using all WA produce and the best he can find, he's not particularly organic because he believes WA meat doesn't really need to be, although he will get organic meat on request. 'WA is one of the best places in the world for produce, with very strict health laws: we just strive for very consistent quality in everything we do.'

Also @:
Shop 68, Floreat Forum Shopping Centre
Floreat WA 6014
9387 4044

Monday-Friday 8.00-5.30 Thursday 8.00-7.30
Saturday 8.00-5.00 Closed Sundays and public holidays

M. & M. PRINCI BUTCHERS

527 Fitzgerald St
North Perth WA 6006
9242 5442

Monday-Friday 7.00-5.30
Saturday 7.00-1.00 Closed Sundays
Off-street car parking immediately outside shop

The sign outside says 'Macelleria Italiana' and this is, indeed, a very Italian butchers' shop, both in its attitude and in its clientele. This is a family business – and proud of it.

The customers, many of whom speak Italian for preference, do not come here for self-service, pre-packaged, value-added, heat-and-eat dishes. They wish to discuss thoughtfully and at length with Pasquale Princi, or one of his staff, their requirements and choices, and then have him cut precisely what they need from the joint they have carefully selected, to take it home and cook themselves in the proper, Italian, way. So the service can be a bit slow, but no one seems to mind. It is the way they've always done it. 'They're prepared to wait and have a chat. I know each and every customer, what they want and how they want it cut,' Pasquale told us.

The Princi family have been butchers here for 37 years (and for many generations in Calabria before coming to Australia), and play an important role in the WA food industry. Pasquale's uncle Michael, the head of the Princi family, buys and raises the animals on his 360-acre (146-ha) beef farm at Gingin and personally selects, each week, those to be slaughtered in the family abattoir: 'You can't buy on the phone from a wholesaler. You have to go to the farm and see for yourself. I still go every week. In the last two or three years many people, such as young married couples, have been coming back to butchers like us. They seem to want what we provide: old-fashioned service, back to basics, cutting fresh. You can't find what we do in supermarkets.'

At their factory in Malaga – which is run by Pasquale's brother

Giuseppe – they also produce the well-known Princi smallgoods that are found in many good Perth shops and in Melbourne; Princi's have a big export market. Joe Princi in Beaconsfield (see next entry) is Pasquale's cousin and Michael's nephew. La Porchetta, the popular Italian restaurant in Morley, is run by Michael's son, Antonino.

Late one Friday evening, after the last customer had left, we were talking to patriarch Michael and Pasquale in the closed shop. 'We're bred to this,' said Pasquale. 'We've lived meat all our lives. You have to be hands-on. I was first in today – and I'm last out tonight.'

PRINCI BUTCHERS
115 Lefroy Rd
Beaconsfield WA 6162
9314 2494

7 days 7.00-7.00 (7.00-6.00 winter months)
Plenty of free off-street parking

This is very much a family operation, with Joe Princi, his three sisters and brother-in-law all working directly in the business and cooperating closely with his uncle, Michael Princi, and cousins. Princi Butchers is moving to inside Princi's at Romanos, the Italian shop next door, which the family owns and runs.

Although they are not an organic butcher, Joe Princi knows the provenance of everything he sells. 'It's better to have quality than a certificate and we know everything about our animals: the farmer, the soil, the grass. Nowadays, I get people asking me where the meat comes from. I don't buy from the eastern states. I'm not knocking the other states, but the produce out of WA is sensational.'

Joe personally goes down south, as well as to the sales, and buys on the hoof. 'Dad taught me. I buy my meat the same way he did.' As well as the more obvious signs, such as breed, weight, age, structure, musculature and size, Joe looks for animals with a calm temperament, because disturbed, stressed animals don't produce tender meat. 'We buy milk-fed calves in the field with their mums.' For the same reason, Joe insists that animals who have had a long journey to the abattoir are allowed to rest for a day before they are slaughtered to allow them to calm down and relax. As for size, Joe looks for lighter animals – the meat is more tender and his customers don't always like the big cuts of meat which come from heavier animals. He told us he has found very, very good suppliers in Donnybrook and the Porongorups.

Lamb is grown specially for them, as is pork, at Lake Grace. Joe uses and sells the whole animal – including ears, tail and feet.

Three months before Christmas they start collecting legs for ham. They bone them and then cook them at the Princi family smallgoods factory in Malaga. The cooked hams then come back to Princi's to be glazed to their own recipe. They sell about 150 each Christmas: you need to order in advance, as you should with fresh turkeys, either whole or boned and rolled.

Joe and his sisters have been involved with meat for 40 years. They grew up around meat: 'We're a dying race now, the way we handle our meat,' they say. But from what we've seen, these high standards are still alive and well in Perth – if you know where to look.

PRONTO GOURMET BUTCHER

Mosman Park Shopping Centre
Monument St
Mosman Park WA 6012
9384 5062

Monday–Friday 8.00–6.00 Thursday 8.00–7.00
Saturday 8.00–5.00 Closed Sundays and public holidays
Car park in front of shop

Carlos Florenca, originally from a fishing family in Madeira, has a fierce determination to be the very best butcher he can. Starting on the bottom rung of the meat trade, skinning lambs on the line at the meatworks, he's worked his way up the ladder, via spells at Continental Meat Supply and the Boatshed, before acquiring his own shop in May 2000. Since then he has lifted this previously rather ordinary butcher's shop onto the top rung of that ladder.

This is now an affluent area where many of his customers are time poor, so about 60 per cent of his stock has had value added – in the form of marinades, skewers, stuffings, etc – and he expects this trend will continue. Carlos already makes his own pâtés, spring rolls, beef Wellingtons and sausage rolls, and his wife, Karen, adapts recipes and helps to create new ones.

Carlos' sisters, Maria and Lucia, are with him in the shop, as is his right-hand man forever, John. Beef is from Dandaragan. It is often organic and is always hung for at least 10 days – usually 14. A shoulder of Amelia Park lamb we bought was swiftly boned out for us. We also saw organic osso bucco, French-style pork cutlets, lean pork T-bones (he leaves a little bit of the fat on both of these, otherwise they are too dry when you've cooked them), homemade Cumberland sausages and pure pork chipolatas (as well as beef, chicken and lamb) – some gluten-free. All the chicken is Mt Barker free-range.

You will hear more of Carlos. Watch this space.

REID'S MEATS AND DELICATESSEN

Shop 3, 30–32 Ardross St
Applecross WA 6153
9364 1142

Monday–Friday 8.00–6.30
Saturday 8.00–4.00
Closed Sundays, public holidays and between
Christmas and New Year
Ample parking by the shop

This is a traditional butcher's shop, without too many superfluous frills, serving a discerning and quite demanding clientele. 'I just want to be a little village butcher,' says Brett Reid. As the village in question is a charming enclave in wealthy Applecross, his meat is of the highest quality and the excellent service is of the old-fashioned variety – calm and courteous, helpful and friendly.

He sells lamb, grain-fed yearling beef (some certified organic and all aged in Cryovac, which now seems to be the trend in Perth) and pork (from female pigs only) from Dardanup, and genuinely free-range, hormone and antibiotic-free chickens from a small supplier in Baldivis. His homemade sausages include the bestselling organic beef, plus English-style pork, Italian, free-range chicken, lamb and rosemary, garlic and herb. There are also some gluten-free sausages.

Brett cures his own silverside and bakes his own hams, selling around 200 each Christmas.

There are homemade lasagne, hot, roasted, free-range chickens, salads, coleslaw and potato salad on offer too. During the winter months, homemade soups (minestrone, chicken and vegetable, ham and pea) are very popular with the regular, mainly local, clients.

There's a small range of frozen fish and meat too, including rabbit, kangaroo, duck breasts and rack of goat.

Reid's Meats and Delicatessen offer a Cryovac-packing service for boating or caravan holidays, and will even sharpen your knives for you. That's the sort of personal service you'd expect here.

ROSSMOYNE FAMILY MEATS

55 Central Rd
Rossmoyne WA 6148
9457 2464

Monday-Friday 8.00-6.00
Saturday 8.00-1.00 Closed Sundays
Ample parking by shop

Go to where Bull Creek flows into the Canning River, Rossmoyne, and there you'll find an excellent Polish butcher who specialises in high quality pork, who smokes all his own meat and makes all his own smallgoods on the premises. His name is Stan Czarniecki, and with his wife, Diana, he has been running Rossmoyne Family Meats for the last 5 years.

Regular customers come from far and wide for their produce: beef fillet and sirloin, osso bucco, T-bone, rump, porterhouse and round steaks; pork loin, belly, chops, schinken, speck and bacon.

You'll find kassler, kabanosy double-smoked sausage, black pudding, white sausage, Nuernberger sausage, Vienna sausage and much more. The kabanosy we tried was wonderful, and keeps for up to a month in the fridge.

Some chicken is sold here, but no lamb.

Free-range eggs and a variety of imported Polish sauces and groceries are also available.

SCARFO'S MEATING PLACE

Melville Central
Marshall St (cnr Leach Hwy and North Lake Rd)
Myaree WA 6154
9330 9377

www.scarfo.com.au
7 days 7.00–7.00
Closed Good Friday, Easter Sunday, Christmas Day
Ample parking in car park

Tony Scarfo and his father Joe work side by side at this very user-friendly butchery in Melville Central shopping complex.

Harvey beef, Bunbury lamb, milk-fed veal from Gingin, ten different kinds of house sausage (many award winning), capretto, farmed rabbit, quail, spatchcocks, chickens – all free-range – are on offer to their 2000 customers each week, of whom at least half are regulars.

Father Joe comes up with recipes for the pre-prepared dishes they specialise in, based on the food of his native Italy. Among the regular dishes he masterminds and prepares are: Calabrese veal rolls (stuffed with Italian sausage, sun-dried tomato and cheese), beef with olives, chicken parcels (Tuscan – stuffed with prosciutto and cheese, or Josephine – stuffed with spinach and ricotta), huge Italian rissoles and succulent and delicious garlic chicken, which we tried. All the pre-prepared chicken dishes begin with a whole, fresh, free-range Mt Barker chicken, of which there is very little left at the end: the carcasses are sold for stock.

The meat cabinets are specially designed: they have a low central section so there is a no feeling of a barrier between the butchers and the customers. The service at this high quality, budget-conscious butcher's shop is both friendly and efficient, and there is a very positive feeling about the place.

SEBASTIAN BUTCHERS

41 Haynes St
Kalamunda 6076
9293 1224

Monday–Friday 8.00–5.00
Saturday 8.00–2.00 Closed Sundays
Parking on the street and car parks

Kalamunda, up in the Perth Hills, is not really within the geographical limits of this book, but there are two family-run food shops there that are so outstanding that we decided to break our own rules (if you make 'em, you can break 'em). One is Collodel Ice Cream and Sorbet (see page 286). The other is Sebastian Butchers. We will drive to Kalamunda just to buy Giuseppe's – aka 'Pip' – pure pork sausages … though, of course, once we are there we always find ourselves buying a few other things as well.

All the homemade sausages here are excellent, but the pork sausages, plump and pink, the minced pork still with some texture, with the correct balance between fat and lean, just faintly redolent of herbs, are close to perfection: we think they are a real find. Their Campagnola sausage is a favourite too and their marinated pork chops are fit for a feast. All their pork comes from Linley Valley and is free-range, as are their chickens, which come from Mt Barker. And they use only rice flour in their products, not wheat flour.

Pip buys his own meat on the hoof (we have met him at the cattle market when we've been selling and he's been buying); all low-stress, free-range and hormone-free. The beef is all hung on the premises before a team of seven butchers start work on it. Everything here is homemade: smallgoods like pancetta, coppa and their bestselling off-the-bone leg ham, oven-ready joints and pre-prepared, marinated dishes (Pip makes all his own marinades). They are renowned for their Christmas hams. There's a good selection of game meats too: quail, duck, spatchcock, pheasant and rabbit in season.

A small selection of in-season fruit and vegetables, grown by Pip's orchardist brothers-in-law Frank and Ben, and some gourmet groceries are also available: cheese, pasta, antipasto, olive oil and dried spices.

Sebastian Caltanisetta, Pip's father, who started the shop in 1973 with his wife Teresa, still comes into the shop every day. His daughters, Lilly and Sandra, are never far away, particularly on high days and holidays. 'We're old-style here,' says Pip unashamedly, 'and we treasure our customers.' We have found the service here wonderful; and *all* the staff seem to be a part of this small, tightly knit family business.

If you are planning a day out in the Hills – and why wouldn't you? Kalamunda is beautiful and the views are spectacular – you'd be making a big mistake if you didn't call into Sebastian Butchers. Worth a detour, as the *Guide Michelin* would say. If you're coming from Perth, don't forget they close at 2.00 on Saturdays, even on market days.

THE MAD BUTCHER

Shop 4, 639 Rockingham Rd
Munster WA 6166
9418 1326

Monday–Saturday 7.00–6.00
Sunday 8.00–4.00 Closed public holidays
Off-street parking

The Mad Butcher is endeavouring to sell high-quality meat at almost wholesale prices by eliminating the middle-man. Opened in August 2006, it's managed by Tony Violanti, whose previous experience includes managing Peter's Choice in Claremont.

A quarter of their meat comes from their own animals in the southwest, which they feed up, slaughter, bone and vacuum-pack. Beef is held for a month before sale and can be kept for up to 2 months, depending on the efficiency of your domestic fridge. The remainder of their meat comes from Harvey and the southwest.

Their bestsellers are whole rump, sirloin and scotch fillet; rump, porterhouse, T-bone and Scotch fillet steaks are also available. Boned, marinated and butterflied legs of lamb and spatchcocked marinated chicken come vacuum-packed. All bone-in lamb is offered fresh rather than vacuum-packed. Experience has shown that the bones can pierce the packaging.

They make their own Italian sausages; competitively priced free-range eggs come from their own hens. There are freezer chests full of frozen fish fillets and shellfish; a small selection of cheese and some groceries are also available.

This is not an area which demands 'very manicured meat', says Tony. The clients prefer plain, high quality meat presented in an unadorned way so their money goes further.

This would be an excellent place to stop on your way to the southwest, as would Tony Ale & Co. (see page 230).

THE MEAT SAFE

Shop 3b, Crossways Shopping Centre
196 Rokeby Rd
Subiaco WA 6008
9381 6661

7 days 7.00–7.00
Closed Christmas Day and New Year's Day
Parking in shopping centre car park

The Meat Safe is the sister shop of Boatshed Quality Meats in Cottesloe (see page 47) and joint managers Terry Hanna and Tom Barton, both of whom previously worked at the Boatshed, aspire to the same high standards of produce and service as that excellent shop.

Much of the produce has been pre-prepared and is ready to cook. The Indian resident chef, Amar, is constantly experimenting with new curries and Indian dishes. It is a very friendly shop: 'We aim for the atmosphere of the local social club and the excellence of a five-star hotel,' says Terry.

Among the pre-prepared dishes, the Tuscan chicken (free-range breasts stuffed with feta cheese, basil, sun-dried tomatoes and marinated in a tomato-based Italian sauce) is one of their bestsellers. Of the plain, unadorned meat, the Scotch fillet from Harvey looked excellent. They will order in organic beef if requested, otherwise all the meat is MSA-approved. Their lamb is from Amelia Park; all the chicken is Mt Barker free-range, which they buy in as whole birds and bone out themselves.

Amazingly, this is the only butcher in prosperous Subiaco; luckily, it is a very good one.

THE MEAT SHOWCASE
Claremont Fresh Growers Market
333 Stirling Hwy
Claremont WA 6010
9284 5103

7.00-7.00 364 days
Closed Christmas Day
There is a ground level car park by Claremont Fresh. There is also an upper level car park: turn left immediately after Avion St on St Quentin Ave and go up the ramp.

The Meat Showcase is a shop within a shop. Many of Gary Perrin's customers are 'time poor ... they just need to drop in and buy'. To accommodate them, the same meat he sells over his counter is available, already cut and packaged, in the fridge cabinet in the main Claremont Fresh shop. If you're *really* in a hurry, you can phone ahead and he'll have whatever you want fully prepared and ready to go: cooked to order and wrapped in foil if that's what you want. To use this free service, simply phone by lunchtime and collect your cooked roast on the way home.

Their pure pork chipolatas are a very firm favourite with the authors of this book. 'Simply delicious ... the best' was the unanimous verdict at an autumnal Sunday brunch party. Twelve guests, with an age range from 18 months old to croquet-playing 75 years young, devoured the lot with huge enthusiasm (not to be confused with greed).

Gary Perrin is an MSA-registered butcher, so all the meat here is hormone-free, antibiotic-free and of a very consistently high quality.

TONY'S HOUSE OF TENDER MEATS

Shop 5, 27 Old Great Northern Hwy
Midland WA 6056
9250 2424

Monday-Friday 8.00-5.30
Saturday 8.00-1.00 Closed Sundays
Off-street parking in council car park

Tony's is a hidden treasure in more ways than one. *Hidden,* because it can be hard to find, and a *treasure* because that's what you'll find when you get there. But once found, it will not be forgotten. Virtually all the customers are regulars, and sometimes on a Saturday morning, you can't get through the door.

Tony Palmieri has been a butcher in the Midland area for 28 years, has worked with some of the masters of the trade, and has owned this shop for 18 years. All his meat is sourced from the best local producers – lamb from Narrogin, Harvey beef – with a high proportion pre-prepared by way of marinating, stuffing or wrapping in pastry: there are Tuscan butterfly lamb legs, veal cutlets filled with mushroom risotto and Gruyere cheese, pork Florentine with English spinach and feta cheese, and marinated and herbed rabbit pieces.

Many of his older customers like to have a conversation with Tony or one of the experienced ladies behind the counter about the most appropriate cut and then take it away to do the rest themselves. 'People still like meat cut freshly for them,' he says. Many customers ask for advice and the staff are happy to give it. We were recommended the aged rib-eye beef for roasting.

We found gammon, which we haven't seen in many other Perth butchers, alongside their other homemade smoked products, such as speck, kassler, chorizo, chicken breasts and pork fillet.

Tony also supplies a small number of select restaurants on this side of Perth, in the Swan Valley and the Hills.

TORRE & MORDINI GOURMET MEATS

Shop 17, Carine Glades Shopping Centre
473 Beach Rd (cnr Davallia Rd)
Duncraig WA 6023
9246 2399

7 days 8.00-7.00 (Thursdays 8.00-8.00)
Closed Christmas Day and Good Friday
Parking in car parks

Frank Torre and Silvio Mordini have butchery in their blood. They've been at Carine Glades for over a decade now and, on customer demand, about 80 per cent of their produce is pre-prepared and ready to go. And very good it all looks, too.

'Meals ready to cook – that's the growth area since we started. We keep trying to introduce new lines, keep innovating and changing,' says Silvio. 'If everyone is putting pâté around the fillet in a beef Wellington, we might try mustard instead.' We saw chicken Parmigiana, chicken mignon, Italian roll-ups, chicken with basil and pesto, schnitzels, lamb with herbs, spices and honey, satays and kebabs. Meat wrapped in pastry is increasingly popular here, particularly in the winter months, so as well as individual beef Wellingtons, there are chicken parcels and beef and lamb curry pies.

Apart from top quality Amelia Park lamb, Harvey beef from the southwest, infused Watsonia pork and free-range chickens from Mt Barker and Liberty, there's wagyu beef from Margaret River, White Rocks veal, rabbits, duck, goat and nine different kinds of handmade sausage on offer. Venison and buffalo can be ordered on request.

Most of their customers are regulars, some coming in each day to buy that day's meal.

WEIR'S BUTCHERS

Shop 31, Broadway Fair
Nedlands WA 6009
9386 1105

Monday–Friday 7.00–7.00
Saturday–Sunday 8.00–5.00
Closed Christmas Day, Boxing Day, Good Friday
Parking in the shopping centre car park

Tucked away upstairs at Broadway Fair, Ted Weir is continuing his family tradition of butchery, offering a wide variety of quality meat and food-to-go combined with excellent service. He believes that 'self-service is no service'. Staffed by Ted, his wife Val, four butchers (including Laurie, who's been with them for nearly 35 years), this is a small family business which became a 7-day-a-week operation.

In the meat section, there is WA beef, lamb and pork, sourced mainly from the southwest, 30 different lines of chicken, all with homemade, home-devised marinades and a good selection of offal – lambs' brains, lambs' kidneys and oxtail. There's a full range of homemade sausages, some gluten-free. Everything is of the high and consistent standard that MSA registration ensures.

But it's in the food-to-go department that Val Weir comes into her own. Everything is individually made to recipes devised by Val and the family. 'We like to make things like you would at home … home recipes,' she says. Pies include: Aussie, steak and kidney, beef and Guinness, beef and burgundy, chicken and vegetable in creamy sauce. There's also beef stroganoff in pastry, rogan josh, chicken and mushroom fettucine, shepherd's pie and much more. By customer request (or was it demand?) lasagne – ready to pop into the oven – has just gone back onto the menu. Val also makes a couple of vegetarian slices on puff pastry.

Joints are cooked to order for clients: phone and speak to Ted or Laurie. Home-smoked and glazed hams are very popular at Christmas: phone your order in early, because when the book's full, it's closed.

CAKE DECORATING SUPPLIES AND SERVICES

Even though there are only two listings in this category – you will find everything you could ever need for cake baking and decorating.

MAJOR CAKES

900 Albany Hwy
East Victoria Park WA 6101
9362 5202
www.majorcakes.com.au

Monday-Friday 9.00-5.00
Saturday 9.00-2.00. Closed Sundays and all public holidays
Parking in Westminster or Hampshire Sts

You might want to make your own cake and decorate it in any way imaginable. You might even want to be taught how to do it all yourself. Or you might just want to have an expert do it all for you. Whichever – if it's cakes and cake decoration, this is the place to come.

Rosemary Scalzi's shop is a like a warren, housing every piece of cake-baking equipment, aid or decorating ingredient you might ever need: cake and tart tins of all shapes and sizes to hire or to buy; readymade icing to roll out and use; food flavourings and colours of every description; and hundreds of different decorations to put on cakes – cherubs, cupids, roses, little brides and grooms, footballers, cricketers, baseball players, fairies, cute animals.

If you want to learn how to decorate cakes yourself, Major Cakes runs a variety of classes: beginners, intermediate and advanced; flower work; Royal icing; Christmas cakes (beginners and advanced).

Upstairs, above the shop, there is the kitchen and workspace where the professional cake decorating takes place. They make the large variety of cakes themselves in an ordinary domestic oven and pride themselves on the homemade taste of their range: rich fruit cake; light chocolate cake; butter cakes, torte and croquembouche. Rosemary told us: 'We make here and we decorate here.' There are many different styles of cake decoration to choose from: elaborate or simple designs for weddings, corporate events, birthdays and other celebrations.

THE HOME PROVEDORE BAKING ESSENTIALS

35 Market St
Fremantle WA 6160
9430 9334

Monday-Friday 9.00-5.30
Saturday 9.00-5.00 Sunday 10.00-5.00
Ticket parking on Market St, High St, railway station car park

The Home Provedore Baking Essentials is just that: the new corner shop a couple of doors away from its parent, Kitchen Essentials, stocking just about everything the most ambitious home cook could want when it comes to home baking.

Bakeware and cake tins of every conceivable shape and size, plus scales, whisks, bowls, spatulas, piping bags, spoons, thermometers, paper baking cups, sieves, cutters, jelly moulds and rolling pins are all here.

And when you've made your cake, there are beautiful cake stands, serving plates and platters, paper napkins, candles (the ice cream cone candles are huge fun!), cake bases and cake slices to help you serve it beautifully.

You'll also find aprons, oven gloves, mesh dome-shaped food covers, tea-towels, table mats and a good selection of cookbooks focusing on baking, cake decoration and desserts.

CAKES AND PATISSERIE

Before World War II, it was not quite the done thing for a respectable WA housewife to buy a cake; cakes were made at home. Possession of a shop-bought cake would get you some sideways looks from the ladies of the CWA. Luckily most Europeans have never shared this view and have always gone to the patisserie or pasticceria in the old country and, thanks largely to post-war immigration from Europe (including a good few skilled pastry cooks), they carried on doing so here.

Perth now has an excellent selection of patisseries and Perth shoppers are no longer shy about patronising them. We've sampled as wide a range of their wares as our waistlines would permit and, where possible, have used a lemon tart as our benchmark. The difference between a factory-made lemon tart and a freshly made tarte au citron with real lemons and free-range eggs is immediately apparent. All the patisseries in this book have passed the lemon tart test.

CAKES DELIGHT

Shop 5, 893 Canning Hwy
Mt Pleasant WA 6153
9316 9922

Tuesday–Friday 8.00–6.00
Saturday–Sunday 8.00–5.00 Closed Mondays
CASH only
Ample off-street parking

Walking into Cakes Delight, we realised what an appropriately named placed this is. Nothing but delightful cakes!

Jimmy Hoe is a slightly larger-than-life character and obviously a consummate baker of vast experience. Born in Indonesia but brought up in Singapore, where he started his baking career, he's worked in France, Switzerland, Japan and Shanghai, often as executive pastry chef in large hotel groups. After a time in Northbridge, he's now across the river on Canning Highway, producing a very large variety of excellent cakes and pastries.

Using quality ingredients including Swiss chocolate, best WA butter, imported French flavourings, Pioneer free-range eggs and locally sourced fruit, Jimmy – aided by his wife Julia, son Gabriel and a couple of apprentices – is busy busy.

Many cakes are made to order: their new vanilla soufflé cake and chestnut soufflé cake; cakes for weddings, birthdays and christenings; croquembouche; blow sugar work; chocolate carving. Almost anything you want is possible.

'We have to keep everyone happy, so that's why we open on Christmas Day and holidays,' says Jimmy.

Place special orders as far in advance as you can: so as not to lose the high quality at peak times, Jimmy does close his special order book when it is full.

CHEZ JEAN-CLAUDE PATISSERIE

333 Rokeby Rd
Subiaco WA 6008
9381 7968

Monday-Friday 6.00-6.30
Closed Saturdays and Sundays
CASH: surcharge on EFTPOS and credit cards
Parking on street

When we called in to see Jean-Claude Sterchi he was busily peeling Pink Lady apples to make apple pies; that's how very hands-on he is. It is necessary to pay great attention to detail, he says, particularly when it comes to baking baguettes, which are extremely vulnerable to tiny fluctuations in temperature and flour quality: 'It is a daily fight to get them right,' he says. But it is a fight he usually wins, because his baguettes are justly famous.

Jean-Claude learned his trade in his native Switzerland and bought this shop from another Swiss baker when he and his wife and children came to live here 10 years ago. He is trying, successfully, to re-create a European style of bakery: the Swiss Art of Baking. 'Everything is made from scratch, the same as in Grandma's time,' he says.

At the front of the shop is a beautiful display of the bread, cakes, sandwiches, pastries, biscuits and petits fours. The little gift-wrapped presentation boxes of petits fours are proving very popular; people take them as 'thank you' presents instead of flowers.

He makes about 20 different kinds of loaf, mainly European-style bread – including their Vitafit bread, which is high fibre, cholesterol-free and low fat, and a wheat-free 100 per cent rye bread – in the bakery which is visible from the shop.

The award-winning cakes can all be ordered in advance: St Honoré, Grand Marnier, Black Forest Gateau, Millefeuilles and Strawberry-Chocolate Diploma or Zuger Kirsch.

Jean-Claude employs about 35 bakers and cooks who prepare all

CAKES AND PATISSERIE

the goodies in a warren of rooms behind the shop during the day for the night staff of three bakers to bake. He trains all his staff and insists that 'they must be passionate about what they do'.

Please note that Chez Jean-Claude Patisserie is no longer open on weekends.

Also @:

26 Oxford Close
West Leederville WA 6004
9381 1235

Monday–Friday 7.30–3.30

The West Leederville gourmet café serves light lunches, coffee, fresh fruit or vegetable juice and, of course, all the breads, cakes and pastries from the Subiaco bakery.

CHOUX

93 Shenton Rd
Swanbourne WA 6010
9385 4227

Monday–Friday 7.00–5.00
Saturday 7.00–2.30 Sunday 7.00–12.30
Closed all public holidays and from Christmas Eve until
the end of January
Limited 15 minute parking in front of shop

Choux has very much the feel of a patisserie or boulangerie in a provincial town in France. It has an inviting atmosphere, quaint rather than Paris chic, and they produce excellent cakes, fine pastries both sweet and savoury, to eat in or take away, plus coffee, baguette sandwiches and wonderful pissaladiere.

All the patisserie, sweet and savoury, including the pastry, is made from scratch by co-owner and head chef Emmanuel Mollois, who is rapidly establishing a major reputation here.

The quiche Lorraine and the tarte au citron here are truly delicious and as authentic as you will ever taste outside France. The macaroons – Choux are the only people in Perth making them and they are fast becoming their trademark – and the escargots stand comparison with the best.

The whole range comes in large, medium and small sizes and most things are available daily although everything can be pre-ordered. If your special order is very specific, 4 days' notice is appreciated.

The baguettes and bread are excellent, too. There is also a small range of fine groceries available: à la Perruche sugar cubes, cassis, cornichons and meringues large and small.

This is a place to shop early in the day if you can.

Emmanuel runs French Pastry cooking classes @:

DKA
145 Hay St
Subiaco WA 6008
Call Choux for details.

CORICA

106 Aberdeen St
Northbridge WA 6003
9328 8196

Monday-Friday 8.00-5.30
Saturday 8.00-12.30 Closed Sundays and public holidays
Ticket parking in Lake St, Aberdeen St

Corica – or Giuseppe Corica Pastries – have been producing continental-style strudels, cakes, tortes and pastries for half a century now: they specialise in traditional Sicilian sweets and biscuits, but it's their apple strudel for which they are most famous.

The long, oblong strudel is made from puff pastry, filled with alternate layers of smooth apple puree, creamy custard and whipped fresh cream, and it's as light as light can be. When you buy one, it's given to you in a long, oblong brown cardboard box which is quite sturdy – just the thing to protect the delicate gastronomic icon of Perth contained within.

Renowned for their wedding croquembouche, Corica also make celebration cakes for all occasions: these include the ever-popular St Honoré, Torta Liqueur, Moka, Black Forest, chocolate, rum and cherry cakes, not to mention their custard-filled pastry horns.

DOLCE & SALATO

19 Collie St
Fremantle WA 6160
9336 5266
www.dolcesalato.com.au

Monday, Wednesday, Thursday 7.00–5.00 Closed Tuesday
Friday, Saturday, Sunday 7.00–6.00
CASH only
Park in the Collie St car park

Dolce & Salato is trying to re-create, in Australia, some of the traditional family food and cooking of Italy, using Australian ingredients. 'Dolce' means 'sweet' and 'salato' means 'savoury': the two sides of this business are the handmade Italian sweet cakes and pastries and the savoury, regionally named pizzas and breads.

Two of the four partners, Piero and Nino, originate from Vasto in the Abruzzi region of Italy – Vasto is a sister city of Perth – and most of the cakes and pastries are Abruzzo specialities, many derived from the family recipes of Piero, who with his Neopolitan wife Alba, runs the kitchen.

The clinical modernity of the sparkling glass-fronted cabinets belies the traditional nature of their contents. In them you will find handmade bocconotti, pasta di Mandorla, mignon cakes, fresh pastries including cannoli Siciliana and cannoli filled with either chocolate or custard. The same pastry is used to make chiacchiere – 'to chat' in Italian – which you nibble with your coffee.

Delicious sfogliatella, a very pretty, shell-shaped pastry filled with ricotta, orange, sugar and cinnamon, is available in two sizes. Tiramisu, zabaglione, apple strudel, nougat and beautiful-looking semifreddo cakes of various kinds are all available to eat in or takehome.

The savoury pizza comes in big slabs (80 x 25cm) and is sold by the slice: there are about a dozen different toppings, including prosciutto, Italian sausage, pancetta, speck and Italian ham and cheeses such as provolone and bocconcini. Uncooked pizza dough is available for purchase, to take home, if you ask.

Although they are 'trying to give our customers something different; something very authentically Italian and traditional in how it's produced', Dolce & Salato use only WA and Australian ingredients, sourced locally where possible. No artificial ingredients or preservatives are used.

Some recipes have been slightly adapted to take account of the different qualities of Australian flour, for example, but this is the only concession they make to being away from Italy, so when a customer asks for cheesecake, they will get baked ricotta with sultana on a shortbread crust.

Special orders and catering are undertaken; phone and ask to speak to Alba.

Also @:

497 Walter Rd
Morley WA 6062
9378 3020

FOR THE COFFEE TABLE
436 Cambridge St
Floreat WA 6014
9383 7341
www.forthecoffeetable.com

Monday-Friday 8.00-5.00
Saturday 8.30-12.00 Closed Sundays
Parking in front of the shop

Ex-banker Graham Baker and his wife Carol own and run this excellent small family business which makes and sells handmade biscuits, slices and cakes.

High quality, natural ingredients – real butter, whole fresh eggs, sugar, fresh lemon juice, good chocolate – are the order of the day here. Everything is made from scratch and the whole operation seems to epitomise our idea of 'small is beautiful'. Whatever the size of your order, it will be handmade.

There are 23 different kinds of biscuit on offer, including almond bread, coffee biscotti, yo-yos, hazelnut chocs and their bestselling Florentines. Meringues, raspberry shortcakes and melting moments are all hand-piped.

Biscuits are baked in different sizes.

They make fourteen varieties of slice, using chocolate, caramel, fudge, nuts and fruit. These include chocolate hazelnut slice, ginger slice and lemon with coconut.

For Christmas, there are fruit mince pies, tarts and rich fruit cakes which come in five sizes, from 250g up to 1.5kg.

For the Coffee Table is a largely wholesale business, supplying many leading hotels, cafés and shops in the Perth area, but all their products are available to the general public at the retail shop in front of their production facility in Floreat. Orders can be placed by phone or through their website.

FRANÇOIS

Unit 10, 663 Newcastle St
Leederville WA 6007
9227 8088

Tuesday–Friday 7.00–5.00
Saturday 7.00–4.00 Closed Sundays and Mondays
Closed after Christmas each year for 3 weeks
Parking in nearby car parks

This very pretty, elegant little café and patisserie is owned and run by François and Michele Rebetez: François is the pastry chef, chocolatier, ice cream maker and baker, and Michele, his wife and partner, runs front of house with great style and panache. On the outside, it looks like the industrial warehouse it is, situated in a nondescript car park – 'a real ugly duckling,' says Michele – but cross the threshold and you are transported into a beautiful space which has a very French look and feel about it, with large gilt mirrors, small tables and bentwood chairs, glass-fronted cabinets full of handmade chocolate, truffles, cakes and patisserie and a couple of occasional tables displaying carefully chosen giftware.

The café menu changes four times a year, because Michele and François believe in using seasonal ingredients as much as possible. 'There's nothing nicer than something in its season,' says Michele. But the menu is only a small part of what they provide. 'You eat with your eyes. I want people to get up and look in the cabinets; to see the produce and say: "Oh! That would be nice."'

Michele collects cookbooks, and if she finds a recipe she likes, she tries it at home and then in the café as a special. Only if it proves popular does it get onto the menu.

François does most of the baking. He learned his craft in Switzerland and France; Michele trained in hotel management in Lausanne in Switzerland. Both worked in grand hotels the world over before settling here. 'It was our dream to work for ourselves in the place we love.'

The mousse cakes, made with fresh fruits in season, are very popular and something of a speciality – there are mango, passionfruit, blackberry and chocolate. The tarts looked gorgeous and François' handmade chocolates are famous with the regular customers. Everything here, apart from the bread, is handmade by François.

The bread on sale here is actually made in France by Lenôtre (where François did part of his training), then imported frozen for François to prove and bake. It is superb – proper French baguettes. Given that Australian flours are not ideal for baguettes, and have to be specially mixed even to come close, importing bread of this quality may be a sensible step until someone here perfects the right kind of flour … and plenty are trying.

They have no plans to expand: 'We want to stay small and be in control. That's the only way to keep the quality consistent.'

(This is the same François who was previously on Waratah Ave in Dalkeith. In January 2006, victims of hugely rising rents, François and Michele decided to move to Leederville. They ran two shops for a year before closing the Dalkeith shop in February 2007. So if you live in the western suburbs and are still suffering from withdrawal symptoms – like one of the authors of this book – this is where to find them now.)

LA GALETTE DE FRANCE SOUTH PERTH

Shop 3, 35 Mends Street
South Perth WA 6151
9474 9730

Tuesday–Sunday 7.30–5.30 Closed Monday
Parking meters on street

Eric Masure and his wife Nadia opened this delightful, newly-renovated small patisserie in August 2007. We had tried his superb almond croissant in Subiaco Market so we were very happy to learn that his produce was going to be available 6 days a week.

Eric wants to introduce the beautiful French food about which he is passionate to Australians: 'We are not in Paris but the West Australian audience can be reassured that they can get authentic French classics, unaltered, simple but tasty.'

The burgundy-coloured walls are adorned with famous black-and-white photographs depicting French life and underneath a very pretty chandelier, the glass-fronted counter is divided into three sections: cold, ambient and warm.

In the cold section are small cakes, *petits gateaux*, and a good selection of small sweet tarts, and one or two larger cakes. Eric prefers customers to pre-order full-size cakes (only 1 or 2 days' notice required) so that they are freshly-made and to your specification. He hates seeing cabinets full of stale cakes! The ambient section contains the *Viennoiserie*, the croissants, plain, almond, chocolate; escargots and pastries, brioche and pithiviers. Eric loves small pies and quiches so the warm section houses just that: beef burgundy pies, chicken pies and small quiches.

Eric told us: 'Working in this industry is already very rewarding. When you know that you have provoked a great sense of enjoyment, it becomes a privilege.'

Top-quality Braziliano coffee is served French demi-tasse size. Eric is testing different Australian flours to achieve the authentic French baguette without importing flour from Europe. Bonne chance!

CAKES AND PATISSERIE

PATISSERIE LA VESPA

247 South Tce
South Fremantle WA 6162
9433 5277

Tuesday–Saturday 7.30–4.00
Sunday 8.00–12.00 Closed Mondays
CASH only
Parking in South Tce and side streets

La Vespa's cakes, croissants and pastries are made using a mixture of flours specifically blended by owner Andrea Pruneddu for each item. When he came here from Sicily, where he trained as a pastrycook with his father, he found the off-the-shelf Australian flours subtly different from those he'd been accustomed to use in Italy, so he adapted. That attention to detail and his obvious passion for his craft shows in the very high quality of his produce.

The eggs he uses in his cakes come from his own hens on his property at Roleystone; the lemon tarts he makes with real lemons (and those eggs again) – we tried one, and it was the genuine article, all right. The hot weather in WA can be a problem for pastrycooks, so Andrea makes sure his work bench and all his equipment is kept as cool as possible.

His object, he says, is just to make the best quality handmade food that he can, rather than to make a lot of money. La Vespa, formerly a corner shop, was set up with second-hand equipment shipped out to him from Sicily by his father. Although the shop is quite simple – 'What you see is what you get,' he says – it is tremendously popular with his regulars.

Croissants are his biggest seller. He also makes traditional handmade gnocchi, which is sold frozen.

About half of what La Vespa make is eaten on the premises: the other half is takeaway tarts, desserts, cakes, gelati and special orders.

PICOBELLO PATISSERIE

Shop 22, Bicton Shopping Centre
260 Canning Hwy
Bicton WA 6157
9339 4122

7 days 7.00–5.30
Ample parking in front of shop

Duy Nguyen took over the Picobello Patisserie early in 2007; he makes everything he sells on the premises himself and his wife Anh runs front of house.

Using free-range eggs and fresh ingredients, his range of beautiful-looking whole cakes includes hazelnut and sour cherry, cheesecake, chocolate gateau, strawberry, plaisir double-layered mousse and lemon tart. He also makes a small range of gluten-free tarts (passionfruit and lemon) and will do more if demand increases.

Celebration cakes, made and decorated to order, include wedding cakes, christening cakes and confirmation cakes, St Honoré and croquembouche.

Picobello has a few tables for coffee and eat-in snacks.

There is a small but attractive range of gift-wrapped shortbread, fruit mince slice, caramel slice, chocolate hedgehog and miniature meringues.

PRINZ OF VIENNA

90 Moreing Rd
Attadale WA 6156
9330 3321 or 6364 3525
www.prinzofvienna.com.au

Monday-Friday 7.30-5.30
Saturday-Sunday 7.00-1.00
Closed some public holidays, open Easter Sunday,
closed Good Friday
Parking on street in Moreing Rd

The Prinz of Vienna is Michael Prinz and his wife Margie. Everything sold here is handmade, from scratch, on the premises: bread, cakes, strudel, sandwiches, cookies ... the lot. The semi-open aspect of the bakery allows you to spy on the baker at work.

All the cakes and pastries are either products you'd find in a traditional café in Vienna (strudel, Sachertorte, Mozart torte, some miniature cakes and pastries) or Australian favourites with a Viennese twist (such as the vanilla slice which looked more like millefeuille). The strong Austrian influence here means you won't find muffins, chocolate éclairs or Anzac biscuits.

The breads have a strong European flavour too: German rye, rustic rye, siebenfelder (the seven fields multigrain) as well as wholemeal, soy and linseed and some Italian breads.

In keeping with European tradition, this café is very child-friendly. There's a low, sunny, yellow table with little blue and orange chairs for toddlers, and toys and games to amuse them.

Cakes can be made to order.

PUSEY'S PUFFS

Cnr Dalkeith & Princess Rds
Nedlands WA 6009
9389 5152

Monday–Friday 7.00–5.30 Saturday 7.00–3.00
Closed Christmas Day, Boxing Day, Good Friday
Limited street parking

As you enter this delightful shop, the bell tinkling on the door transports you back to a time when everyone had their favourite pie-and-cake shop run by a family using recipes handed down through generations. This was a time when additives were unheard of and flavour enhancers meant real eggs, milk, cream, butter and bacon – Pusey's Puffs recaptures that bygone era.

The man behind the puff, John Pusey, doesn't mince his words or his meat – what you see is what you get, and what you get is a product that is consistently of the highest standard – straightforward, tasty, honest food baked daily by John with the help of his wife Sonya.

Pusey's Puffs is full of all those little cakes and pies like grandma used to make. And that's exactly where John's inspiration and love of cooking came from. His old, family recipes use the freshest ingredients and local free-range eggs with everything made from scratch. The pies are stuffed with chunky meat and fresh mushrooms and made with crisp, homemade shortcrust pastry. His sausage rolls are meaty with just enough spices – no need for sauce with these tasty morsels! The spinach, pinenut and fetta quiches, a breakfast favourite, are both light and eggy. And then there are Pusey's signature Powder Puffs – light, airy pillows of sponge sandwiched together with fresh cream and homemade strawberry jam, dusted with icing sugar – need we say more?

CAKES AND PATISSERIE

ROCHELLE ADONIS

PO Box 357
Subiaco WA 6904
0410 584 774

Rochelle@rochelleadonis.com
www.rochelleadonis.com

Commissioning a classic, bespoke wedding cake from this internationally highly regarded pastrychef is very much like asking a top couturier to make your wedding dress. It is going to project her design skills, artistry and flair — that's why you've chosen her — but it must also reflect your concept of what a wedding gown should be. So it is with Rochelle Adonis. You phone for an appointment and then, in her kitchen north of the CBD, have a discussion about the nature of the occasion, your ideas for the cake, your budget, the number of tiers, and any likes and dislikes … and then she will interpret them into a perfect cake.

'I love my work and every product I make is for those occasions when only the best will do,' Rochelle told us. Her basic signature cake is made from dark, rich, dense chocolate, layered up with ganache made from imported French Valrhona chocolate. This is the building block — or 'the house'. The next step is 'rendering the walls' (covering the cake with whatever delectable icing you choose), and then 'we decorate', which often means beautiful, freshly cut flowers, and then the whole creation is completed with silk ribbon. (If you want Thomas The Tank Engine or a West Coast Eagle, you've come to the wrong place: there are several places in Perth doing excellent novelty cakes, but this isn't one of them.)

Rochelle also makes decadent, delectable nougat, which you can buy at many of the good food shops in this book, including Wine Liaisons, Liquorice Gourmet Foods and the Boatshed.

We are very fortunate to have her here in Perth.

ROOM FOR DESSERT

290B Cambridge Street
Wembley WA 6014
08 9383 7420

Summer: Monday-Friday 9.00-4.30 Saturday 8.00-4.30
Winter: Monday 9.00-2.00 Tuesday-Friday 9.00-4.30
Saturday 8.00-4.30 Closed Sundays and public holidays
CASH only
Limited parking in Cambridge Street by shop

Room for Dessert, a small European-style patisserie, has only been established for a couple of years but we are not surprised that Will Muellner, the proprietor/pastry chef, is quietly building up a loyal following. This place is very special and Will, obviously passionate about his work, is producing excellent patisserie of the highest quality.

The extensive range of petits fours are attractively displayed on white plates in a glass-fronted cabinet. We sampled six of his range of sixteen – lemon curd, a very rich ganache, a mixed berry, a Paris Brest, a chocolate éclair and a beautifully piped, very dense, chocolate mousse tartlet. They were all exquisite and had a real taste of France, rather than just a hint of one.

There is a range of quiches and pies; fruit tarts, including classics like lemon and lime brulee or apricot; and croissants, pastries and muffins.

The speciality cakes include mousse cakes, which are made with natural fruit purees; a duo of white and dark chocolate mousse cake; tiramisu; chocolate gateaux and orange almond syrup cake.

At the moment this is a small operation – everything here is hand made from scratch and Will only has one assistant in the kitchen – so 3 days' notice is required for special orders. Quiche, tarts and cakes are all available in three different sizes.

There are a few tables inside this charming shop where you can have a coffee and perhaps try one of the miniature Florentines.

RUBY'S PATISSERIE

89A Wanneroo Rd
Tuart Hill WA 6060
9345 0612

Tuesday 8.00–2.30 Wednesday–Friday 8.00–5.00
Saturday 8.00–3.00 Closed Sundays and Monday
CASH only
Off-street parking

Paul Skinner loves making cakes. His little shop, with a big stainless steel and tiled bakery at the back, is full of very beautiful and delicious cakes, pies, tarts – the tarte au citron, which we always try, was a satisfying contrast of sweet crisp pastry and soft, not quite runny, lemony filling – and cabinets full of fresh fruit flans, slices, petits fours and biscotti. He will decorate any of his birthday or wedding cakes with eye-catchingly original designs, including a version of a croquembouche made with Parisian-style macaroons, which we hadn't encountered before, instead of the traditional cream-filled, toffee-coated choux puffs.

But it is the actual, basic, cake-making process – the blending of flour, sugar, butter and eggs to produce a perfect sponge – that he still most enjoys, 10 years after he first opened here. The wedding and novelty birthday cakes are the mainstay of the business, and when we were there the big walk-in fridges had several of each (Caribbean pirate cakes were all the rage with 4-year-olds just then), and there were also more than a dozen white confirmation cakes.

Paul will turn out a celebratory cake in a hurry in an emergency for a regular customer, but very much prefers a week's notice. He is not modest about his cake-making skills: 'This is the best cake shop in Perth ... in WA ... maybe even in Australia. That's God's truth.' So there.

CAKES AND PATISSERIE

SIMPLY BEAUTIFUL BISCUITS
Shop 13, Mosman Park Shopping Centre
50 Harvey St
Mosman Park WA 6012
9385 4085

Monday-Friday 8.00-5.30
Saturday 8.00-12.30
Closed Sundays and public holidays
Car park in front of the shop

This shop has the delightful feeling of an old-fashioned grocer. Cakes, pastries, biscuits and slices are displayed under clear glass cloches on ceramic stands on old scrubbed pine tables, dressers and shelves. They are surrounded by racks of brightly coloured linen aprons and tea-towels, tins and packets of many varieties of traditional-looking tea, jars of jams and preserves, oils, coffee, cooking implements, some of the more serious cookbooks and culinary gifts of many kinds. Stewart Buchanan and his wife Marlene took over this much-loved patisserie in 2007 and have kept it exactly as it always was.

Behind all this, in the back room, the serious business of baking gets underway at 4.00 each morning. A wide range of biscuits (32 varieties in various sizes), slices (twelve varieties), cakes and some savoury items are made here, nearly all by hand. Much of their output is wholesale, but everything is available in the retail shop and special orders are welcomed.

'Local people love coming in and looking around,' says Stewart. From time to time a neighbour will drop in with a bag of lemons or limes which soon get incorporated into the produce.

At Christmas time, the festive range includes stained glass fruit cake, plum pudding wrapped in a tea-towel or cellophane, Siena cake and fruit cakes in many shapes and sizes.

The special gift bags of shortbread, Florentines, sesame cheese rounds and cheese straws are very popular as presents at any time of the year.

CAKES AND PATISSERIE

SUGAR CUBE

Shop 1/45 Ardross St
Applecross WA 6153
9315 3252
www.sugar-cube.com.au

Tuesday–Friday 8.00–5.00
Saturday 8.00–2.00 Closed Sundays, Mondays and public holidays
Parking in Ardross St

This is a little jewel box of a shop. The cakes and pastries are so beautiful you don't know whether to eat them or take them home and display them as works of art. We ate them; sorry.

Peter Cox is the pastrychef, and Darren Agar, the cake concierge, looks after the business. He's helped in the shop by the very efficient and friendly Cheryl. Their speciality is cupcakes, which have become very trendy, and which Peter decorates topically for any and every occasion: daylight saving, shamrocks for St Patrick's Day and some for a local book club meeting when we were there.

Their bestselling line, though, is their near-perfect lemon tart, which is made with free-range eggs and the best butter, of course, using lemons grown in a customer's garden when they are in season. Not too much sugar, so these tarts are tart.

We've tasted lots recently, and Sugar Cube's are up there with the frontrunners. They are available in all shapes and sizes.

Sugar Cube also make those divine little Portuguese custard tarts called panatas using a friend's mother's recipe. The individual tower cakes looked divine; the traditional Christmas cakes, made using Peter's granny's recipe, as good as you'd expect and the rocky road ... well.

On the savoury front, there is quiche of all kinds: double-smoked bacon and egg; English spinach, mushroom and pinenuts; pumpkin and sweet chilli sauce with peppered pastry.

Many products are gluten-free and they will make gluten-free bread to order. They are listed by the Coeliac Foundation.

They also sell a big range of flavoured T2 teas, which you can sample before you buy, and Toby's Estate coffee. In the confectionery line there's Rochelle Adonis nougat and Pariya Turkish delight – only the best here.

As with many excellent small shops selling handmade food of a high standard, the earlier you place your special order, the less chance there is of disappointment.

Worth a detour.

THE PEARL OF HIGHGATE

189 Lincoln St
Highgate WA 6003
9228 9100

Tuesday-Friday 7.00-4.00
Saturday-Sunday 7.00-1.00 Closed Sundays and all public holidays
CASH only
Parking on Lincoln St

You'll have to go looking for The Pearl of Highgate, because you won't find it by accident. This small, unprepossessing shop doesn't even have a sign with its name on to help newcomers. But seek it out you should, because once you find it, you will discover what a gem of a patisserie it is.

Proprietor Nick Niederberger trained and worked in his native Switzerland and in hotels in France, Austria and the UAE before coming to Australia. After 3 years at No. 44 King Street, he realised his dream by opening his own bakery over 8 years ago.

Ninety per cent of his customers are regulars – whom Nick describes as 'unique, challenging and knowledgable' – and they keep coming back for his wonderful cakes and tarts, slices and biscuits. You'll find gluten-free orange and almond jaffa cake, raspberry and rhubarb cake, gluten-free chocolate and Kahlua cake, pear, white wine and polenta cake alongside the Plumtastic, bread and butter pudding, crème brulee and his bestselling flaky, traditional Swiss apple tart. On the day we visited, the 'special' which Nick had made – a cinnamon, ricotta and dried fig tart – looked wonderful. There's an emphasis here on using seasonal local produce whenever possible.

Apart from all the wonderful patisserie, Nick makes his own brioche and there is some Barrett's bread available too.

Nick Niederberger is passionate about what he's creating here: 'I just strive to be better every day.' He has an excellent reputation for consistently high standards. Go and see for yourself.

The following bread shops also sell their own cakes and patisserie:

Abhi's Bread (see page 30)

Annie's Bread Shop (see page 32)

Bayview Bakery (see page 34)

Fresh 'n Crusty (see page 35)

Lawley's (see page 310)

New Norcia Bakeries (see page 39)

No. 44 King Street (see page 258)

Temptations Bakehouse and Patisserie (see page 41)

The Kosher Food Centre (see page 225)

CATERERS

As much as you may love cooking and entertaining, there are times when it is more convenient and more cost effective to call in the services of a professional caterer so that you can sit back with a glass of wine and enjoy yourself.

When choosing a caterer it is important that you feel comfortable with them and that they understand your needs. Finding one that complements your ideas and enhances the style of your function is essential. If you have recently been to a catered party or event and enjoyed the food, atmosphere, service, music ... find out who the caterer was and give them a call.

A good caterer will ask you the right questions and offer you a variety of suggestions, but it's a good idea to know a few basics about what you want before you start ringing around: information like venue, number of people, budget, and theme or style of function – formal/informal, indoor/outdoor, sit down/ buffet or cocktail food for instance. When thinking about your budget, keep in mind that staff and the hire of equipment and tableware are on top of the food costs. And like anything – you get what you pay for.

This is by no means a comprehensive list of Perth's caterers, just a few of the more established and reputable companies and some talented newcomers to give you a good starting point.

BEAUMONDE CATERING
1/129 Broadway
Bassendean WA 6054
9377 2947
www.beaumondecatering.com.au

Fine food, imaginative and innovative menus of superior quality and exceptional service are what you can expect from this award-winning caterer. Established in 1990, Beaumonde Catering is owned and operated by Mark Dimmitt and Gary Payne and specialises in high-quality, fine-dining plate service and cocktail functions. From catering for intimate dinner parties to opening nights at the Art Gallery for 500 people, their attention to detail and service makes them highly regarded in the industry. Beaumonde prides itself on creating events that are distinctive and individual and guaranteed to leave a lasting impression.

BRUSH FORK + PENCIL
885 Wellington Street
Perth WA 6000
9324 3488

Exquisite food and presentation uphold Brush Fork + Pencil's reputation as one of Perth's foremost catering companies, using the best and freshest of local produce. They provide corporate and private party catering with modern, fresh flavours.

BY WORD OF MOUTH CATERING
9381 6993/0412 626 878

'Individually inspired food' is how chef Lee Martin describes his style of catering. With 20 years' experience in the restaurant industry and currently Executive Chef at No. 44 King Street, he also runs his own successful catering business – By Word of Mouth Catering.

From finger food, cocktail parties, weddings and intimate dinners at home, Lee provides contemporary restaurant-style food and service of the highest quality. Apart from some preparation, which is done at his commercial kitchen in Mosman Park, everything is cooked fresh in your home or at the function. 'It's like inviting the restaurant to your home,' says Lee.

Lee aims to keep his business small and personal and ensures each function is individually catered.

FORNO WOOD FIRED OVENS

Unit 9/125 Rockingham Road
Hamilton Hill WA 6163
9418 5741
www.forno.com.au

Since 1994, Pat Gaffney has been perfecting wood-fired oven design to combine tradition with modern technology. He has created a fabulous range of domestic and commercial ovens suitable for indoor and outdoor alfresco areas.

About 5 years ago, a friend of a friend was having a party and was planning to get take away pizzas. Pat already had an oven on a trailer and offered to cook gourmet pizzas at the house. It was a huge success and inspired him to develop the woodfired catering side of his business, which has continued to grow through word of mouth. He does lots of birthday parties and has even catered for a wake.

You can hire out an oven, complete with equipment and instructions on how to do the cooking yourself – or sit back, relax and have Pat do it all for you. He'll bring the oven, pizza dough, fresh ingredients and expertise to your home, and produce beautiful wood-fired pizzas before your very eyes. Just add some good chianti and you have the makings of a fabulous party.

GEORGES

Shop 13, The Boulevard Shopping Centre
31 Gayton Road
City Beach WA 6015
9285 0240
www.georgescatering.com

Georges, in City Beach, provides a full catering service and delights in producing innovative cuisine as exquisite to the eye as it is to the palate. Offering stylish, innovative and quality food, using the best produce available, they can cater for any occasion – dinner parties, buffets, morning and afternoon teas, family get-togethers, weddings, cocktail parties and corporate events – and will specially design menus to suit your individual needs. (See page 252.)

GOOD MOOD FOOD

11/1 Baden Street
Osborne Park WA 6017
9242 5660
www.goodmoodfood.com.au

This vibrant young catering company was started by chef/owner David Philipsz in 2003 and specialises in corporate functions – from formal boardroom luncheons, casual stylish snacks and signature platters, to cocktail parties – private celebrations and weddings. David and his team are conscious of the need to eat healthily and try to be a little different, offering seasonal menus, quality fresh ingredients and friendly helpful service.

HEYDER & SHEARS

Nelson Crescent
East Perth WA 6004
9221 4110
www.heydershears.com.au

By combining exquisite food with excellent staff and fabulous event styling, Heyder & Shears aim to provide their clients with the best function experience possible. They can do anything, anywhere, whether it's a family wedding in the garden, a sandwich lunch for six, a formal dinner at the State Library or an upmarket bush barbecue to entertain Japanese businessmen. They never fail to impress.

Established in 1987 and widely regarded as an icon in the industry, Heyder & Shears are innovative and creative and specialise in sourcing the right equipment to tailor the function. They have specialist event managers and co-ordinators who focus on different areas of the function — lighting, theme, food, service and staff. 'Tell us what you want and we'll tailor the event to match your needs and budget. It really helps to have an idea of budget. We can give you exactly what you want then,' say owners Andrew Gaby and Athan Mirmikidis, 'Our business is having a party and helping people have a party.'

IL PAIOLO WOOD FIRED OVEN CATERING

8 Weston Drive
Swan View WA 6056
9294 3293
0417 943 211
www.perthcatering.com.au

People are drawn to wood fires. So, with this kind of catering, the fire provides the focus: 'People can see what we're cooking so there is a lot of interaction. It adds a real talking point to any party,' says Vince Velletri, the Italian-trained chef and co-owner, with wife Rosalba, of this unique and entertaining business. They bake a selection of gourmet pizzas, seafood, meat, vegetables and bread in their wood-fired ovens, which they bring to your house or business premises, full of Mediterranean flavours, simple, tasty and fresh. Vince is a firm believer in the Slow Food movement and sources the freshest and best foods from local suppliers.

LAWLESS COOKING

Subiaco Village
8/531 Hay Street
Subiaco WA 6008
0419 090 903
www.lawlesscooking.com

'lawless – not governed by or obedient to laws.'

This could well describe Iain Lawless, the Scottish-trained chef and owner of Lawless Cooking, who doesn't think of his business as caterering but as bringing a restaurant to your home. Having spent many years in Thailand, his cooking is deliciously eclectic with a distinctive Asian influence: 'We had a Thai lady tell us once that our food was more authentic than in Thailand,' he says. This may be because everything they cook is made from scratch: the aromatic pastes and marinades are ground by hand in stone mortars and pestles from fresh ingredients. This is delicious, innovative food, stunningly presented.

As well as proving his skills as a chef, Lawless comes as an entire cooking package – providing not only food but also an eating experience. He loves to encourage clients to try new things and show them how to eat and enjoy the food he cooks. Iain believes your function should be all about you and your guests and will do whatever he can to help make the process easy and stress free – helping to choose the food you want and like to eat, themes, venue and music. From boardroom lunches to banqueting, dinner parties to cocktail food, Lawless Cooking provides a personalised service with clients continuing to challenge them with interesting requests and obscure locations.

'We just really love cooking and food, a lot of love goes into it. We're happy just to chug along and cook what we want and that gives us a lot of satisfaction because people trust us and want to try new food and be inspired.'

MEDITERRANEAN WOODFIRED OVENS

14 James Street
Fremantle WA 6160
08 93352525
www.woodfiredovens.com.au

Mediterranean Woodfired Ovens, based near Fremantle Arts Centre, offers oven hire for a unique and relaxing catering alternative.

Depending on the number of guests, you can choose from the medium-sized 'Family' oven which cooks 2–3 pizzas at a time, to the large 'Entertainer' which can cook 4–5 pizzas/2 large roasting trays. Both oven sizes come on trolleys and are designed to easily access standard side-gate openings and be wheeled straight in to the party or function area. If you are planning a really large party, try the 'Don' all purpose oven that comes on a trailer.

The ovens can be hired out for the night or weekend, with pick-up on Friday and return on Monday. Hire includes wood, long handled pizza peel, pusher and pizza boards, user guide, basic tuition and recipes. To make your party really easy, you can also hire a pizza chef, pizza dough, any additional equipment you may need and have the oven delivered to your doorstep. Now it can't get any easier than that!

THE URBAN PANTRY

452 Newcastle Street
West Perth WA 6005
9228 9433
www.urbanpantry.com.au

From elegant cocktail or dinner parties, weddings, birthdays and corporate events, The Urban Pantry can cater for any celebration you are planning. Owner/chef, Craig Young, will design a menu to reflect your individual tastes or you can design your own from their extensive choice of menus. To make it even easier to organise, they can co-ordinate the hire of staff and equipment, flowers and table styling.

To take the stress out of home entertaining or office functions, The Urban Pantry has created a fabulous selection of Urban Bites, Plates and Salads, which you can order, pick up, and take home. All come packaged in ready-to-use containers or you can supply your own platters and bowls. They also make their own range of Urban Produce for gift hampers, which include chutneys, jams, pickles, syrups, sauces and dressings.

TRAMPS FOOD, TASTES & TRENDS
Damon Rubery
0421 565 026

Damon Rubery has only recently branched out on his own with Tramps Food, Tastes & Trends. After an apprenticeship with Heyder & Shears, he travelled overseas working in a number of catering jobs in France, the UK and the USA, before returning to Perth where he became head chef at Zest Catering.

Now, with wife Paula in charge of front of house, wine and service, Damon is making a name for himself specialising in small, intimate occasions including dinner parties, weddings and functions serving cocktail-style food, bowl or plate-and-fork food, which is proving to be very popular in Perth. He believes food should be honest and consistent and from start to finish it's all about personal service. 'Catering gives me a buzz. We like to walk away from a function knowing we have given the client a great night and exactly what they hoped for.'

ULTIMO CATERING
Unit 3/285 Great Eastern Hwy
Burswood WA 6100
9355 1533
www.ultimogroup.com.au

Ultimo Catering began 8 years ago as a café in West Perth. Through word of mouth and a growing corporate client base, they have continued to grow to become one of Perth's successful catering companies.

Awarded the 2006 Restaurant and Catering Industry Association Award for Off-Site Full Service Caterer of the Year, Ultimo can provide a complete range of catering and services for you including innovative menus and food, liquor, equipment, staff, party theming and decorating, for all styles of celebrations and events.

CHOCOLATES AND CONFECTIONERY

A small amount of very high-quality chocolate can be good for you. The trouble is that it is hard to find real chocolate. It has usually been adulterated with too much sugar, vegetable fat and powdered milk. Real chocolate is made of cocoa butter and is deliciously and richly bitter with a lingering aftertaste.

When buying chocolate look for the cocoa content, it should be at least 70 percent and preferably higher, and the colour should be dark brown – chocolate brown.

On your behalf we have tracked down some of the places where you can buy real chocolate in Perth.

JOHN WALKER CHOCOLATIER
Shop 40, London Court
Perth WA 6000
9221 2704
www.johnwalkerchocolatier.com.au

Monday–Saturday 9.00–5.00
Closed Sundays and public holidays

The cacao tree's fruit – *Theobroma cacao* – translates as 'food of the gods' and this is how John Walker describes his large range of delectable-looking chocolates and truffles. They are freshly made according to recipes refined over many years. This is classical chocolate making, using real flavourings, such as Cointreau, whisky, coffee, Grand Marnier, vanilla bean, dried fruit and nuts. The 50-odd gracefully shaped varieties of chocolates and truffles come in dark, milk and white.

The couverture is specially made for John Walker in Belgium. Some flavourings have to be imported, but wherever possible, Australian products are used: macadamias and ginger from Queensland and wildflower honey from WA. No preservatives or stabilisers used here.

And guess what? It seems that we buy chocolate as gifts for high days and holidays, so there are special lines and a huge range of novelties for birthdays, Christmas, Easter (of course, all those bunnies), Valentine's Day, Mother's Day, Father's Day and weddings. Special orders welcome.

Also @:
Shop 300, Garden City Shopping Centre
Booragoon WA 6154
9364 7939

Shop G70B, Karrinyup Shopping Centre
Karrinyup WA 6018
9446 4300

Shop 75, Galleria Shopping Centre
Morley WA 6062
9276 3606

LEONIDAS – LES PRALINES BELGE

Shop 204, Trinity Arcade
72 St George's Tce
Perth WA 6000
9324 3100

Monday–Thursday 9.00–5.30 Friday 9.00–7.00
Saturday 10.00–4.00 Closed public holidays

Any lover of fine Belgian chocolate will find this beautiful little shop irresistible. All the chocolates here are made in Belgium, where all *chocolatiers* are strictly monitored in terms of the quality of their confectionery by the government, and flown into Australia weekly. They are very fresh: an exclusive, niche product.

Leonidas, who make the chocolates, do not box them until they are ordered, so they don't sit around in a warehouse in Brussels for weeks. It is recommended that they be eaten within 3 weeks of buying them. Three weeks! We were lucky to get them home.

Like all Belgian chocolates, they are made with cocoa butter – no vegetable fats or shortening are used. Robert Pijls, the Belgian owner of this alluring shop, trained as a hotel manager in Europe but has become an evangelist for his enticing products and can talk about them at length.

The exclusive range is made up of more than 120 distinctive pieces: truffles, praline, caramel, ganache, marzipan, orange and lemon peel, liquor-filled chocolates, and fine solid chocolate. You can buy them loose or in very elegant packages ranging in size from heart-shaped gift boxes containing one perfect praline to jewellery boxes of twelve or 30.

There are eleven different pralines suitable for diabetics; kosher, vegan, gluten-free and sulphite-free pralines are also always available. Robert will direct customers who have special dietary requirements or allergies to the right chocolate.

White, milk and dark Callebaut couverture and cocoa powder are also on sale here.

THE CHOCOLATE FACTORY, FREMANTLE

312 South Tce
Fremantle WA 66162
9335 5529
www.freochoc.com.au

7 days 10.00–5.00
Off-street parking on forecourt

The Chocolate Factory, a small family business run by Derek Wyers and his son Andrew, employs two full-time chocolatiers – one a Belgian, the other Belgian-trained – whom you can watch working their magic through a window in the back of the shop.

Derek imports the chocolate (milk, dark and white) as buttons from Tasmania and his chocolatiers turn them into rocky road, chocolate-covered ginger, handmade truffles, pralines, logs, hearts, bars, medallions, champagne bottles and a giant 3kg chocolate rabbit called Sir Walter, though nobody remembers why. They crush orange, mango and cashew nut toffee and coat the rubble with chocolate. They even mix chocolate with chilli (at first you don't notice, then hmm …). In all they make and stock 150 different varieties of chocolate product. Willie Wonka would be in his element here.

Although chocolate has a long shelf life, Derek says it is much better eaten fresh. The Fremantle Chocolate Factory is on the tourist itinerary but they sell mainly to other retailers. Derek also runs the Margaret River Fudge Company, so the fudge is on sale here; Mondo nougat from the Swan Valley is available too. Eighty per cent of sales are still of milk chocolate, 15 per cent of dark and 5 per cent of white chocolate.

COOKING SCHOOLS

We both knew how to cook before we went to cooking school – the same one, coincidentally, Leith's, in London – but we still learnt a huge amount.

The cooking techniques you learn from your mother or just pick up along the way from cookbooks and friends are just fine as far as they go but as in all professions, there are tricks of the trade – smart ways of doing things that you can only learn from a master.

But you need to choose your cooking course carefully. They are not all the same and some will be more suitable for you than others.

Some schools are demonstration only and some are hands-on, and there are many different styles of teaching. Some are light-hearted and just for fun – more like a dinner party than a schoolroom – while others are serious and are designed for the serious food lover. There is a place for them all.

We have selected a few disparate ones from the many available, mostly on the basis of personal knowledge and choice of cuisine, instruction-styles or personalities.

Before choosing we suggest you phone and have a conversation with the owner to see if the particular course you are thinking of joining is the best one for you.

The following businesses also offer classes and tours:

Choux (see page 97)
Major Cakes (see page 91)
Wandering Wok Tours (see page 20)
Western Australian Barista Academy (see page 330)
Wine Education Centre (see page 343)

AMANO COOKING SCHOOL AND KITCHENWARE SPECIALIST

12 Station Street
Cottesloe WA 6011
9380 4799
www.amano.com.au

Free angle parking outside the shop

Complementing the specialist cookware store at Amano and celebrating its twentieth year is the Amano Cooking School where culinary enthusiasts are taught by a renowned faculty of local, national and international guest chefs.

Classes are held in a large modern purpose-built demonstration kitchen behind the store and include Italian with John Maiorana, 'Pub Culture' with Brad Burton and Paul Cherry from the Subiaco Hotel, Seasonal Cooking with Kate Lamont, the Art of Pastry with Rochelle Adonis, Sophie's Choice with Sophie Zalokar, fabulous Everyday Cooking with Marg Johnson and Vegetarian Delights with Kurma Dasa. Guest chefs have included Tony Tan, Christine Manfield and Greg Malouf. The talented chefs and cooks are enthusiastic and generously share their passion for food with students.

The classes are mostly demonstration format although some, like bread making, are hands-on and include a set of recipes and generous tastings of all dishes prepared. The classes are mostly held in the evening with the occasional daytime or weekend class. No particular level of expertise is required to attend, just a keen interest in food.

LAWLESS COOKING

Subiaco Village
Shop 8/531 Hay Street (inside Epicurious)
Subiaco WA 6008
0419 090 903
www.lawlesscooking.com

Ticketed car parks between Forrest and Barker Sts

Lawless Cooking is the creation of chef Iain Lawless, whose overwhelming passion for food and cooking is reflected in his unique hands-on cooking classes.

Classically trained in Scotland, Iain says he really learnt to cook in Australia where he worked in a 100-year-old Barossa Valley bakery just because they made good, naturally fermented bread. His travels have included teaching chefs and restaurant consultation in Thailand. He continually seeks out opportunities to learn and loves to inspire and share that knowledge with others.

Hands-on classes are held in a large, bright kitchen inside Epicurious and include Essential Thai, Hot Woks for Hectic Workers, Spanish Tapas and Mediterranean. Classes are limited to sixteen 'apprentices' and include fresh ingredients, easy-to-follow recipes, lunch and equipment. Ingredients for the classes are sourced from some of Perth's best suppliers and from Northbridge's Chinatown.

The Saturday classes are held over several hours and feature cooking, dining and sipping wine with Iain's colourful sense of humour thrown in for good measure. Everything is made in the class from scratch – the Thai pastes are ground in large stone mortars and pestles, the pasta is hand made from fresh eggs and flour and rolled out in a pasta machine – and all done by you! In the evening, classes are geared towards a more relaxed atmosphere for those who have been working during the day and are popular with corporate clients.

'A lot of people walk in feeling quite intimidated, but we try to make it fun and accessible and they always walk out feeling dead chuffed – brilliant,' says Iain in his Scottish brogue.

MATTERS OF TASTE

103 Harris Road, cnr Pembroke Street
Bicton WA 6157
9319 1097
www.mattersoftaste.com.au
Monday–Saturday 9.00–5.00
Plenty of off-street parking outside the shop

Chef Tracey Cotterell has been sharing her love of food and wealth of knowledge with culinary enthusiasts through her cooking classes for more than a decade. What began in her home kitchen in 1997 has developed into a kitchenware and fine grocer store complete with a purpose-built demonstration kitchen. However, it still retains that feeling of sitting around the kitchen workbench, cooking, chatting and eating the delicious dishes being demonstrated in front of you.

Tracey's down-to-earth teaching style and approach to cooking give students the confidence to easily replicate the demonstrated recipes in their own kitchen. The seasonally inspired recipes and classes are created by Tracey and her team of experienced professional staff.

Classes are designed as a 'Seasonal Series' – Summer, Autumn, Winter, or Spring,. Each season includes Easy Entertaining, Mid-Week Cooking and Classic Recipe classes. Choose single classes or complete the Series. There is a maximum of fourteen per class, which includes demonstrations, generous tastings, refreshments and a set of laminated recipes to add to your Matters of Taste cooking folder. Other classes include Real Cooking for Kids, cheese-wine-cook, and the popular Christmas ones, as well as free Saturday Event classes.

If exploring another city with other food lovers and kindred spirits appeals, then Matters of Taste is the place to look. They offer culinary tours that are fun and informative and include destinations like Melbourne, Sydney and Margaret River – and hopefully in the future, other countries, like Italy.

At Matters of Taste, their passion is food and, whether you are an experienced cook or a complete novice, you're bound to come away feeling inspired.

UPPER CRUST COOKING CLASSES

Shop 1, 77 Colin Street (cnr Hay Street)
West Perth WA
0421 697 727 9481 4149

Parking in Colin St

Upper Crust Cooking Classes is situated in the heart of the West Perth business district, in what may seem like an unlikely venue for a cooking school. But because of its unique location, Upper Crust has a large corporate client base and attracts many enthusiastic individuals.

Owner Gabriel Zahra and manager Helen Slattery – who owned the business until quite recently – have both worked in the hospitality industry for many years. Regular weekly, as well as corporate and private, classes are held in the demonstration kitchen and cover a wide range of cooking styles and techniques. They run a monthly program that highlights some of Perth's leading chefs – Tapas with Justin Peters from Duende, Darlington Estate Winery head Chef Ben Toye, Finger Food with Lee Martin from No. 44 King Street and Sam Southall from Frasers Restaurant. Clients often suggest chefs they would like to see in the classes.

Recipes are devised to be seasonal, fresh, quick and easy, using ingredients that are readily available. The chefs are big supporters of WA produce – 'We are spoilt with such good food here in WA, it's a shame not to use it,' says Helen. Classes of not more than twenty people are typically held in the evening and include three recipes, local wine, tastings of all the fantastic food prepared by the chefs and lots of helpful hints and tips.

URBAN PROVIDER, COOKING PASSIONS

267 Vincent Street
Leederville WA 6007
9228 0507
www.urbanprovider.com.au

Parking in Vincent St

Nico Moretti, an Italian-born Canadian, grew up in London, Canada where his father, Vito Moretti, started the city's first Italian restaurant in the 1950s. Nico's background is in chemical engineering but his passion has always been food. In 2002 he decided to pursue his love of food and entertaining and established his own cooking school, Urban Provider, Cooking Passions.

Nico is self-taught but travels extensively to learn more about authentic cuisine. 'I love food, any food, and I love cooking and sharing my passion for food with other people,' he says. Classes are conducted from his open-plan gourmet kitchen, which overlooks a beautiful Bali-inspired garden. Nico's classes are fun, laidback and very entertaining with recipes that are simple, easy to prepare, delicious and can be replicated effortlessly at home.

Cooking Passions offers participants more than fourteen different cooking class experiences ranging from Balinese, Gourmet Brunch, Indian, Dressed to Grill BBQ, Asian, Tapas, Thai, Moroccan and of course Italian, Pasta or Risotto. The cooking classes are limited to ten people, 'so everyone gets a front row seat'. Join one of the scheduled classes yourself or get a group of friends or workmates together, bring along a bottle of wine and enjoy what people are calling the 'dinner party cooking class'. It's a great way to celebrate a birthday or other occasion.

Nico also escorts small groups of travellers on culinary tours: luxury gourmet retreats to Bali, food and wine discovery tours of Tuscany and, in the near future, Puglia, and weekend escapes to Margaret River.

WHOLE FOOD COOKING

13 Janet Street
West Perth WA
0411 886 614
www.wholefoodcooking.com.au

Parking in Janet St

Whole Food Cooking, as the name suggests, are classes designed to help you understand how to cook wholesome, health-supportive and delicious meals. Jude Blereau, a natural-foods chef, food coach and cooking teacher, founded Whole Food Cooking in 2001. Her focus is on helping people learn about good food and giving them the tools and information they need to make healthy eating a part of their everyday lives.

Jude's classes are predominantly vegetarian cooking but she uses fish and organic, grass-fed meat where applicable. And she offers dairy-, wheat- and gluten-free options.

There are many interesting classes to choose from including Mastering the Basics of Wholefood Cooking – an intensive 5-week core program that helps you understand the foundations of healthy food and eating; Nourishing Young Children; Pretty Cakes – Both Large and Small; and a variety of seasonal cooking classes for family feasts; stocks and soups and fish. Organic ingredients and a variety of wholefoods are used wherever possible. Classes run for approximately 3 hours and include all recipes and generous tastings. Private (individual and group) and corporate classes are also available.

Join Jude in her kitchen in West Perth and be inspired by her passion to broaden your knowledge and make wholesome food a part of your everyday life.

DELICATESSENS AND CHEESE SHOPS

Australian laws require all cheese made here to be made from pasteurised milk, even though the pasteurisation results in less flavour. However, it is now legal to import the French Roquefort cheese, made from unpasteurised ewes' milk, so some small Australian cheesemakers, like WA's own Gabrielle Kervella, are wondering why they can't make cheese using their own unpasteurised milk. Hopefully the law will change eventually but the next best thing is to find someone who knows about cheese, cares about it and keeps it in good condition. There are several in Perth and they are well worth a visit. There's all the difference in the world between supermarket cheese and cheese from a specialist shop.

Many good cheese shops and delicatessens in Perth are an integral part of larger food stores. They include:

Antonio's Fresh Continental Store, Mt Lawley (see page 184)
Boatshed Fresh Food, Cottesloe (see page 186)
Brighton Road Food Market, Scarborough (see page 189)
Carine Cuisine Gourmet Foods, Duncraig (see page 194)
Claremont Fresh, Claremont (see page 195)
C LoPresti, East Fremantle (see page 197)
David Jones Food Hall, Perth (see page 200)
Fresh Provisions: Bicton, Claremont and Mt Lawley (see page 202)
Herdsman Fresh Essentials (see page 205)
Gourmet Centro, Melville Central, Myaree (see page 213)
Michael's Gourmet, Broadway Fair, Nedlands (see page 191)
Sorelle Deli, Midland Junction (see page 146)
Peaches, South Fremantle (see page 216)
Princi's at Romano's, Beaconsfield (see page 218)
Scutti – A Taste of Europe, South Perth (see page 219)
Simon Johnson, Subiaco (see page 220)
The Re Store, Lake Street and Oxford Street, Northbridge (see pages 227, 228 and 229)
Tony Ale & Co., Jandakot (see page 230)

BORRELLO CHEESE

59 Rice Rd
Oakford WA 6121
9525 1232

Monday–Saturday 7.00–3.00
Closed Sundays and public holidays
CASH only
Ample parking

Borrello cheese is available at many of the shops featured in this book, but their own retail shop, attached to the newly extended factory, is well worth a visit if you are heading down south and want to see all their other products.

Five or six local dairy farms provide the cows' milk from which the Borrellos make their Italian-style cheeses. Their extensive range includes Romano (a hard, tasty cheese), fresh and baked ricotta; pecorino, fetta, mozzarella, bocconcini and provoletta.

Stracchino is one of their most popular cheeses: not as soft as a brie, it has a unique flavour. On our visit we tried and then bought a very young parmesan cheese which was absolutely delicious.

The Borrello family started out dairy farming and making cheeses for themselves. They have now grown into a large and award-winning cheesemaking concern, but when you visit and see Vince and Teresa Borrello, aided by all three of their daughters, you realise that it is still a family business, albeit not so small now.

DELICATESSENS AND CHEESE SHOPS

DELI DI MONDO
12 Hislop St
Attadale WA 6156
9330 3771

Monday–Friday 7.30–6.30
Saturday 7.30–5.00 Closed Sundays and public holidays
Possibly closed between Christmas and New Year

Walking into Deli di Mondo is like taking a trip down memory lane.

There's a wall of shelves full of tubs of the kind of lollies that were all the range in the 1950s and 1960s: humbugs, barley sugar, aniseed balls, licorice allsorts, wine gums and rock candy. Not only that, but they sell curried egg sandwiches and potato salad like the one Mum used to make. And that was owner Sherry and John Renna's intention. 'We're pitching towards a generation that remembers the lollies I had when I was young; things for kids that look good and taste good. And the most popular sandwiches are the ones we had as kids,' says Sherry.

Of course they sell a lot more than lollies. There's a big range of readymade food-to-go: curries, pies and lasagne to take home to heat and eat, freshly made pasta sauces, their own arancini, salads, sandwiches, rolls and wonderful-looking homemade smoothies made with fresh fruit, and of course coffee to take away or drink outside at a couple of pavement tables.

The wide and excellent range of groceries they sell include Goan Cuisine chutneys and sauces, French Bonne Maman jams and preserves, a big range of dried and fresh pasta, some Maggie Beer products, cakes and biscuits, chocolate, coffee and tea.

In the fridges you'll find antipasto, a selection of cheeses, olives, King Island cream and yoghurt.

Sherry's intention was 'to do a really good food shop that makes people feel good when they come in. I'm selling all the things that I love.' We just wanted to take the whole lot home.

DELICATESSENS AND CHEESE SHOPS

FIG JAM

Shop 13, The Mezz
148 Scarborough Beach Rd
Mt Hawthorn WA 6016
9443 8233

Monday-Friday 8.00-6.00 Thursday 8.00-9.00
Saturday 8.00-5.00 Closed Sundays and public holidays
Car park under The Mezz

Phoebe Flinn, co-owner of this smart little gourmet deli, really cares about cheese. She chooses it, buys it, looks after it and sells it, cut to order. Her selection, on raffia mats under glass, is comprehensive rather than large; thoughtfully chosen and carefully maintained. It looks a picture. 'You have to have a passion for it,' she says, 'I go round straightening up the edges.' Funny; some husbands do that at home.

As well as cheese, Phoebe and her business partner Ralph Einsaar sell fresh Golden ravioli and handmade gnocchi, and all the best brands of preserves, sauces, oils and dips. There are also pies and pastries from Jean Claude, a mouth-watering array of locally chargrilled antipasti, and some unusual products from The Grocer, such as gold leaf, gelatine sheets and glutinous black rice.

In the smallgoods section, there are products from Princis and Elmar's alongside some beautiful leg ham, some boned and rolled Mt Barker chicken and Ralph's very rare cold roast beef, all of which are freshly sliced to order. Again, not a huge selection, but what there is is carefully sourced, carefully kept, and of high quality.

GEORGE STREET MERCHANTS

75 George St
East Fremantle WA 6158
9339 7175

7 days 8.00–6.00
Closed public holidays
Parking in George St

George Street Merchants is a new addition to the heritage-listed charming enclave of streets in the Plympton Ward of East Fremantle. This European-style gourmet food shop is managed and part-owned by Alison Thorburn. It adjoins the award-winning George Street Bistro (Soren Koberstein and Sabine Treder) and is a joint business venture with them.

All the bread, patisserie, cakes, dips and food-to-go is made by the in-house chefs, using much of the produce that is for sale in the shop: the pâté en croute (duck, apricot, prunes, green peppercorns and pistachio nuts, wrapped in bacon and a golden pastry case) looked superb, as did a blue cheese dip we sampled.

There's a small selection of fruit and vegetables, including some organic produce; a large selection of biscuits and cakes, many of them gluten-free; chocolates, Norfolk Island and Kili coffee; a selection of tea; an English grocery range including Bird's Custard and Lyle's Golden Syrup; and produce from Germany, Denmark, Croatia and Italy. Four Peter Gordon (of Sugar Club fame) products are available, including his famous sweet chilli jam.

In the deli fridge there are smoked and roasted meats, salamis and hams from Elmar's; their own roasted beef, pork and lamb, tins of foie gras; and a good cheese selection, including some excellent Brie de Nangis and Bresse Bleu. Free-range and biodynamic yoghurts, milk, butter and eggs are available.

The shop is full of high quality, unusual and carefully selected items. Many of their products are unique and exclusive to them in WA, and some, like MarieBelle chocolates from New York, are unique to them in Australia.

DELICATESSENS AND CHEESE SHOPS

OLIVER'S FINE FOODS
Shop 1, 13-15 James St (cnr Quarry St)
Fremantle WA 6160
9335 5800
www.oliversfinefoods.com.au

Tuesday-Sunday 9.00-6.00
Closed Mondays
Parking in James St

Mark and Nancy Oliver had not long opened this corner shop when we came across them, and it will probably evolve a little, in line with the preferences of their new customers. Oliver's is chic (simple but elegant shelving and islands), comfortable (several squashy sofas to relax on with a drink) and well stocked with good local WA brands of gourmet groceries such as bottles of olive oils from Fini, Dash and Oliver's (no relation), jars (Food Symphony relishes) and packets (Aussie Bush Tucker spices). Smallgoods from local suppliers, fresh fish fillets from Sea Diamond, Five Senses, Naked Bean and Rubra coffee, Borrello and Capel Valley cheeses as well as confectionery including Rochelle Adonis nougat from North Perth fill the cabinets and shelves.

There are high quality curries, soups and pasta dishes from Portobello to take-home and reheat.

For local residents and nearby office workers, there's takeaway coffee, fresh milk, Abhi's wonderful bread and some freshly made sandwiches.

Oliver's is on the way to the Fremantle Arts Centre, so keep an eye out for it if you are down that way; there's not another deli quite like this one in Fremantle.

DELICATESSENS AND CHEESE SHOPS

SAS'S
Shop 1A, Crossway Shopping Centre
Cnr Rokeby and Bagot Rds
Subiaco WA 6008
9388 3122

Monday–Saturday 8.00–7.00 Closed Sundays
Shopping centre car park

When Sas Javanoski used to come to Perth on holiday, he always grumbled that he couldn't find a good, old-fashioned, exciting deli selling wonderful food of the kind he was used to in Melbourne. So when he came to live in Perth he set about creating what he felt was missing – Sas's was born in 2002. And what a triumph it is.

The shop is in two parts. The counter side has whole cheeses, hams (including fabulous-looking prosciutto from Parma) and salamis, which Sas will cut to order. The other side of the shop has shelves of pre-cut and wrapped cheese and smallgoods, for convenience, all of it cut and vacuum-packed on the premises. 'We're all about freshness here', he says. Whether you buy your salami pre-packed or have it cut to order, 'it's all the same product'. Sas only sells smallgoods made from Australian pork.

It is worth a visit just for the cheese. There is an excellent range of whole hard, soft and blue cheeses, Australian and imported from France, Spain and Italy, all in perfect condition and including lots of our favourites: St Agur, d'Affinois, Brie de Meaux and Pont L'Eveque. When Sas sells his cheese he presents it to you as he says it should be: wrapped in waxed paper, not cling film or plastic.

Sas firmly believes there is not much difference in price between wonderful, high quality, good cheese and awful factory-made bad cheese. As most people only buy in small quantities of, say, 100g or so at a time, the actual payment price will only be a few cents more for the vastly superior product – so why not buy the best?

And there are some wonderful grocery products: fourteen kinds of olives, beautiful-looking pates, Wattle Valley dips and sauces, nuts, olive oil, balsamic vinegars, Duchy Original biscuits, Good Girl Muesli and lots more.

SORELLE DELI

**Shop 2, Midland Junction
380 Great Eastern Hwy
Midland WA 6056
9274 1401**

7 days 7.30–6.00
Off-street parking in car park

Sarah Howlett and Kylie Monaghan are neither Italian nor sisters. They are, however, great friends and vastly experienced in the food world. This year they took over this landmark continental deli in Midland – which Sarah had been trying to buy for the last 10 years – and transformed it.

They specialise in coffee, olives, antipasto, ham, prosciutto and mortadella and cheese, all cut to order. Mindful of their longstanding Italian and Croatian regular customers, they continue to carry the kinds of regional specialities and traditional baby foods that they expect to find here.

Kylie started as a pot-scrubber at the famous River Café in London and worked her way up through some pretty prestigious restaurants in the UK before fetching up at the cellar door of Houghton's Winery in the Swan Valley in 1996, where she met Sarah. The two became fast friends and have since developed a number of ventures in the food and hospitality line, into which Sorelle Deli is currently being slotted. We have encountered their travelling catering service, Vanti Pasto, and look forward to its integration into Sorelle – and vice versa. The two businesses look certain to become more than the sum of their parts. Sarah says, 'It's great. We love it. It's wonderful.' We think it is, too.

They stock fresh Vastese bread during the week, and at the weekend, several kinds of New Norcia bread. Come early and you won't be disappointed.

THE GINGER PIG
40 Angove St
North Perth WA 6006
9227 8729
www.thegingerpig.com.au

Tuesday-Friday 9.30-6.00
Saturday 9.00-4.00 Closed Sundays
Parking in Angove St

Angove St has become a food destination in its own right: first with Milkd, in 2005, and a year later, with The Ginger Pig. Owned by Michelle Rolle and Jeanne Deneulain, this tasteful, high-ceilinged, compact shop has a collection of classy comestibles and high quality food products on its shelves. Small can be beautiful, and that is what The Ginger Pig is.

There is a select array of cheeses – perhaps up to 20 different kinds – which are cut from the piece: Italian, Swiss, French and Australian, all in perfect condition. In the delicatessen section, there's prosciutto and smallgoods from Princi. They also sell the very good Punch coffee; look out for it in its classy gold bags.

Shelves of top-branded groceries by Peter Watson, Stefano de Pieri, Tetsuya, Simon Johnson, Marie Claire, Jamie Oliver and Duchy Originals huddle alongside handmade products from *ooh la lah*, another small business, who only use seasonal fruits in their preserves, jams and chutney.

Ginger Pig's own food-to-go range is aimed at professionals who work long hours and have little time for shopping and cooking: delicious and healthy dishes such as butter chicken curry with fluffy steamed rice, panfried salmon with coriander and ginger, roasted vegetable couscous, risotto and lamb shanks which you either boil in the bag (which retains the most flavour), microwave or reheat on the stove top or in the oven (read the careful instructions on each item). These are also now available in a very few good shops, such as Herdsman Fresh, Boatshed Fresh Foods and Claremont Fresh.

Bread is from New Norcia Bakeries; Dorper lamb and wagyu beef from the Dorper Lamb Company can be ordered from here.

Picnic hampers, in stylish wooden Ginger Pig boxes, come in four sizes – Simple Picnic, Picnic Delight, Vegetarian Delight or Deluxe. A mid-range hamper would contain, as a starter, Ginger Pig Lavosh crackers, Barossa Valley camembert cheese, Port Salut cheese, caramelised onions and French green olives; as main course, luscious lamb pattie, salmon and dill frittata, green garden salad with cherry tomatoes and vinaigrette dressing; and as dessert, two Limar nougats and two chocolate-coated figs, all complete with table cloth and Ginger Pig essential utensil kit – even a bag for your rubbish. Or you can order a hamper as a present; choose your own or specify a price and they will make one up and gift-wrap it for you.

DELICATESSENS AND CHEESE SHOPS

THE GOURMET DELI

Shop T16, Midland Gate Shopping Centre
Midland WA 6056
9274 8778
www.thegourmetdeli.com.au

Monday–Wednesday and Friday 9.00–5.30 Thursday 9.00–9.00
Saturday 9.00–5.00 Closed Sundays and public holidays

If you are in Midland, the Swan Valley or the Hills, and are looking for a diverse, select range of fine foods, including the pre-eminent brands like Stefano de Pieri, Peter Watson, Tetsuya's and Simon Johnson, this would be the place to come. Taken over and reinvented by Andrew Baker and Margaret Cruikshank in 2006, The Gourmet Deli is a pretty little shop with open stainless steel shelves along one side and island racks in the middle, all full of elegantly packaged and branded goods. There are glass-fronted counters on the other side, with cheeses – both local and imported – and cakes and confectionery. At the far end, there's a cold cabinet of packaged smallgoods from Elmar's and Mondo D'Oro.

They stock the Rochelle Adonis nougat, handmade in North Perth, and the Pariya range from Iran, including the fashionable pashmak Persian fairy floss, made with sesame oil and pulled sugar, which looks great as a decoration on a cake or dessert.

They stock coffee by Five Senses and Illy and tea by, among others, T2. There are Swan Valley-produced olive oils and branded goods, and homemade chocolates too. They will make up a gift hamper for you, and if they don't have what you need they will order it in for you.

By the entrance is a cabinet of pretty tea and coffee cups and saucers.

ECLECTIC SHOPS

The shops included in this chapter were simply too good to be missed. They had to go into our book – but where? They could happily fit into any of several categories but we decided to give them one all of their own.

SWEETS OF LONDON
Shop 12, London Court
Hay St Mall
Perth WA 6000
9218 8305

Monday-Saturday 9.30-5.00
Closed Sundays and public holidays
CBD car parks and meters

Question: where would you go if you wanted to buy:

Heinz Tomato Soup

Colman's Mustard

Typhoo Tea

Branston Relish

PG Tips

A Cadbury Flake

Bird's Custard

Paxo Stuffing

Bisto

Smash

Scotts Porridge Oats

Camp Coffee

HP Sauce

Bassett's Liquorice All Sorts

Thornton's Toffee

Ambrosia Creamed Rice

Marmite

or a Mars Bar?

Answer: Sweets of London, London Court. (Not as expensive as an airfare to the UK.)

THE GOOD STORE

Shop 2, 363-367 Albany Hwy
Victoria Park WA 6100
9361 8271
www.thegoodstore.com.au

6 days 10.00-5.30
Thursday 10.00-9.00
Parking in side streets and in front of shop

The Good Store is a gift shop – with a difference. They specialise in being what Marshall Martin, the proprietor, describes as 'the one-stop shop for useful presents over an eclectic range. We specialise in useful rather than dust collectors.'

Apart from the World's Best Potato Peeler, The Good Store does sell one or two premium food products, because Marshall feels that 'food always makes a good present'.

From WA, you'll find Passionate Passionfruit Preserve, Eden Gate Blueberry Jam and The Olive Factory Stone-Pressed Olive Oil. Rochelle Adonis', delectable nougat is here too, as is Max Brenner Drinking Chocolate and a HUGE mug to drink it out of.

This place is fun.

WINE LIAISONS

48 George St
East Fremantle WA 6158
6424 9400

Monday 9.30–5.00 Tuesday–Thursday 9.30–7.00:
Friday–Saturday 9.30–8.00 Closed Sundays
Parking in George, Hubble, Glyde, Sewell Sts

This unique and exciting shop is a must. It sells an eclectic mix of beautiful products associated with wine and good living. Founded in 2005 by mother and daughter team Dee and Liza Jones, it is adjacent to and part of The Wine Store.

There is a wide selection of fine, carefully selected food: olive oil, vinegar, chocolate, antipasto, nuts, preserves and jams, crackers, biscuits and sauces from a variety of high quality suppliers including Maggie Beer, Christine Manfield, Simon Johnson, Peter Watson, James Oliver, Stefano de Pieri, Bitton, Ogilvie & Co., the WA Berry Farm and Crunch. Phillippa's Herbed Spiced Nuts and Dukka are on sale, along with a small selection of fresh daily bread from Abhi's (except on Mondays).

In the deli fridge you'll find the excellent Paradise Beach Purveyors range of dips, including hummus, tzatziki and baba ganoush; smoked and sliced meats from the Margaret River Deli Art; cheeses from Blue Cow; and Rochelle Adonis nougat. A new fridge stocks Dorper lamb and wagyu beef, sold in Cryovac packages or cartons.

Apart from the fine food selection, Wine Liaisons stock exclusive ranges of many European collections of stemware, decanters, art, wine accessories and some beautiful tableware.

There is also a large selection of wine books, cookery books, elegant table linen, napkins, aprons, tea-towels and excellent small, inexpensive gifts. Wine Liaisons will make up gift baskets and hampers to order: consult the very friendly staff.

FISHMONGERS

Fish is better fresh; everyone agrees. But how fresh is fresh? Some say a herring straight out of the sea at Rottnest, into a frying pan and onto your plate is to die for, whereas a herring two days old you can give to the cat.

However some experts say fish are better if they are allowed to rest a while after they're caught: one day for a small fish like a herring, two days for bigger fish like a dhufish and up to five days for an 80-kilo monster. They say it's all to do with rigor mortis. Either way you can buy wonderfully fresh fish from the fish shops in Perth and Fremantle.

But lots of the fish and shellfish we eat are caught in the north west, or down in the Southern Ocean by trawlers which may stay at sea for a week at a time. If these are snap frozen on board, are they better or worse than if they were trucked two thousand kilometres to Perth when the trawler returns to port and sold 'fresh'?

Squid and cuttlefish, we're told are definitely better frozen. Some say fish frozen whole on the trawler is better than fish that's been filleted immediately after death and then frozen.

So don't be afraid of fish that's been frozen and, when fish is sold fresh, scrutinise it to see if it looks fresh and smells fresh (eyes bright, pupils black or bluish-black, gills red and smells of the sea) — and above all, talk to your fishmonger. The fishmongers in this book have been chosen because they know about fish, care about what they sell and are happy to answer your questions.

BOATSHED FISH CO.

36 Jarrad St
Cottesloe WA 6010
9385 0611

364 days 6.30–8.00
Closed Christmas Day
Boatshed car park

Owner Tim Pappas has a simple philosophy, which he may just have inherited from Kim and Cath Potter at Partridge's with whom he worked for 5 years: just aim for a high turnover of a smallish selection of fresh, local fish, line-caught if possible; sell fresh if bought fresh; sell frozen if frozen.

On the day we visited, a local fisherman had just brought in some herring he'd caught on a line just a few hours earlier. They were shiny and silver with eyes like jet, smelling as fresh as the sea; about as good as they get.

Many of the regular customers come in and say, 'What's best today?' ... and 100 per cent of those who ask buy whatever is recommended. Tim is very happy to talk to customers, advise them and point to what is especially good. When we were there he had displayed some marinated Spanish mackerel very prominently to draw attention to it, and was pleased that customers were asking about it and buying it.

Boatshed Fish do not have a huge range, but what they do have is more than adequate for anything up to and including a very smart dinner party. If you want something unusual, perhaps for a special recipe you want to try, ask in advance and they will do their best to get it for you. One customer recently asked Tim for squid ink and he tracked it down. Buying fresh equals buying best: this is absolutely what the authors of this book recommend.

Michael Pember, co-owner of the Boatshed, had told us earlier that day, 'Cooking fish is simple but people are frightened of it. We need to take away that fear and make people confident. We have to give them the information they need.' Tim very much agrees.

CORAL SEAFOOD

Unit 5, 1 McNeece Pl
O'Connor WA 6163
9314 2033

Monday–Friday 8.00–5.00
Closed Saturdays and Sundays
CASH only
Free off-street parking in front of unit

All the seafood sold here is frozen, mostly at sea, and much of it goes wholesale to regular clients including restaurants and cafés. But Chris Dermer will welcome retail customers who can find their way here. Those who do – and he has a coterie of faithful regulars who spread his fame by word of mouth – benefit from being able to buy at wholesale prices, which are 30–40 per cent below retail. However, Chris believes that 'continuity and consistency are more important than price'.

Prawns and squid are seasonal, but many of his clients have become used to being able to buy them all year round. Because the fish here is frozen, most varieties are available most of the time.

Chris Dermer has been selling frozen fish in the Fremantle area (originally from the old iceworks in Marine Terrace) for 26 years and has been buying from the same fishermen for the last 25 years.

The day we visited, the frozen scampi from the northwest, in 3kg boxes, looked beautiful. Scallops, smoked salmon, squid and prawns are all available in 1kg size. Only whole boxes available.

This would be a good place to telephone before you go.

FESTIVAL FISH

Herdsman Fresh Essentials
9 Flynn St
Churchlands WA 6018
9284 0781

7 days 8.00-8.00
Parking in Herdsman Fresh Essentials car park

Festival Fish is next to Creative Meats, inside the Herdsman Fresh Essentials building. Like the butcher, though, it operates as a separate business. This open-fronted shop is one of the two retail outlets of Festival Fish, a big fresh fish wholesaler who sells mainly to restaurants.

Proprietor Gavin Glauert – grandson of one-time curator of Perth Museum Ludwig Glauert – has been in the business for the past 25 years. He sources his fresh fish from all over WA, but particularly from Broome and Darwin; his tuna comes from the Port Lincoln area in South Australia and Cairns in Far North Queensland.

On a typical winter Saturday morning, we spied some lovely fresh fish: sashimi tuna and salmon, bar cod, coral trout, red emperor, king snapper, pink snapper and some cooked tiger prawns.

In the frozen department, there were green prawns, squid, scallops and thawed smoked salmon.

Also @:

Shop 1, 391 Fitzgerald St
North Perth WA 6006
9228 1109

Wholesale @:
Unit 1
13 Hunt St
Malaga WA 6090
9248 9013/8916

FISHERMEN'S BASKET

Shop 2B, Midland Junction Markets
380 Great Eastern Hwy
Midland WA 6056
9274 1311
www.fishermensbasket.com

7 days 8.00–6.00
Open most public holidays
Off-street parking in car park

Murray McGorlick, a butcher by trade, buys whole fish, mostly from Kailis, and fillets them every day to ensure freshness. He leaves some whole in case you want it on the bone.

The Rankin cod, red emperor, saddletail snapper and deep sea mullet we saw all had the bright, black eyes that speak of freshness. There were some in-season fresh prawns which had never been frozen.

Garlic prawns, made to their own recipe, are a big seller, as is Tasmanian salmon. which comes whole, filleted or smoked. There is also a large selection of frozen fish.

Murray provides a lot of written information, including cooking tips, about his stock, and if you have a sizeable order he will deliver. You can order on the internet.

FRESHOCEAN

787 Canning Hwy
Applecross WA 6153
9316 9316

7 days 8.00–7.00
Closed Christmas Day
Ample parking at the side and round back of the shop

Enterprising fishmonger and architect Edward Ho opened Freshocean late in 2006 in order to fill the demand he noticed for daily fresh fish in this area.

It's a beautiful spacious shop, white-tiled and squeaky clean, with five big fish counters – two for whole fish, one for shellfish, one for fish fillets and one gourmet – and walls emblazoned with blown-up photographs of fish and sea creatures.

Freshocean sells only fresh whole fish and fish fillets; the freshness of their fish is their speciality. Some of the shellfish has been frozen at source and defrosted for sale in the shop.

The fishermen supplying Freshocean are from Carnarvon, Geraldton, Albany, Exmouth and Broome. The day we visited, the Rankin cod from Exmouth looked superb.

The marinara mix, which is made fresh daily and usually includes pieces of the freshest fish of the day, salmon, pink snapper, swordfish, Exmouth prawns, Carnarvon scallops, local squid and fresh parsley, has become a firm favourite with the regular clients. The smoked salmon, which they smoke themselves, is made from fresh salmon which has never been frozen.

Helpful and friendly staff were able to answer all our queries.

Special orders can be filled, and there are some recipe cards, books and DVDs on sale.

KAILIS BROS

101 Oxford St
Leederville WA 6007
9443 6300
www.kailisbrosleederville.com.au

7 days 7.00-6.00
Closed Christmas Day and Boxing Day
Car park opposite shop and café

Kailis Bros had its origins in Perth nearly 100 years ago, when a Greek immigrant called George Kailis began selling fish from a basket. A couple of generations later this very popular fish market and café at the lively end of Leederville is just a tiny part of his huge legacy to the seafood industry in WA.

It is a big shop with high ceilings with marble-fronted counters of whole fish, looking bright-eyed and shiny in their icy beds, and glass-fronted cabinets of fillets and value-added fish and shellfish of every kind. (It even has its own waterfall cascading down the back wall.) According to their publicity, most of these fish were swimming in the Indian Ocean the previous day; the best of the overnight catch comes in first thing each morning.

Kailis Bros now also offer many fishy dishes which have been prepared by their chefs ready to eat or to cook and serve, including prawn kebabs, marinated and sauced seafood of many kinds, salads and chowders. They make a speciality of seafood platters of several sizes to take to picnics or parties. A typical one would include prawns, lobster, smoked salmon and crusty bread. They also sell the acclaimed Kailis organic olive oil, New Norcia and Barrett's bread and a small selection of cookbooks. Next door is the café.

LARNER'S OYSTER SUPPLIES
Unit 1, 85 Forsyth St
O'Connor WA 6163
9314 5411

Monday-Friday 6.30-3.00
Saturday 6.30-12.00 Closed Sundays
CASH only
Free off-street parking in front of unit

This small, unprepossessing shop, run by former stockbroker Jeremy Pearce and his brother Simon, is THE place for oysters. Myriads of them arrive, still alive and tightly closed, mostly in the traditional hessian sacks, from SA and Tasmania (and, in the hottest months, from cooler Albany). They are shucked by hand, but with compressed air-powered oyster knives, in a huge, spotlessly clean, stainless steel and concrete coolroom at the back. The open oysters are then stacked onto film-covered plastic trays ready for sale. The overwhelming majority are sold wholesale: if you have an oyster in a restaurant in Perth it probably came from here.

Larners is also open to retail shoppers, but wholesale buyers have preference if stocks are ever low. Larners also sell fish – the Atlantic salmon from Tasmania looked superb – and scallops and blue swimmer crabs, caught in Shark Bay and steamed on the crab-boats at sea, are also very popular. After 10 years in North Fremantle, Larners moved here about 2 years ago. If you haven't tracked them down yet, they are well worth a visit.

MELVILLE SEAFOODS

Shop 12, Melville Central
7 Marshall St (cnr Leach Hwy and North Lake Rd)
Myaree WA 6154
9317 7788

7 days 7.00-7.00
Closed Good Friday, Easter Sunday, Christmas Day
Parking in adjoining car parks

There's a wealth of experience in and around WA fish, so it's very heartening to see a young man in his early twenties making the kind of impression that Kevin White is doing at Melville Seafoods.

The speciality here is the Shark Bay crabs, which are either steamed as soon as they are caught or sent to him alive and kicking. And very beautiful and fresh they look too.

Apart from his bestselling fresh Tasmanian salmon (of the quality you can eat raw), there's plenty of top quality choice here: whole fish, filleted fish, garfish, swordfish, tuna, shark, snapper, whiting; prawns, oysters and crayfish; scallops, octopus, squid and mussels; and three separate stands of free recipes.

A very large variety of live fish are available from the tank, and the staff will prepare them for you ... that's about as fresh as it gets. We saw blue manna crabs, pink snapper, yellowtail kingfish, mud crabs, live bugs, mulloway, black bream, live crays, king prawns, snow crabs, marron, river trout, eels, yabbies, barramundi and silver perch.

Sushi is made daily by their sushi chef Margaret Chong, and there is a value-added cabinet containing a large variety of pre-prepared and marinated seafood, made on the premises by the staff.

Kevin started his career at Peel Fisheries, then moved into Melville to work for the two previous owners of this business, which he then bought in 2004. He's keen to educate his customers about the seasonality of fish and to encourage them to 'try something new and different'.

MY LITTLE FISH SHOP

Shop 20, Bicton Shopping Centre
258 Canning Hwy (cnr Petra St)
Bicton WA 6153
9339 3800

7 days 9.00-6.30
Closed Christmas Day
Ample off-street parking

Ben Sheridan definitely believes that 'frozen is the new fresh' when it comes to selling fish in WA. His gleaming white antiseptically clean shop is lined with fifteen glass-topped chest freezers containing a massive selection – 150 varieties – of frozen fish and seafood. We saw crayfish, lobster, crabs, tuna, snapper, trout, trevally, cod, pomfret, dhufish, groper, orange roughy and swordfish and many different kinds of prawns, both cooked and raw, as well as a selection of crumbed products. A Chinese section included soft-shell crabs.

He has a small selection of fresh, locally caught fish including, on the day of our visit, red emperor fillets, crimson snapper fillets, mussels, oysters and fresh Tasmanian salmon, all of which looked sparklingly fresh.

There's a cabinet containing jars of marinated octopus, yabbies, imported crab meat, salmon caviar, and Maggie Beer smoked salmon pâté. Shelves of Zephyr olive oil, Maggie Beer verjuice, mayo, batter mixes and sauces to accompany fish complete the display.

PANSINI SEAFOODS

137 Carrington St (cnr of Hope St)
White Gum Valley WA 6162
9335 5095

Wednesday–Sunday 9.00–5.00
Closed Mondays and Tuesdays
CASH only
Plenty of parking on slip road in front of house

Con Pansini's Fish Shop, which he owns and runs with his wife Chiara, is in the basement of their family home.

After 20 years in Fremantle Markets, he had hoped for a quieter life, working from home. But no, 5 years on, he's busier than ever.

The small shop is packed with fridges, full of locally caught fresh fish, much of it filleted and prepared. If it's labelled FRESH, it means it has never been frozen – 'The biggest thing with the customers is to be honest with them.'

Supplied by ten individual fishermen, all Con's produce is of the highest quality: local crabs and crays, oysters from Albany, Ceduna and Tasmania, fresh fish fillets including coral cod, boneless pearl perch, baby snapper, scarlet perch, pink snapper, boneless groper, dhufish, red emperor and deep sea mullet, fresh salmon and smoked salmon from Tasmania, locally smoked whole trout, local herring, garfish, Freo sardines (cleaned or whole), fresh whiting, and cooked crabs. Large whole fish will be cleaned on request.

We sampled a deep sea mullet, which we baked whole, and some fresh Tasmanian salmon which we mixed with smoked salmon and served raw as salmon tartar. Only the freshest fish stands the test of being served raw: this passed with flying colours.

They also sell frozen crab meat, prawns, shellfish and fillets.

Christmas and Easter are the busiest times: last year they packed nearly 400 orders and Con shucked 1400 dozen oysters over the pre-Christmas weekend. They offer an old-fashioned, personal service of very high quality.

PARTRIDGES

Unit 1, 2a Loch St
Nedlands WA 6009
9389 9600

Monday-Friday 2.00-6.00
Saturday 10.00-2.00 Closed Sundays and public holidays
Parking across the road in Grosvenor St

Partridges has a tiny shopfront, tucked away behind the cemetery, and is attached to the wholesale business which supplies hotels and restaurants. They offer a limited range – eight or ten fish, which change pretty well daily, but what they have is the absolute tops.

Kim and Cathy Potter deal in wet line-caught fish which has been properly handled and bled. Because the fish is line-caught, it is not all the same size, and customers are sometimes a bit surprised to discover that if they buy half a dozen King George whiting, no two are identical. But that's one of the joys of buying at this kind of shop. All their fish is sashimi quality, because they supply a number of Japanese restaurants.

We suggest that you come here with an open mind rather than pre-conceived ideas of a specific fish you might want for a special recipe – there are plenty of other good places around with larger selections – and ask their knowledgeable and experienced staff: 'What have you got? What's best today? What should I buy?' We did just that and came away with a couple of fresh baldchin groper fillets (sometimes called bluebone groper) from Kalbarri. It was a big-flaked, white, firm fish, and was one of the most delicious fish-eating experiences ever.

When the Potters set up their business 20 years ago they were the first to import Tassie salmon into WA, and it's still a big seller. Partridges also sell fish and shellfish frozen at sea, including prawns, squid and scallops. 'If it comes in fresh, we sell it fresh. If it comes in frozen, we sell it frozen.' Whole ducks, poussin and French-style magret of duck, in packs of five or ten, are available frozen.

SEAFOOD SECRETS

Shop 306, Garden City Shopping Centre
125 Riseley St
Booragoon WA 6154
9315 5931
www.seafoodsecrets.com.au

Monday–Wednesday + Friday 9.00–5.30 Thursday 9.00–9.00
Saturday 9.00–5.00 Closed Sundays and public holidays
Ample, shady, car parks

This is the new way to buy fish, particularly for anyone who is not confident about it ... and there's no smell.

Seafood Secrets is a clean, bright, white space with glass-topped and glass-fronted freezers and accessible chilled open shelving containing many kinds of fish, ready portioned and in transparent packaging. But it's the labels that are so helpful and which answer many of the questions one would normally ask a fishmonger.

Each fish label gives you: the name of the fish; the best by or use by date; whether it's bone in or 100 per cent boneless or de-boned; the place of origin; how the fish was caught (by line or by trawl); grading specifications (weight and price to you and me); the Omega oil levels; and process branding (for example: Chilled – Never Frozen, or Cryo-Tech, or Opti-freeze).

After selecting your fish, there is further help available, if you want it. Decide how you want to cook your fish (bake, shallow fry, grill, steam etc). Then select how and when you wish to flavour your fish. The options are: before cooking (marinades, spices, pastes or crumb coatings); during cooking (cook-in sauces and oils for liquids); and after cooking (finishing sauces and oils). All of this range, called Ocean Flavours, is colour coded and has easy-to-follow instructions on the packet.

If you are using this label method for the first time, there's a Seafood Consultant and friendly staff to help you.

There's also a selection of healthy seafood meals, ready to go and be reheated at home.

SEAFRESH CLAREMONT

26 St Quentin Ave
Claremont WA 6010
9383 2031

7 days 8.00–6.30
Closed Christmas Day
Car park outside shop

After 23 years in the fish business Peter Lynch proudly boasts that he's never bought a product out of a fish market. 'We source everything ourselves. I want every customer of mine to have an experience. I want to sell them the best fish, which they can take home and cook well. It's our job to source that product.' Peter shows the same determination as his brother Louis (see next entry) to sell only the very best fresh fish.

Peter thinks there are many people who would like to eat fish, but because they have either had one bad experience buying and cooking it or are a bit frightened of it, they tend to go to restaurants instead. However, he firmly believes that if they bought the best, freshest fish available, took it home and cooked it simply, they wouldn't need to go to restaurants. Peter only stocks Grade A, in-season fresh fish – 'fat, healthy and sweet'. Buying anything other than the freshest and best means 'all you are doing is a rescue job'.

There is a counter of 30 or more varieties of fresh fish fillets and steaks, a counter of about ten types of whole WA fish (and some very fresh-looking whole Tasmanian salmon), a cabinet full of different varieties of smoked fish, one of oriental-style cuts and accompaniments to sashimi, plus cooked crabs and crays, Ceduna mussels and oysters, and one of pre-prepared seafood.

When we visited, Peter recommended either the scallops from Shark Bay, the 'beautiful, beautiful squid from up north' or the Exmouth prawns which had just 'hit Perth'.

SEAFRESH INNALOO

Innaloo Shopping Village
Cnr Scarborough Beach Rd and Ellen Stirling Bvd
Innaloo WA 6018
9445 2451

364 days 9.00–6.30
Parking in shopping centre car park

Louis Lynch had just completed a tour of 60 fish markets and shops throughout Australia when we met him, and was understandably pleased to discover that his shop 'had the largest variety of seafood in Australia'. We had no trouble at all believing that when we visited this paragon among fish shops. Counter after spotless counter displayed row on row of whole fish and fish fillets, nestling on crushed ice – far too many to count, all fresh and mostly local. The Atlantic Tasmanian salmon was farmed, of course, but almost everything else was wild. Louis' prawns, six or eight varieties, are caught at sea, cooked on board the trawlers in salt water and sent south. He says they are far superior to prawns farmed in Asia. They certainly looked beautiful, blushing pink on their frosty beds.

Louis and his partner hold one of the last commercial fishing licences for the Swan River, so there were blue manna crabs, black bream, mullet and whiting from Point Walter and other fruitful fishing spots. 'There's plenty of fish in the river,' he says. 'This must mean the water is still clean and salty.'

As well as the huge variety of fresh fish, we saw an unusually large and enticing selection of seafood to which value had been added in the form of marinades and sauces, plus sashimi, sushi and kebabs, as well as ready-cooked meals such as fish soups and chowders. Both the tom yum and the seafood chowder we tried were delicious. There are fishy dips, too, all made by the resident full-time chef.

Since Louis took over, in a very hands-on way, his staff has grown from three to 45, and his turnover is now about 30 times greater than it was in 1989. He attributes his success, in part at least, to his 'dedication to buying correctly' and to his real passion for providing a standard that is 'just a little bit higher than the public is expecting'. As a result, though many customers initially just come in for a piece of fillet, most leave with much more.

Louis, his wife Naomi and his brother Peter (see previous entry) have thought long and hard about fish, fishing and fishmongering, and very much want to pass on this knowledge to their customers via the staff: 'Fish is seasonal,' he says, 'but not everyone knows that. For example, pink snapper is not really available all year round. In April and May, before the breeding season, they eat as much as they can and are fat and superb, but by August and September they have lost that condition and are not as good. We'd like customers to buy something else then.'

Go there and ask their advice; you won't regret it.

SEALANES

178 Marine Tce
South Fremantle WA 6959
9432 8851

7 days 8.00–6.00
Closed Christmas Day
Ample parking

Walking through the door at Sealanes and seeing their sparkling array of beautifully fresh fish and seafood ahead of you, you know instantly that you have entered a very classy establishment. Everything here is at the peak of freshness, the staff are professional and helpful, and the spacious shop is well designed to enable you to walk around and see everything that is on offer before you choose what to have.

You can buy whole fish, which they will clean and scale for you. There is a very good selection of fresh fish fillets: king, red and baby snapper, Tasmanian salmon (skin on or off), swordfish from Geraldton, orange roughy from Albany. There is also a large range of prawns, crays, scallops, crabs, smoked salmon and an increasing number of pre-prepared dishes. Dai, their in-house Japanese chef, is in charge: there's sushi, Thai fish parcels, marinated mussels on the half-shell, seafood omelette, fish kebabs and lots more. The shop manager, Manuel Canada, says that as much as 25 per cent of their sales are now of pre-prepared fish; he encourages feedback from his many regular customers.

Sealanes have recently extended their stock of gourmet products: accompaniments for fish, sauces, vinaigrettes, dressings, olive oils, honey and chocolate. These are sourced locally where possible.

Friendly advice is on offer to customers who are planning a party or a barbecue: what will be in season, what to buy, how much to buy and how to cook it.

Barbecue packs, ice and a small quantity of frozen fish and shellfish are also available.

SOUTH PERTH SEAFOODS
298 Mill Point Rd
South Perth WA 6151
9474 3112

7 days 9.30-7.00
Closed some public holidays (phone to check)
Car park outside shop

Bruno Bini started his career as a professional fisherman 23 years ago and still has many friends on the boats who phone him when they have caught something they think he and his wife, Kylie, would like to sell in this light, bright shop with its murals of undersea life on the walls.

So about half their stock is freshly caught local fish, some direct from the fishermen and some from wholesalers. They sell whole fish, freshly filleted fish, frozen and Cryovac fish and fillets. There is also a big tank of live crayfish, crabs, mussels and oysters and – his speciality – Bruno will shuck the oysters for you while you wait.

Bruno and Kylie had just taken over this shop when we visited in early 2007. They are planning a few changes, so by the time you read this, they will probably have increased the size of the fresh fish display while maintaining the size and quality of the frozen.

Bruno is passionate about obtaining the freshest local fish possible. If there is anything you particularly want, just ring and ask and he will very likely be able to source it. Otherwise, this is the sort of place to come and ask: 'What's best today?'

SPLASH'S FISH HOUSE

Shop 16, Carine Glades Shopping Centre
473 Beach Rd
Duncraig WA 6023
9447 7133

7 days 8.00–8.00
Closed Christmas Day
Parking in car park

Sasha Spasevski, who owns and runs Splash's Fish House, is the longest serving tenant at Carine Glades. His long glass-fronted L-shaped counter displays the fish — both wet and gourmet prepared — to good advantage. Everything is done in store here and it all looks appetising and interesting.

Home, hot-smoked Tasmanian salmon, first soaked in brine then smoked over jarrah sawdust for 30 minutes, is a speciality. Sasha gives the salmon a very light smoke so that the delicate taste isn't swamped. The piece we sampled — still very moist inside and a beautiful rosy pink colour like salmon gum — was seriously good.

Uncooked fresh wet fish, bought whole daily from the markets and filleted on the premises, includes: yellow fin tuna, Darwin barramundi, Rankin cod, saddletail snapper, dhufish, red emperor and Tasmanian salmon. Other varieties are available according to the seasons.

In the cold, cooked department there's gourmet salmon shepherd's pie, snapper mornay, several kinds of fish cakes and fish balls, salmon risotto, chilli mussels, squid and cuttlefish, garlic octopus, tuna bake pasta, snapper and crab Scotch egg (invented by Sasha's mother, Tina). There's a complementary selection of prepared salads: chargrilled vegies, rice, potato, and coleslaw, plus a pretty seafood one.

We took home some chilli-marinated wings of red emperor: quick, easy, and very yummy.

And of course, fish and chips, cooked to order.

SWISH 'N' CHIPS

Alexander Buildings
Unit 5, 71 Walcott St (cnr Beaufort St)
Mt Lawley WA 6050
9227 8132

Fresh fish: 7 days 9.30–7.00
Food-to-go: 7 days 11.30–2.30; 4.30–8.30
Car park behind shop in Raglan Rd

Swish 'n' Chips is much more than an award-winning fish and chip shop: their selection of fresh fish and shellfish, pre-prepared seafood meals to go, salads and daily specials are aimed at those who have little time to produce a healthy fish meal themselves but who are happy to have former professional chefs (and brothers) Jason and Graeme Robertson do the work for them.

In the fresh fish department, there is an emphasis on seasonal and local fish: fillets of red emperor, pink snapper, Tasmanian salmon, red throat emperor, swordfish, saddletail snapper and swordfish. The fresh crab meat, prepared sardines, live crays, freshly cooked tiger prawns and wild barramundi all looked wonderful.

In the value-added section we saw garlic prawn skewers, scallops wrapped in bacon, fish parcels and Thai fish cakes. Their home hot-smoked salmon is a big seller.

In the food-to-go section, the daily specials were seafood risotto, teriyaki fish, chilli mussels, seafood chowders and pasta.

Eight different prepared salads, beautifully displayed on large white plates, make up the salad cabinet. These are some of the very best we have seen and it was easy to spot that they had been made by professional chefs. They included rice, beetroot, Mediterranean, Greek and green bean salads and ratatouille and coleslaw.

Jason and Graeme are helped in the running of this small family business by their wives Anita and Kylie. Everything here is handmade on the premises – as Jason says, 'From the mayo upwards ...' And very good it all is too.

THE FREMANTLE FISH MARKET

Stalls 11/12, Fremantle Markets
Cnr Henderson St and South Tce
Fremantle WA 6160

Friday 9.00-9.00
Saturday 9.00-5.00 Sunday 10.00-5.00
Mondays and public holidays 10.00-5.00
Closed Good Friday
CASH only
Parking in surrounding car parks: Henderson St, Parry St

Bob Williams, a veteran of all aspects of Freo maritime life, took over the Fish Market stalls in early 2007 and has since extensively refurbished this corner of the market.

He's concentrating on selling fresh, local fish and shellfish, prawns and oysters, sourced from Canning Vale Market, Sealanes and a few local fishermen.

He's had a sardine business for many years, which is now run by his son; they catch, fillet, smoke and marinate their own sardines, prawns and octopus – all of which are on sale here.

THE GROPER AND HIS WIFE

Shop 14, The Boulevard Shopping Centre
31 Gayton Rd
City Beach WA 6015
9385 7384

Monday, Wednesday–Sunday 11.00–8.00 Closed Tuesdays
Closed Christmas Day and Boxing Day
Ample parking in shopping centre car park

This is a famous fish and chip shop but it also offers a unique service: you can buy raw – to take home and cook yourself – any of the fresh fish which they are cooking that day for takeaway fish and chips.

For the last 3 years, The Groper and His Wife has been Joe and Fiona Drabble: 'Fiona and I just love good food – fresh, local produce, with no preservatives – yummy food!' So all the fish for sale is local and fresh. Joe told us when we were there that 'today, the pink snapper is sensational'.

Not only can you buy this wonderful fresh fish here; they also sell a very extensive selection of salads, made daily on the premises by Trang, who uses WA produce wherever possible. There's garden salad, seafood, Greek, potato, pasta, wild rice, coleslaw, and Caesar salads, plus grilled pumpkin, couscous, Moroccan chick pea, artichoke, marinated prawn and marinated octopus salads.

Joe and Fiona make all the marinades, mayonnaise and dressings themselves.

The Groper and His Wife has a large number of very regular customers, some of whom travel far to buy their consistently high quality produce: 'If we wouldn't eat it or serve it to our guests at home, we don't sell it.'

WORLDWIDE SEAFOODS

1 Pritchard Rd
O'Connor WA 6163
9331 1677

Monday–Saturday 8.00–5.00
Sunday 8.00–4.00
CASH only
Parking by shop adjacent to wholesale operation

Jim Nikoloudis and his friend, the late Ricky Merlino, opened this small shop, next to his wholesale fresh and frozen seafood business, almost by accident, but now, after more years than he wishes to remember, it's still there. He says: 'Like a mousetrap, it's easy to get in but hard to get out.'

The live blue manna crabs from Mandurah, on the day we went in March, were as big and beautiful as we've ever seen in a WA fish shop. Jim told us that they were the best he'd ever sold. The nanny gai which we bought – just in from Albany, as fresh as can be, with their glass-like scales shining crimson and their big, bright, black eyes – were a picture, and tasted delicious, simply grilled with a drizzle of lemon, cracked black pepper and a sprinkling of lake salt.

A big tub of fat black mussels from SA was tempting, and there were prawns, both raw and cooked, lovely-looking fresh octopus, whole pink snapper, some very fresh local herrings and a smallish range of fish already filleted.

Our visit was early in the week, and a day or two after Cyclone George had kept the northwest trawlers in port, but this information was offered as an explanation for his limited stock, rather than an apology. Even at the best of times, Jim Nikoloudis, a somewhat reluctant entrant in this book but one we very much wanted to include because of the high quality of his product, pointed out that he normally has only a small range available, and while retail customers are welcome (many are friends), his is essentially a wholesale business – the retail shop attached to his cold stores very much takes second place.

FLORISTS

Flowers are a fresh product and are subject to nature's whims – some seasons are better than others, one crop can be a dud, the next a delight.

Fresh flowers may seem expensive in WA and to a degree they are – a result of a small population, few local growers and transport costs. And, like most things, you get what you pay for.

If you want to buy a bunch of a single type of flower, such as lilies or irises, a supermarket that stocks fresh flowers is a convenient option. Remember, though the flowers may be slightly cheaper, they may not have been processed to purchase – stripped of leaves below the tying point, trimmed and placed into clean buckets of fresh water and refrigerated at the end of the day. A good tip is to find out the day the flowers are delivered and purchase on that day or the day after.

For quality assurance and personal service, find a florist you like and become a regular client. Like your favourite butcher or baker, your florist can supply you not only with fresh flowers, but also with information on flower care and inspiration for a special occasion. And your florist will try to source your favourite blooms. A good florist will help you choose the right flowers to suit the occasion and your budget.

A FEW TIPS TO CONSIDER WHEN CHOOSING A FLORIST:

- Look for a style that complements your own, as well as the design skills to offer a variety of styles to suit a variety of occasions.

- How are the flowers presented? Look for clean buckets and vases, clean water, free of loose debris.

- Check that bunches are stripped of leaves below the tying point.

- Check that flowers are stored correctly, for example in a coolroom for most flowers and at room temperature for tropicals.

- Check the amount of flowers on display. Having lots may look wonderful, but don't be fooled. It could mean the florist puts all the stock out at once and doesn't keep the bulk of it properly stored. If their turnover isn't great, the flowers could have been around for a while, especially if they are in full bloom.

- Don't be tempted to buy flowers that have been sitting outside all day, especially close to the road or in direct sunlight.

- Pre-order. It gives your florist time to source the flowers and buy them in fresh for you.

- If you are on a budget, do as you would do with any fresh produce: buy flowers that are naturally in season and locally grown rather than hot-house grown or imported.

- And, finally, ask questions about the flowers – the best way to care for them and where they are from (local, interstate or overseas). The florist should be knowledgeable about the names, care and seasonality of the flowers he or she sells.

FLORISTS

ABSOLUTE FLOWERS
627 Beaufort St
Mt Lawley WA 6050
9328 8468
www.absoluteflowers.com.au

BAYVIEW FLOWERS
Ground Floor, Bayview Centre
Leura Ave
Claremont WA 6010
9385 6464
www.flowerswa.com

BLOOM BY DESIGN
Shop 26, Subiaco Pavilion
Rokeby Rd
Subiaco WA 6008
9380 9101
www.bloombydesign.com.au

BOATSHED FLOWERS
40 Jarrad St
Cottesloe WA 6011
9284 5176

ESSENTIAL BLOOMS
Herdsman Fresh Essentials
9 Flynn St
Churchlands WA 6018
9387 3414

EUFLORIA
Shop 7, Glengarry Shopping Centre
Cnr Glengarry Drv
Duncraig WA 6023
1300 308 614
www.eufloria.com.au

FLEURTATIOUS
134a Stirling Hwy
Nedlands WA 6009
9386 8010
www.fleurtatious.com.au

FLOWERS AND UNIQUE DESIGNS
972 Albany Hwy
East Victoria Park WA 6101
9355 3993

FRESH PROVISIONS
Bicton Shopping Centre
262 Canning Hwy
Bicton
WA 6153
9339 5333

FUNKY BUNCHES
109 Oxford St
Leederville WA 6007
9443 2600
www.funkybunches.com.au

Also @:

Shop 2, 175 Labouchere Rd
Como WA 6152
9367 3844

LIME FLOWERS
164 Canning Hwy
East Fremantle WA 6158
9319 1837

MAGNOLIAS OF CENTRAL PARK
Shop 11, 152 St Georges Tce
Perth WA 6000
9486 9220

FLORISTS

MANIC BOTANIC
225 Oxford St
Leederville WA 6007
9242 4552
www.manicbotanic.com.au

MISS MINNIE'S GARDEN
129 Claremont Cres
Swanbourne WA 6010
9384 5099
Also @:

71A Princess Road
Nedlands WA 6009
6389 1600

POPPY'S FLOWERS
45a Hampden Rd
Nedlands WA 6009
9386 1623
www.poppysflowers.com.au

SWEET VIOLETS FLORIST
242 Hay St
East Perth WA 6004
9221 7772
www.sweetvioletflorist.com

THE RAINFOREST
Carine Glades Shopping Centre
473 Beach Rd
Carine WA 6020
9447 2607
www.therainforest.com.au

VEGETAL
200 Hay St
Subiaco WA 6008
9388 2454

FOOD STORES AND GROCERS

Food Stores are often several shops – bread, butcher, fishmonger, florist, fruit and vegetables – under one roof, which are run either as separately owned businesses or as part of the whole. They are all slightly different and are a unique and distinctive part of the Perth food shopping scene. The standards are very high. They offer some of the range of a supermarket but with produce that has been carefully selected specifically for that shop rather than bought in bulk over the telephone.

Food Stores tend to employ a lot of people – keeping those shelves of fresh produce looking as beautiful as they do requires constant attention – so there is always someone on the floor who knows what they are talking about. We love them.

The Grocers in this category all appealed to us because of their individual personalities and the high quality of their products.

ANGRY ALMOND

71 Princess Rd
Nedlands WA 6009
9389 7950
www.angryalmond.com.au

Monday-Friday 9.00-6.00
Saturday 9.00-1.00
Limited parking on Princess Rd

From humble beginnings at the Station Street Markets in Subiaco, owner Brett Ling recently opened this store on Princess Road to give shoppers who didn't want to be confined to the limited hours of the market 7-day access to his products.

The Angry Almond specialises in wholefoods, health foods, cheeses and dips (including those by Paradise Beach Purveyors, Meredith Dairy and Maggie Beer) and olive oil, both local and European, and has a huge range of dried fruit, nuts and snacks – all big sellers – and an ever-expanding variety of grocery lines. Scoop as much or as little as you like from the immaculate buckets and boxes of flour, rice, cereals and grains, dried beans and pulses, Puy lentils, Gaby's muesli, confectionery and even loose Belgian chocolate.

Brett's mother Kerry Ling manages this bright, friendly store, while brother Ryan oversees their expanding online food shopping store, servicing the metropolitan and regional areas of WA.

The Angry Almond is able to source unusual products and a wide range of hard-to-find ingredients. The Lings' aim is to provide their customers with a sense of old-world merchant-style shopping, where people can come in and try new things.

Also @:

Station Street Markets
Subiaco WA 6008
Friday-Sunday and public holidays 7.00-6.00

ANTONIO'S FRESH CONTINENTAL STORE

Shop 7, 623 Beaufort St
Mt Lawley WA
9227 5551

Monday–Friday 8.00–7.00
Saturday–Sunday 8.00–6.00
Public holidays 8.00–4.00 except Closed Christmas Day, Boxing Day, New Year's Day, Good Friday and Easter Sunday
Parking at small car park behind the arcade off Walcott St

Tucked away in an arcade off Beaufort Street, it would be easy to miss this all-embracing Continental grocer. But it would be a great mistake not to make the effort to find them. Owned and run by Mel and Marie Tindiglia with daughter Donna and sons David and Mark, it yields more surprising delights the closer you look.

The biggest turnover here is ham, cold meats, prosciutto, salamis and smallgoods – mostly cut to order but some pre-packed – and a very large and interesting cheese selection. There are over 230 cheeses – goat, cow and sheep – some of which are quite hard to find elsewhere; they are either cut from the wheel or pre-packed. Most of the produce in this section is locally sourced. The fast turnover means FRESH.

The main glass-fronted counter contains long lines of stainless tubs of antipasti, most of them devised and made by the family, such as pesto wrapped in prosciutto and marinated in oil; salmon-wrapped white Castello cheese in oil; several kinds of home-cured olives, including barbecued, cracked and stuffed with prosciutto. A speciality is their octopus: it is home cleaned and marinated, and home cooked, and they sell up to 1000kg a year. There were many more antipasti, far too many for us to taste (although they do encourage tasting), but including marinated eggplant, roasted capsicum and sun-dried tomatoes.

The family are particularly proud of their homemade fig and almond cake and apricot and walnut cake, which are both very dense and concentrated. They used to buy these in but now make them themselves.

They have fresh ravioli and a very big selection of dried pasta plus sauces to accompany it. The shop is crammed with packaged groceries and tins, jars and bottles of sauces, preserves, oils – both bulk and boutique – and many kinds of vinegar, including aged balsamic. Spices, nuts and seeds are all pre-packed and individually priced.

There is a big range of organic groceries, including baby foods, and a wide range of gluten-free and wheat-free products, and there's a freezer cabinet containing quails, squid, sardines, spatchcocks and Mahogany Creek turkey breast.

The customers, mostly Europeans and professionals, are very loyal, and after 10 years here, many are on first name terms with the shop owners. Influenced by these regular clients, the family does not try to compete with supermarkets; nor are there any plans to expand. It is very much a family business, specialising in quality, fresh products, many of which they make themselves.

Marie says: 'We enjoy it. The kids are with us. If I stayed at home on Mother's Day, I'd be on my own, but if I come to work I'm with my family.'

BOATSHED FRESH FOOD

40 Jarrad St
Cottesloe WA 6011
9284 5176
www.boatshedfresh.com.au

7 days 6.30–8.00
Closed Christmas Day

Parking at the Boatshed car park in Jarrad St

This is the very boatshed where the America's Cup-winning yacht *Australia Two* was built, and very high quality products are still coming out of it, in the form of some of Western Australia's finest foodstuffs. It is, in fact, four independently owned food shops, under one roof. The main shop, the centre of the complex, sells a big range of exceptionally fresh fruit and vegetables, beautifully presented, and a range of luxury groceries. There's a delicatessen, a large cheese section, a food-to-go counter and a florist. Except for the deli, it's self-service, but don't worry, self-service does not mean no-service: in our experience, there are always floor staff available to ask for help.

The Boatshed grew out of the farmers' or growers' markets which sprang up here in Western Australia about 20 years ago as an alternative to supermarkets. The food was fresher, and more of it was locally sourced, often direct from the growers. The markets stayed open longer, and rather than do a weekly shop, you were encouraged to come several times a week and buy in smaller quantities. It was rather like shopping in a European city, except instead of visiting several shops and a couple of market stalls, you could get all your food under one roof. The Boatshed has changed a lot since then, mainly in the direction of adding value to the produce and making life even easier for the cook, but it still follows that general market-based approach.

In the fresh produce department – fruit and vegetables – the quality is superb, and the range is very comprehensive: there'll be nine or ten varieties of tomatoes, fifteen different salad leaves, all as fresh at the end of the day as they were at the beginning and mostly grown specially for the Boatshed. 'You'd struggle to find an imported fruit or vegetable in our store,' says part-owner Michael Pember, who takes a very hands-on approach to sourcing and buying. Michael deals directly with all the growers, believing that a personal relationship with them is critical. Seasonal, spanking-fresh WA produce is the order of the day.

The Boatshed pre-prepares, cuts and very attractively packages some of their fruit and vegetables, so that they're ready to cook or serve. The proportions change with the seasons – in winter there are more root vegies prepped for soup, in summer there are fruit salads and platters.

With dry groceries, the Boatshed is moving away from the convenience-store style and more into the kind of place where you'd come to find an unusual ingredient or the very best example of a product. They carry many top brands: the complete Marie Claire range, which includes teas, jams, pastes and mustards, Jamie Oliver's oils and sauces, Duchy Original biscuits and shortbreads, and Maggie Beer's products. There's also a good selection of gelato, ice cream and some frozen goods.

The cheese selection is enormous: there are more than 100 different kinds of cheese. They are mainly pre-packaged by the Boatshed, but if you ask, they will cut to order for you.

From simple to grand, the florist offers cut flowers, in-season plants, hand-ties and potted bulbs. Looking down onto the beautiful display of flowers is one of the joys of shopping here.

The food-to-go section offers dishes prepared by their four chefs, including delicious family-sized pies and hot soup.

The delicatessen counter has an excellent range of smallgoods, hams, prosciutto – all cut to order – and prepared salads, marinated vegetables, olives and pâtés.

'We want to be a food lovers' shop,' says Michael. Many food lovers would agree that they already are. Amazingly, though,

Michael and his South African partner Craig Skead still believe they have a long way to go to get the Boatshed exactly the way they want it. 'On a scale of one to ten we are still around three,' he told us. The mind boggles – what would ten be like?

BOATSHED QUALITY MEATS
It's quality all the way here. They stock a huge variety and number of different cuts of meat, poultry and game. If it is available, they have probably got it – or will get it for you. There are friendly, knowledgeable staff all smartly kitted-out in black uniforms, caps and aprons. (See page 47.)

BOATSHED FISH CO.
The fish area at the Boatshed was previously just a small section inside the main store, but like the butcher, it has now moved into its own, much larger space and carries a bigger range. Nearly all the fish on sale here are local, fresh and line-caught. (See page 155.)

TEMPTATIONS BAKEHOUSE AND PATISSERIE
This is the flagship store of Temptations, a small chain producing good sourdough and yeasted breads, many varieties of different cakes and some quiches. (See page 41.)

BRIGHTON ROAD FOOD MARKET

111 Brighton Rd
Scarborough WA 6019
9341 6213

7 days 6.00–9.00
Closed Christmas Day
Off-street parking in front of shop

This shop is an oasis in a culinary desert. There is a wide range of high quality fresh food and produce in every section of the shop.

The fruit and vegetables, beautifully displayed on refrigerated, mirrored shelves, are up there with the frontrunners when it comes to freshness and variety.

A comprehensive range of smallgoods, including Elmar's sausages, many kinds of stuffed olives and peppers, marinated octopus and prawns, and homemade food-to-go, fill up the long deli cabinet.

In the bread department, there is New Norcia, Abhi's and Bodhi's, some organic loaves and some spelt. In the patisserie cabinet, we saw an attractive range of petits fours.

In the egg department, there are free-range and organics from Forrestfield and Kalbarri in WA and Ovaston in Queensland, and in the cheese department, Borrello, King Island, Margaret River and imported French roquefort. The yoghurts, fresh salsas and sauces are made especially for them, and there is a fridge of Mt Barker free-range chicken.

There is a very wide range of dried pasta, beans, peas, lentils, nuts and dried fruit, herbs and spices. Among the packaged groceries, there are good names like Five Senses coffee, Il Gelato and Maggie Beer pâtés.

In this price-sensitive locality, proprietor Sam Hondros is managing to offer some excellent produce at supermarket prices.

The excellent range of fresh-cut flowers is displayed attractively just inside the main door.

FOOD STORES AND GROCERS

BROADWAY FAIR SHOPPING CENTRE
88 Broadway
Nedlands WA 6009
9386 3390

Broadway Fair is a long-established and very busy shopping centre in the heart of Nedlands, near the university. It looks a bit tired and slightly shabby (but, then, after 40 years of shopping, who wouldn't?), but don't be deceived. It is well worth a visit, because in here are some very good food shops indeed.

BROADWAY FRESH
Shop 32
9389 8054

Broadway Fresh is where some of the best and more serious restaurateurs buy their fruit and vegetables. When you walk in, the heady scents alone are reward enough. Come here for the best local produce and old-fashioned, honest service. (See page 270).

KONG'S ORIENTAL SUPERMARKET
Shop 9
9386 1939

Kong's Oriental Supermarket has a cave-like feeling with high shelves packed full of exotic produce bordering narrow aisles down which homesick overseas students wander, looking for – and finding – the foods their mothers cooked back home. (See page 23.)

WEIR'S BUTCHERS
Shop 31
9386 1105

This is the current shop run by the famous Weir family, top-class Perth butchers for more than 65 years. The standard is high, and there is a great emphasis on service, in the form of pre-preparation and a wonderful selection of food-to-go, homemade by Val Weir. (See page 89.)

Also @ Broadway Fair Shopping Centre:

ARARAT KEBABS
Shop 6
9389 1063

7 days 10.00-10.00

Customers come from far and wide for the fresh Turkish bread which comes out of the oven each day at 10.30 and 4.00. And very good it is too.

Turkish pide (filled with beef, chicken and salad), kebabs, pizza and doner kebab are also available.

BROADWAY FAIR HEALTH FOODS
Shop 28
9386 7670

Monday-Friday 9.00-6.00
Saturday 9.00-5.00 Closed Sundays

This shop stocks a comprehensive range of health foods: grains, mueslis, dried fruit, beans, rices, nuts and seeds, some of which are organic. Scoop what you want yourself from the transparent plastic bins.

MICHAEL'S GOURMET
Shop 26
9386 3367

Monday-Friday 7.00-5.00
Saturday 7.00-4.00 Closed Sundays

Marija has been serving her family of customers homemade soup and pâté, sandwiches and snacks for over 30 years. There is a good selection of cut to order cheese, including roquefort, and smallgoods, which are sliced to order.

CARINE GLADES SHOPPING CENTRE
473 Beach Rd
Duncraig WA 6023
9243 0608 (Centre Management)

Shopping Centre hours: 8.00–8.00 364 days a year
Closed Christmas Day See individual entries for opening times
Off-street parking in car park

Carine Glades is a fairly small shopping centre which punches far above its weight. Per square metre, more people go through here every week than they do in far bigger centres. You might think this is because there are not very many shopping alternatives in this part of suburbia, but actually, as we discovered, it is more because there are enough really good shops here to make this a food destination in its own right.

FRESH 'N CRUSTY
Shop 18
9246 1167

There's no bakery here, but Damien Duffield carries a huge range of genuinely different bread and rolls. Buying from many different bakers, he selects from each the varieties which they do best: from one, ciabatta, from another sourdough, another Cape seed. He sells 32 different kinds of bread rolls, plus cakes, tarts and flans. (See page 35.)

LIQUORICE GOURMET FOODS
Shop 7
9448 9993

A delightfully eclectic shop selling a relatively small number of kinds of not particularly related products – lollies, nuts, tea, coffee, olive oil, spices, jams and cereals, chocolate, grains and seeds – but with a huge range in each category: 150 different teas, for example, and 32 different types of hand-mixed breakfast cereal. If there is a spice they don't have, we haven't heard of it. Most of this is help-yourself-with-a-scoop-from-a-transparent-bin type of shopping: great for small or large amounts of these top quality products. This is the older but littler sister of Liquorice in Mt Hawthorn (see page 211).

MR FRESH GROWERS MARKET
Shop 12
9447 4066

Right up there with the frontrunners: fruit and veg doesn't come much better than this. This sparklingly clean shop is stacked full of beautifully displayed produce of the highest quality. Mr Fresh is a most apt name for this great shop. (See page 277.)

SPLASH'S FISH HOUSE
Shop 16
9447 7133

More than half their output is either fresh wet fish, fishy food-to-go (well, so is fish 'n chips, but this is something else) or gourmet seafood dishes. The faithful regulars still come for their fish 'n chips, but many now leave with a gourmet dish as well. (See page 172.)

TORRE & MORDINI GOURMET MEATS
Shop 17
9246 2399

Think pedigree. These blokes have butchery in their blood; both their dads were very well respected butchers. Their shop is very much in the value-added school of butchery, in which Perth excels. (See page 88.)

Also @ Carine Glades Shopping Centre:

BEAN THERE CAFÉ
Shop 1
9246 2333

The in-house café of the shopping centre, serving breakfast, freshly made toasted sandwiches, focaccias, wraps in pitta bread, cakes and quiche, coffee, smoothies. There's a short lunch menu, including burgers and a couple of salads.

CARINE CUISINE GOURMET FOODS
Shop 27
9447 4433

A comprehensive and busy deli, part-owned (with the butchers, Torre & Mordini) and managed by former Young Retailer of the Year, David Sard-Infiri. Freshly made salads (beautiful tabouli, Greek, three bean, creamy potato, crunchy coleslaw), stuffed and marinated olives and peppers, smallgoods and cheese cut to order or ready sliced and some ready-to-go desserts fill the big L-shaped glass-fronted cabinets. There's also a good selection of groceries and dips.

FOOD STORES AND GROCERS

CLAREMONT FRESH
333 Stirling Hwy
Claremont WA 6010
9383 3066

7 days 7.00–7.00
Closed Christmas Day
Car park by store

When this food shop was opened in 1983 it was as a Farmers' Market, selling fresh fruit and vegetables direct from the grower, in a style that had recently taken off in America. It was one of the first of its kind in WA and was an instant hit.

Brothers Peter and John Dafinkas have owned and run Claremont Fresh – 'more than a market' – for the last 10 years: it has changed and evolved, but it still has beautiful displays of fresh WA produce, mostly now from Canning Vale Market but some still direct from the grower, particularly on weekends and public holidays when the markets are closed. 'We are in one of the most fortunate places on Earth as far as growing our own produce. The majority of the produce on the shelves in WA is fantastic.' Salad leaves and some herbs are grown specially for them, and John will do his best to hunt down scarce or rare fresh herbs for you.

A long display of carefully labelled fruit and vegetables takes up the left-hand side of the shop. We picked out fennel, celeriac, Kipfler potatoes, Asian vegetables and leeks from Wanneroo – all looking in tip-top condition.

At the far end there's a large fridge of cut and prepared fruit and vegetables, gourmet salads, Asian vegetable mixes with noodles, stuffed capsicums, prepared stirfries, casseroles, soups and steaming vegetables. There's also a very good selection of herbs, both loose and packaged.

The old deli counter has gone: it's been replaced by an extremely well-stocked cabinet of beautifully pre-packed smallgoods, sliced meats and salamis, pâtés, olives, dips and sauces. There is an excellent selection of different cheese, much of it from Blue Cow.

In the bread department, you'll find New Norcia bread – pain de campagne, dark rye, ciabatta and baguette – and Barrett's, Lebanese and Turkish breads.

The food-to-go cabinet stocks their own brand hearty soup alongside Pitango low-fat soup and some prepared meals from The Ginger Pig.

The grocery section of the shop has a comprehensive selection of goods from some of the top brand names. Claremont Fresh now package all the dried fruit, nuts and wholefoods which they previously sold loose.

The in-house butcher is The Meat Showcase (see page 86), but if you're in a hurry, there's a cabinet of their pre-packed meat – steaks, chops, sausages and chicken pieces – near the checkouts.

Tucked away in a corner is Claremont Cleanskins, who sell WA wines in unlabelled bottles at very competitive prices.

The consistent high quality of the produce and service over many years make Claremont Fresh the firm favourite of many in the western suburbs.

FOOD STORES AND GROCERS

C. LoPRESTI & SON
170 Canning Hwy
East Fremantle WA 6158
9339 6523

Monday–Friday 9.00–5.00
Saturday 9.00–1.00 Closed Sundays
Parking at rear

The LoPresti family have run food stores in Fremantle since the mid-1920s and this delightful continental-style general food store, reminiscent of a neighbourhood shop in an Italian side-street, since the 1960s. The traditional atmosphere attracts second and even third-generation regulars.

The shelves are crammed with dried pasta, anchovies, passata; the front counter with large bowls of marinated, prepared olives, sun-dried tomatoes and stuffed bell-peppers. Down the centre of the cosy room run open sacks of dried legumes and pulses, rice, polenta and salt. Behind them, on the shelves are Australian nuts and dried fruits, coffee beans and bottled vegetables.

Cheese and olive oil are the star-turns here. Patriarch Claude LoPresti (who has written a book about olive oil and lectured on cheese) or any of his charming and helpful family will advise you on which cheese to choose and why; how to use it, store it, cut it, cook it and serve it. Ask! Their wealth of knowledge about all the products they sell is readily available to you. The day-to-day running of the shop is done by Frank and Maria, Claude's son and daughter-in-law and his daughter, Angelina Ingrilli – but Claude and his wife Mary are there every day.

Claude LoPresti died in May 2007. With the agreement of his wife Mary and the LoPresti family, we have left this entry as a tribute to him.

CROSSWAYS SHOPPING CENTRE
196 Rokeby Rd (cnr Bagot Rd)
Subiaco WA 6008
9288 0288 (Administration)

Shopping hours vary for each shop

BREW-HA
Shops 3-4
9388 7272

Brew-Ha is not really an official part of the Crossways Shopping Centre but it's so close that we felt we couldn't miss them out. When exhausted from shopping at the food destinations listed above, pop into Brew-Ha for a wonderful coffee at the most sophisticated but relaxed community café around. (See page 331.)

MOE SUSHI
Shop 3A
08 9380 9911

We love Moe (see page 236).

NIPPON FOOD SUPPLIES
Shop 26
9380 6783

Japanese food goodies. (See page 24.)

SAS'S
Shop 1A
9388 3122

The Big Boy on the block. High class, great quality, big variety and with seriously serious cheese. And everything is offered two ways: self-service pre-packed (by Sas) on one side, or the same products, over the counter across the way, cut to order. This is a must-do shop. (See page 145.)

THE MEAT SAFE
Shop 3b
9381 6661

The only family butcher in Subiaco. How lucky the Subi locals are that the only one is this good. (See page 85.)

Also @ Crossways Shopping Centre:

SUBI FRESH
9381 2794

Supermarkets are not what this guide book is about, but if you want to do a one-stop shop, the fruit and vegies at Subi Fresh are the best bit of this supermarket. While we are recommending so many of Crossways' independent shops, it would appear a bit perverse not to tell our readers that good quality, fresh, carefully maintained produce is also available here.

BREAD
If you need good bread to go with your newly purchased goodies, Do Not Pass Go, Do Not Collect £200 and Do Not Take the Easiest Option. Just dash across the road to the Subi branch of New Norcia Bakeries (see page 39), where they're selling hand-crafted artisan loaves to die for, or rush up Rokeby Road to Chez Jean-Claude Patisserie (Monday to Friday only – see page 95) for a different slice of true heaven.

FOOD STORES AND GROCERS

DAVID JONES FOOD HALL

Hay St Mall
Perth WA 6000
9210 4000
www.davidjones.com.au

Monday–Wednesday 9.30–6.00 Thursday 9.30–7.00: Friday 9.30–9.00
Saturday 9.00–5.00 Sunday 12.00–6.00
Parking at Pier St car park, or Forrest Pl car park off Wellington St

Whether you are a busy office worker looking for a quick and delicious lunch or have had a hard day's shopping in the CBD and find yourself not knowing what to take home for dinner, you need go no further than the Food Hall at David Jones.

In this large, light and airy space, you will find an exceptional array of carefully selected food in every department, much of which can be eaten in or taken home for your evening meal or dinner party.

Mondo's are the in-store butcher. There is a comprehensive range of beef, lamb, White Rocks veal, pork, poultry, game and sausages, much of it with value added. Pre-prepared portions are marked for one person, two people or four people.

There is an exceptional cheese and antipasto counter, with over 250 different varieties of Australian and imported continental cheese, which are cut to order. There is also a fridge containing pre-packed, pre-cut cheese. 'People can taste and enjoy whatever they like. If they want to sample 20 cheeses, they can sample 20 cheeses,' says Ronnie Colombeen, the Food Hall Supervisor. There is a Cheese of the Month, which runs in conjunction with their Wine Club. David Jones is the biggest seller of French champagne in Perth, and when in season, there are Black Diamond truffles.

The well-stocked smallgoods section includes high quality produce from Italy, France and Germany as well as a good selection of different pâtés from, among others, Pheasant Farm and Barossa Fine Foods. There are fresh pasta and sauces from Ubaldi and local producer Portobello.

Lining the shelves of the large grocery section is an extensive range of gourmet food from some of Australia and the world's top provedores – olive oils, vinegars, condiments, biscuits, sauces, pickles, American and oriental products. Despite this, there is an definite emphasis on WA produce here.

Whole sections are dedicated to tea and coffee, chocolates and confectionery. You'll find Valrhona chocolates from France, Dolfin & Godiva from Belgium and Max Brenner from Israel. An espresso bar serving finger sandwiches, cakes and pastries adjoins the handmade chocolate counter.

The bakery stocks bread from Abhi's and New Norcia, Pusey's Puffs pies and cakes, and Mondo's White Rocks veal pies, as well as cakes, slices, tarts and quiches and pies from the in-house kitchen.

Their catering service includes gourmet hampers, cheese and antipasto platters and sandwiches.

In-house eateries and food-to-go change with the seasons. You'll find Jas Sushi, the Oyster Bar, a new juice bar which serves ice cream in summer, a winter soup bar, Asian noodles, fish and chips, curries, pizza by the slice, pasta and risotto from Portobello and cocktail bites to go.

The food hall no longer sells fresh fruit and vegetables.

FRESH PROVISIONS

Bicton Shopping Centre
262 Canning Hwy
Bicton WA 6153
9339 5333
www.freshprovisions.com.au

365 days a year 7.00–9.00
Parking in shopping centre car park

This is everything a food store should be and it is immediately obvious that great attention has gone into sourcing the produce, displaying it and caring for it. The wide variety of fruit, vegetables and salads, including a smallish organic section, was in perfect condition on refrigerated shelves. Produce comes from Canning Vale Market and direct from small growers – there is passionfruit from Maggie Edmonds in Gingin.

The in-house butcher has Mt Barker free-range chicken, lamb and beef kebabs, fresh duck (from Luv-A-Duck), baby beef Wellingtons, meatballs, steaks, pork fillet and chops, French cutlets, veal rib-eye and much more.

A good bread selection included loaves from New Norcia, Barrett's, Bodhi's and wonderful ciabatta, from Il Panino.

There was a wide range of eggs from several different sources, nearly all organic and free-range; a very comprehensive range of competitively priced pasta; Princi Italian sausages, salamis, hams and prosciutto; and many different kinds of olive oil, several from small, boutique WA groves.

The take-home deli counter featured sixteen fresh, delicious salads, all devised and made by the staff, and excellent cheese, both pre-packed and cut to order; cakes and petits fours are in a small patisserie cabinet next to the deli counter.

In the dairy fridges, you'll find Avon Valley milk, Margaret River organic milk and low-calorie goats' milk. They sell Il Gelato ice cream. The cut flowers, mainly direct from the growers to ensure freshness and to keep the prices down, were in perfect condition.

In every section of the store, there are many organic and gluten-free products on the shelves, including Holle baby food.

A good range of non-alcoholic drinks feature here, including the excellent Warsteiner beer and Ariel wine. A new cookbook stand was being fitted when we visited.

There is an in-store bank (Bank West Community Bank) which is open from 9.00–5.00 Monday to Friday and from 9.00–1.00 on Saturday morning.

The stock is comprehensive, but if you don't see something you want, ask Dorothea, the very efficient and friendly manager. She knows where all the hidden treasure is.

Fresh Provisions in Bicton is the newest of the three stores in the Perth metropolitan area.

Also @:

FRESH PROVISIONS
G15 Bayview Shopping Centre
303 Stirling Hwy (cnr Leura Ave)
Claremont WA 6010
9383 3308

365 days a year 24 hours
Parking in car park

Much of the buying for the three Fresh Provisions stores is done centrally, so most of the produce described above is also available here in Claremont.

The highlight of this store is the very large deli section, with food-to-go either fully or semi-prepared to take home and heat and hot food to take away. Pasta dishes, chicken dishes, meatballs and curries are available round the clock, along with falafels, samosas, patties, pies and sushi, salads and platters.

There is no butcher here but there is fresh packaged meat on sale.

In the middle of the night, this store attracts younger clientele who want good quality hot food-to-go.

FRESH PROVISIONS
Alexander Building
77 Walcott St (cnr Raglan St)
Mt Lawley WA 6050
9227 6309

365 days a year 24 hours
Parking in car park

This was the first Fresh Provisions store to open, in 1989. Closing time was 7.30 in the early days, but customer demand meant that they began extending the opening time, by half an hour each time, until it finally reached 9.00, but there still seemed to be doctors, nurses, truckies, taxi drivers and shift-workers who wanted even longer hours, so the 24-hour operation gradually evolved.

One of the original partners in Fresh Provisions, Zoe Barratt-Hill, a doyenne of the Perth food scene, who is in charge of the gourmet product buying for all three stores and who has done much to push local artisans within the stores – 'I'm a great supporter of WA produce' – told us that this Mt Lawley store is currently undergoing renovations: the major part should be completed by November 2007, the final part by mid-2008.

HERDSMAN FRESH ESSENTIALS

9 Flynn St
Churchlands WA 6018
9383 7733

7 days 8.00-8.00
Parking in Herdsman car park

This outstanding store is a food lover's paradise. It is several stores under one roof, but the heart of it is the fresh food business founded in December 1979 as Herdsman Growers' Market, with 25 staff selling fresh fruit and vegetables from mainly small WA farming families.

Over the years the business expanded into selling groceries and, in 1996, brothers Dennis and Allan Cerenich completely revamped the store and extended it, adding the butchers, fishmongers and florist. During the last decade they have moved into the value-added and ready-meal market, most of it prepared in their own kitchen.

Herdsman now employ more than 300 people, 50 full-timers of whom most have been here for more than 20 years. Dennis told us: 'Our workers are part of our family. It is important to keep them close to the culture. You have to transfer your passion to those who work with you.' So what started as a small family business has grown into a much larger family business, but one which still holds dear the values it had at its inception.

Fresh is still the raison d'être – the fresh fruit and vegetables are of an impeccably high quality, and are nearly all from WA. 'People come to us because we are fresh,' Dennis told us. At Herdsman they have always made a point of buying WA produce and everything is very well labelled as to origin. There is also lots of information about the produce, including nutritional facts and cooking hints.

We saw tree-ripened Pink Lady apples and Granny Smiths as well as two or three other varieties; there were five kinds of pears, including Nashi, Bosc, red d'Anjou (which looked wonderful) – all

FOOD STORES AND GROCERS

from Donnybrook; Mt Barker strawberries – loose, beautifully displayed on dark green cabbage leaves; very fresh-looking green broccoli dusted with crushed ice, and butternut pumpkins both whole and cut open displaying the bright golden-orange flesh; a selection of Australian Certified Organic fruit and veg from White Orchid, straight 'from grower to checkout'; fresh apple and pear juice with no additives or preservatives from the Trigwell family farm (established 1862) in Donnybrook; onions from Myalup; five or six kinds of potatoes and sweet potatoes, including Ruby Lou, Royal Blue and Kipfler; sweet corn from Manjimup; many kinds of tomatoes, including vine-ripened truss tomatoes and the new Japanese variety, momoko.

Staff in the Herdsman kitchens prepare nearly all their salads, fruit platters and meals to go. Everything is hand-done and they are proud of the consistency of standard, style and make-up of their salads. 'We've really gone back to basics; there's no cutting corners, and we use the best and freshest ingredients we have.'

There's a huge cheese selection, with four separate counters. Many local cheeses are cut from the wheel, including Margaret River brie, double cream brie and camembert, and quite a few imported cheeses, including St Agur, Wensleydale, Bresse blue (the French version of gorgonzola), Queso de Manchego from La Mancha in Spain (only recently available here), plus Morbier and Raclette. There are two deli sections, one selling packaged smallgoods, the other cutting to order.

Packaged goods include Maggie Beer pâtés and pastes; Bannister Downs milk; Jamie Oliver pasta sauces; Terra Australia jams and marmalades; Edmond Fallut tarragon vinegar; Guenard walnut oil, and many varieties of other oils and vinegars. They sell Five Senses, Rubra and Braziliano coffees and many teas, including all the usual brands and some more exotic ones. There is a big range of fresh pasta and dried pasta. The Ginger Pig's excellent range of ready-cooked meals are on sale here too.

Goji juice, berries and powder are claimed as the new wonder food, and sure enough, Herdsman had them on display.

A bread section opposite the deli sells Barrett's light sourdough, miche de campagne, olive and rosemary; New Norcia baguettes and ciabatta; and Lawley's Cape seed, panini, ciabatta and pagnotta.

There are cookbooks on wire racks attached to pillars dotted about the place and a rack of recipes by resident chef Dale Sniffen.

In busy periods they will pack for you, and if you need help they will carry your bags to the car for you.

'We are a family of growers who turned into buyers,' says co-founder Dennis Cerenich. 'We want to be an inspiration to people who love food.'

Also @ Herdsman Fresh Essentials:

CREATIVE MEATS
This top-quality butchers' shop opens directly onto the Herdsman shopfloor area but is a separate business. There is a huge variety of meat on sale. For customers in a hurry, there is a counter of packaged meat which you pay for at the main Herdsman check-out. (See page 54.)

ESSENTIAL BLOOMS
A small but good florist. (See page 179.)

FESTIVAL FISH
Squeezed between Creative Meats and Brumby's Bread is this small boutique fishmonger, selling high-quality, mostly-filleted fresh fish and frozen fish and shellfish. (See page 157.)

BRUMBY'S BREAD
Brumby's own breads but also New Norcia 7-grain and sourdough, Il Panino's ciabatta and Sciliano, Bodhi's wuppersoft and cakes and slices.

KAKULAS BROTHERS
183 William St
Nortbridge WA 6003
9328 5285

Monday-Friday 8.00-5.30
Saturday 8.00-5.00 Closed Sundays
Several car parks on Roe St

For more than 70 years this unique emporium just over the famous Horseshoe Bridge has brought the feel of the Mediterranean to Perth. Long before this most isolated of cities had become the cosmopolitan place it is today, Kakulas Brothers reminded us that there was a wider world beyond our shores.

Cousins Evan and George Kakulas, the grandsons of the founder, now preside over this large exotic continental grocery. They stock more than 3000 different foods, many of them in bulk, imported mainly from Italy and Greece, India and Pakistan. There are many varieties of beans, peas, lentils, grains, flours, breakfast cereals and flakes, dried fruits, berries and mushrooms, rice, pulses, spices and herbs; the range is huge. You help yourself, to as little or as much as you want, from the open tubs and sacks arranged throughout this cavernous space. There are also packaged groceries, tins and bottles of olive oils and vinegars, dried fish, olives, cheeses, smallgoods, teas and coffees and exotic sweets.

There is a large stock of health foods and herbal, or natural medicines, which Evan, who is usually on the floor, will happily tell you all about. They have recently started selling dried goji berries and juice: they are an ancient food, said to be the richest source of antioxidant carotenoids of all known foods.

When we visited, George had just returned from a trip to Shanghai, where he had been researching, buying and 'finding things'. We love browsing in shops like this, soaking up the sights and smells; you can almost imagine you are in a warehouse somewhere on the shores of the Mediterranean 100 years ago.

KAKULAS SISTER

29-31 Market St
Fremantle WA 6160
9430 4445

Monday-Friday 9.00-5.30
Saturday 9.00-5.00 Sunday 12.00-5.00
Ticket parking by Post Office on Market St, and in the station car park

Kakulas Sister is a providoring institution located in the heart of Fremantle. Owner Eleni Kakulas is the granddaughter of the founder of the original Kakulas Brothers store, so she has strong links to the grocery business. She and husband Michael Finn run Kakulas Sister and have a second shop in Nollamara.

This shop is like an Aladdin's cave, full of riches and wonderful spicy aromas. Around every corner are hidden treasures waiting to be discovered. Now in its twelfth year, it is ostensibly a grocer's shop, although it has leanings towards a health food shop combined with the feel of a traditional Greek food shop. They carry a huge range of bulk foods, some which seem exotic but which Eleni says she has always carried, and some you won't easily find anywhere else: mastica and mahlepi, for example. Down one side of the large space – which is reminiscent of an old warehouse – are big, open sacks of seeds, pulses, beans, grains, rices, flours and muesli. On the other side are every conceivable kind of dried fruits, nuts and confectionery. The large range of different flours, which they sell in as small or as large a quantity as you want, have always been big sellers: there are wheat, gluten-free, spelt, rye, barley, potato, soya and more.

There's a small delicatessen counter with a range of quality cheeses, olives, prosciutto and salamis. You'll also find an excellent selection of olive oils from WA and elsewhere.

Another big seller is coffee. At the front of the shop are nine or ten open sacks of different varieties of beans which you can grind yourself in-store. Eleni estimates they sell 200–300kg every week.

There's also a diverse range of teas, including flavoured teas from Byron Bay (mango, ginger, orange and vanilla).

They sell some of Perth's best breads, including Abhi's and New Norcia Bakeries (see page 39), and have their own brand of bottled water. Eleni says: 'I like to present interesting and new things, but the shop is not pretentious or gourmet. It just evolved like this.'

Also @:

90 Hillsbrough Dr
Nollamara WA 6061
9440 0642

LIQUORICE GOURMET FOODS

The Mezz
148 Scarborough Beach Rd
Mount Hawthorn WA 6016
9443 7677

Monday–Friday 8.00–6.00 Thursday 8.00–9.00
Saturday 8.00–5.00 Closed Sundays and public holidays
Parking under The Mezz

Liquorice is one of the most delightfully eclectic places we discovered. It is help-yourself-with-a-scoop-from-a-transparent-bin shopping, but the unique thing is the huge variety in each range: so, not ten kinds of tea but 150, not five kinds of nuts but 50; and every kind of spice we have ever heard of and some we haven't.

'Anyone who cooks goes "Wow" when they first come in here,' owner Bronwen Duffield told us. 'We get a lot of people looking in for things they can't find anywhere else. We try to find the very highest quality of what is available – high quality satisfies more. But we would prefer that you just buy a little bit at a time and come back when you need more rather than using it once and throwing the rest out.'

There are also all the lollies you remember from your childhood, including the ones you'd almost forgotten; plus cereals, dried fruits, grains, pulses, herbs, spices, beans, lentils, seeds, and chocolates (including Galler cocoa products); and pasta, Rubra coffee, teas, infusions, pastry cases, jams, sauces, olive oil et al.

Also @:

Shop 7, Carine Glades Shopping Centre
473 Beach Rd
Duncraig WA 6023
9448 9993

7 days 8.00–6.30
Closed main public holidays

FOOD STORES AND GROCERS

MELVILLE CENTRAL
7 Marshall Rd
Leach Hwy and cnr North Lake Rd (by Bunnings)
Myaree WA 6154

7 days 7.00–7.00
Ample car parking

Melville Central is situated on Marshall Road, a slip road off Leach Highway, at the corner of North Lake Road. It is not to be confused with Melville Heights, which is also on Leach Highway but nearer to Fremantle. Bunnings and McDonald's are the landmarks.

LIMES FRESH FRUIT & VEG CO.
9330 2251

A huge shop floor area, which offers a large variety of high quality fruit, vegetables, salads, washed, mixed lettuce leaves, fresh herbs, prepared fruit platters and juices freshly squeezed to order. (See page 273.)

MELVILLE SEAFOODS
9317 7788

There's an excellent range of fresh, frozen and live fish and seafood. Raw and cooked crabs are a speciality; sushi is made daily. There's also a good selection of prepared fish dishes, kebabs and Thai Fish cakes. (See page 162.)

SCARFO'S MEATING PLACE
9330 9377

Harvey beef, Bunbury lamb, free-range chicken, milk-fed veal from Gingin, baby goat, rabbits, quail, spatchcocks and their award-winning sausages are all available at this high quality budget-conscious Meating Place. (See page 81.)

Also @ Melville Central:

BREAD CRAFT
9330 9800 for phone orders

Under the new ownership of Gerhard and Stephanie van Biljon and specialising in the use of spelt flour, four bakers on the premises use stone-soled ovens to bake as many as 30 different breads each day, including an organic spelt loaf, multigrains and sourdough, as well as savouries, cakes, cookies, pizza and handmade Italian continental loaves.

CHAN BROTHERS ORIENTAL SUPERMARKET
9317 6383

The supermarket stocks a wide range of dried, frozen, tinned and fresh oriental provisions. In the fridge, the good selection of oriental leaf greens and their bean sprouts looked particularly fresh. The frozen fish is competitively priced.

GOURMET CENTRO
9330 3451
9330 2054

The sign above the main counter says 'Un Poco di Tutto', meaning 'a little bit of everything', which is an accurate description of this section of Melville Central: owner Pina Casotti offers a range of groceries, including a large cheese selection, natural juices, olives, salamis, prosciutto and hams, frozen berry fruits, Il Gelato and Azzura sorbets and Nonna's pasta. Their food-to-go, which is mostly made on the premises, includes homemade pasta, soups and curries. There's also coffee to have in or take away, and sandwich rolls made to order. There is also a small kitchenware section and a few cut flowers for sale. We think this is a place to watch.

MIDLAND JUNCTION FOOD STORE
380 Great Eastern Hwy (cnr Morrison Rd)
Midland WA 6056

A selection of independent but complementary shops are gathered together here – all under the same roof except for the Junction Ice Creamery. The overall standard is high; they are all open 7 days; it's an excellent one-stop shop for many, particularly since the fire and consequent demise of the Midland Military Markets in 2007.

BARLEYFIELD MEATS
9374 0744

This is the main outlet of Barleyfield Beef, who produce premium quality grain-fed yearling beef from their farm at Gingin: this is beef bred and fed with no antibiotics, no hormone-growth promotants, no chemical treatments and no genetically modified content is used during production. (See page 46.)

FISHERMEN'S BASKET
9274 1311

A daily supply of fresh, good quality WA seafood, both whole or filleted, is available here, as well as frozen shellfish and produce. (See page 158.)

MIDLAND JUNCTION FRESH MARKETS
9250 1205

Fresh, high quality seasonal fruit and vegetables, many of them locally grown, are the order of the day here. There's a good range of dry groceries and a small selection of everyday essentials available as well. (See page 274.)

SORELLE DELI
9274 1401

New girls Sarah Howlett and Kylie Monaghan have transformed the old deli. Many of the old favourites are still here but there are some wonderful new products, including New Norcia bread at the weekends. (See page 146.)

THE JUNCTION ICE CREAMERY
9274 1013

Come here and buy very fresh, homemade, handmade fine ice cream, frozen yoghurt, sorbets and ice cream cakes. There's a small café within the shop for coffee, tea, homemade soup in winter, cakes etc. (See page 290.)

PEACHES

Shop 1, 195 Hampton Rd
South Fremantle WA 6162
9430 5025

7 days 8.00–7.00
Closed Christmas Day, New Year's Day, Easter Sunday
Plenty of parking

Peaches stock some of the best and freshest fruit and vegetables you will find anywhere in WA. This is an outstanding shop, well worth travelling to, and is patronised by people (more than 5000 a week) who know good produce and want the best.

It was started as a simple, old-fashioned greengrocer 20 years ago by Sergio Paparone. A decade later he was joined by Frank Di Tullio, and 5 years ago by Frank's brother Roberto. Sergio says: 'We're passionate about what we do. We just want to sell what we love. We don't want to sell anything we wouldn't want to take home.' And the passion does seem to shine through in the produce.

The fruit and vegetable shelves are all refrigerated, so the stock is always in excellent condition; the lettuce as crisp as if it had just been picked. There is always an excellent variety of fresh herbs. Most of the fruit and vegetables come from WA.

Peaches has a small range of fresh fish from Sea Diamond, including marinated garlic prawns and fillets of fresh local fish and whole fresh Mt Barker chickens and chicken pieces.

Peaches stocks a wide variety of general groceries: bread from various bakeries, including Abhi's, cheeses, Princi smallgoods, some frozen fish, meat and Mt Barker chickens, coffee and tea, Bannister Downs milk, Nudies and fresh juices.

Last year Peaches expanded into the old dress shop premises next door. This new section at the far end of the shop is where you'll find all the organic produce (see page 328). About 30 per cent of their sales are organic and Sergio expects this to grow.

Peaches now has what is probably the biggest range of fresh organic food in Perth.

There are terrific seasonal bargains by the door – one week it might be asparagus, another week, cheese. Outside the shop there are usually 'buckets' of seasonal fruit and one or two exceptional bargains too ... a tray of mangoes or a bag of passionfruit, perhaps.

Peaches' helpful staff will carry shopping to your car: this is usually necessary as we always buy twice as much as we intend.

PRINCI'S AT ROMANO'S

115 Lefroy Rd
Beaconsfield WA 6162
9314 1414

7 days 7.00-7.00 (7.00-6.00 for 3 winter months)
Closed Christmas Day
Off street parking

This very popular deli, owned and run by the Princi family, makes you feel you've stepped through a magical doorway and emerged in Italy. Many of the goods – parmigiano and prosciutto, for example – are imported from Italy, and the rest, though produced locally, are very much in traditional Italian style.

The Princi relatives supply many different types of cold meats, all of which are cut to order. Kat Princi told us: 'We grew up around meat; after school we were always in the butcher's shop. That's where I learned to slice.'

The adjacent Princi family butcher provides fresh sausages and hams.

There's plenty of cheese to choose from, too: provoletta, provolone and fresh mozzarella from local supplier Borrello; cherry bocconcini and ricotta from Rose Valley in Armadale; auricchio, provolone, parmigiano and pecorino from Italy, mostly pre-cut and packaged but they will cut to order if you ask them.

Cakes come from Dolce & Salato and Corica (including their famous apple strudel); there's crusty ciabatta from Il Panino next door and other bread of La Vastese and La Pagnotta.

There are heaps and coils and packets of fresh and dried golden pasta, pyramids of tinned tomatoes and sauces, shelves of coffee as beans or ground, dried beans, peas, lentils, rice, herbs and spices, the dried salt cod called baccala – stiff as planks – and lots of Swiss and Italian chocolates.

If you can't afford a holiday in Tuscany this year, a visit here may do instead.

FOOD STORES AND GROCERS

SCUTTI – A TASTE OF EUROPE

Angelo Street Markets
67 Angelo St
South Perth WA
9367 7688
www.scutti.com.au

Monday-Friday 8.00-7.00 Saturday-Sunday 8.00-6.00
Closed Christmas, Boxing, New Year's Day, Good Friday, Easter Sunday
Parking in street and behind shop

This highly recommended family business, owned and run by Dominic Scutti, with his sons Nick and Mike, for the last 15 years is surprisingly small for the amount of produce it carries; as a result it feels pleasantly packed, with customers squeezing down narrow aisles past shelves stuffed full of scrumptious food.

Cheese, a passion of Nick's, is a speciality, and the long cheese counter contains more than 250, cut and packaged by him on the premises, or cut to the exact amount you want from the wheel. Opposite the cheese counter is the delicatessen section, with local and imported smallgoods of every kind, including hams cooked or smoked by Princi, to which Nick adds a honey glaze of his own invention, plus handmade takeaway dishes such as soup, sauces and meatballs, all made on the premises.

As well as packets, tins, jars and bottles of groceries, shelves full of nuts, sweets, local and imported oils and vinegars, they carry Corica cakes, and pastries and bread from New Norcia, Vastese and Bodhi's.

At the rear is the main business: the beautifully displayed fresh fruit and vegetables, all hand-selected by Dom – 'My father is of the old school; he doesn't buy on the phone saying, "I want this or I want that." He looks at everything before he buys it,' says Nick. This display was sparklingly fresh and right up there with the best.

When we were there the first Chittering Valley citrus came in – mandarins and oranges from Bindoon – they looked a picture.

The Scuttis also sell selected, packaged cuts of meat from Claytons Quality Meats (see page 52).

SIMON JOHNSON

169 Rokeby Rd
Subiaco WA 6008
9388 7780
www.simonjohnson.com

Monday–Wednesday 10.00–6.00
Thursday–Fridday 10.00–7.00
Saturday 9.00–5.00 Closed Sundays
Street parking

The Perth branch of the well-established and stylish Simon Johnson food stores in NSW and Victoria has been open 3 years. It is managed by Kellie Willcock, well known on the Perth food scene. It is a long, elegant shop stocking the large range of Simon Johnson's own-brand products as well as other brands, many imported. Much of the gourmet grocery range is organic.

About a quarter of their sales are of cheese, and there is a separate, temperature-controlled Fromagerie at the far end of the shop which houses the many domestic and imported cheeses, some organic, including the beautiful WA Kervella goats' cheese.

The wide range of sausages includes Toulouse pork, Italian pork, chorizo and lamb merguez. The meat selection includes veal and lamb racks, chicken gremolata and duck confit.

The shop stocks many different types of pasta, some own-brand and others by Benedetto Cavalieri and Latini. Their own pasta sugo (sauce) is ever popular. There is a large and interesting range of olive oils and aged balsamic vinegars.

There is also some very attractive kitchen equipment and apparatus, including gleaming copper pots and pans.

Simon Johnson imports into Australia and distributes and wholesales extensively throughout WA to hotels, restaurants and cafés but is keen to educate people to use his products at home.

FOOD STORES AND GROCERS

SWANSEA STREET FRESH MARKETS

178 Swansea St *
East Victoria Park WA 6101
9361 6234

Monday-Saturday 8.00-6.00
Sunday 8.00-5.00 Closed public holidays
Parking in the car park

The flagship of the Fresh Markets is the fruit and vegetables, with counters of beautifully fresh produce, nearly all from local growers and with a huge emphasis on what's in season.

There are also buckets of produce at bargain prices. There is absolutely nothing wrong with anything sold from these buckets. The only difference is that the fruit is smaller in size. We saw some excellent produce: Pink Lady apples, the first mandarins, good fresh herbs – alongside fresh ginger, galangal, lemongrass, Jerusalem artichokes and a selection of winter root vegetables.

The other half of the space is devoted to a European-style grocery with an emphasis on bulk foods, spices in sacks and clear bins of cereals and grains.

This is a very Italian neighbourhood, which explains the varied range of Italian pasta of all kinds, good cheese, salami and olive oild

Harry Katsamakis, son of Vic Katsamakis – the owner for nearly 30 years with Arthur Psaltis – has managed the Markets for the last decade. It's very much a family business, with longtime employees (including Pat Chua, who has been working here for 28 years) and very loyal customers of many, many different nationalities, some of whom are now third-generation. 'We've been fortunate,' says Harry. 'Our permanent staff have stuck with us.'

* There are two Swansea Streets in this area. The Fresh Markets are, in fact, a huge covered shop, housed in a warehouse-type building on the lower half of Swansea Street, east of Shepperton Road and just north of Welshpool Road.

THE BEAUFORT STREET MERCHANT

488–492 Beaufort St
Highgate WA 6003
9328 6299

Monday–Saturday 8.00–9.00
Sunday 8.00–7.00
Parking: Good luck

The Beaufort Street Merchant is a relative newcomer on the always-changing Highgate and Mt Lawley strip. It is, in fact, four businesses operating under one roof: a liquor store, a food store (which sells gourmet produce, essential everyday grocery items and gift items), a café and a wholesale wine business.

For many customers, this provides an agreeable one-stop shop where a variety of items can be bought, perhaps on the way home from work.

There is a focus on gourmet produce – and there are lots of good brand names in store – alongside essential everyday groceries and fresh fruit and vegetables for customers in the local area.

Products are available from The Grocer, and there is bread from New Norcia, meat from Mondo, Dorper lamb, and Five Senses coffee.

The café offers the full catastrophe breakfast every day of the week. Freshly squeezed juice too ... you can design your own from a choice of watermelon, apple, orange, rockmelon and carrot.

This is a family business, run by Angie Taylor with her brother Scott Taylor.

THE BOULEVARD SHOPPING CENTRE
31 Gayton Rd
City Beach WA 6015

This formerly rather ordinary shopping centre is undergoing a major refurbishment. If you haven't been for a while, it could be worth a visit – you may be pleasantly surprised. This is what we found.

FINESSE BUTCHERY
9385 9761

The new kid on the block is Simon Lawes, who, with his wife Simone, also owns Finesse Butchery in Waratah Avenue, Dalkeith. They sell beautifully prepared and presented meat of the highest quality – you need do hardly anything other than take it home and pop it in the oven. (See page 60.)

GEORGES
9285 0240

This lovely gourmet café has a beautiful range of food-to-go, handmade and cooked on the premises by French chef and proprietor Georges Hombert. He and his wife Sandrine also offer a catering service for all types of events. (See page 252.)

HYPE
9285 2565

Café or shop? What do you call somewhere that's completely organic, largely gluten-free and definitely dairy-free friendly? And which serves and sells homemade soups, risottos, salads, and sells organic groceries, fruit and vegetables, exotic teas and Five Senses coffee. How about HYPE? (See page 320.)

THE GROPER AND HIS WIFE
9385 7384

A much-loved fish and chip shop whose point of difference is that you can buy raw, wet fish here too, and a very extensive range of beautiful, handmade salads. (See page 175.)

THE GROCER

Chelsea Village
145 Stirling Hwy
Nedlands WA 6009
9389 8144
www.thegrocer.com.au

Monday-Friday 10.00-5.00
Saturday 9.00-12.00 Closed Sundays
Off-street parking in front of shop

If you need something really exotic or unusual, such as crystalised violets or flying-fish roe, for a special recipe and you can't get it anywhere else, The Grocer may just have it. Be careful though – that won't be all you come out with. You would need a will of iron to resist the goodies displayed in this exquisite shop.

This small retail shop is the showroom for many of the grocery lines Louise and Andrew Miller provide for their wholesale customers, who make up 90 per cent of the business. This is why products are displayed together by brand, rather than by type.

'Some of the products in the shop are not available anywhere else in WA except in the restaurants that we import them for,' says Louise. It would take too long to give you a comprehensive list of everything they stock, but the range is so eclectic, we thought it might be fun to mention some of their more unusual products. On the day we visited, we spotted edible gold leaf, goose fat, sesame seaweed salad, dried porcini, morels and shiitake mushrooms, pâté de foie gras, all the herbs, spices and extracts, caviar, Brik pastry, quails' eggs, leaf gelatine, Greg Malouf's chermoula and rasel hanout, whole cheeses, handmade, slow-dried pasta, and chocolate made from 99 per cent cocoa.

For dedicated food lovers, The Grocer produces a seasonal newsletter – you can subscribe online, via their website – full of food news, details of any tastings they are having.

We've always had a friendly welcome when we've come in here.

FOOD STORES AND GROCERS

THE KOSHER FOOD CENTRE

15 Plantation St (in the synagogue car park)
Menora WA 6050
9370 3311
www.kosherfoodcentre.com.au

Sunday 8.00-12.30 Monday 8.30-4.30
Tuesday-Thursday 8.30-5.30 Friday 8.00-4.00 Closed Saturdays
Parking in synagogue car park

Ros Bettane, who owns and runs the Kosher Food Centre with her husband, Bernard, joked with us: 'You don't have to be Jewish to shop here; we've got lots of things for everyone to enjoy.' The Jewish dietary laws require that meat and dairy products are not consumed at the same meal, so many of the products they sell, such as ice cream, have been made using soya instead of cows' milk. In fact, much of the food here is dairy-free. There are a lot of gluten-free products as well (most of the smallgoods cabinet, for example), and quite a few vegetarian alternatives, too – including some of the sausages. If you are on a lactose or gluten-free diet and don't already know about the Kosher Food Centre, we're sure it would be worth a visit.

The Kosher Food Centre is not huge, but it is structured like a miniature shopping mall: it has its own butcher, baker, patisserie, deli and grocery. As Bernard, who comes from Lyon, the food capital of France, says: 'No schlepping from shop to shop to purchase your kosher items. Everything is kosher here.'

The butcher sells both fresh meat – beef, veal, lamb and chicken – and some pre-prepared dishes, such as meatloaf and corned brisket. There's also a cold cabinet full of smallgoods, including frankfurters, pastrami, smoked chicken and turkey.

The bakery is famous for its boiled bagels, which are made throughout the day – they are great if you get them fresh out of the oven and still warm. They also bake challah (both small, plaited loaves and upright), as well as rye, pita, Turkish and Italian-style loaves, and pretzels.

The patisserie produces delicious cakes plus Danish pastries, croissants, borrekas and doughnuts for Chanukah. On Thursdays and Fridays there are always special cakes for Shabbat: orange chiffon cake, rich chocolate cake, chocolate mousse cake, Opera gateau, pear frangipani tart and the most delicious-looking apple crumble cake.

In the deli there are dips, spreads and kneidl dumpling mixes; in the freezer there are meals ready to go, such as gefilte fish and chocolate cheese blintzes; and on the shelves there are all sorts of biscuits, plus matzo meal, pickles, and lokshen (noodles).

This is a good place to come if you are a homesick South African. Many of the store's customers emigrated from there and they are well catered for here. It's also a good store to visit if you just want to discover another source of well-made, interesting, world food in Perth.

Bernard Bettane is a graduate of the famous L'Ecole Hoteliere de Paris and has extensive experience in most aspects of the hospitality industry in the south of Europe, America and Israel.

THE RE STORE

The two branches of the Re Store and the big wholesale importer European Foods are all owned and still run by the same family, the descendants of John and Maria Re. John Re opened a shop in Fremantle in 1908 and imported some of the very first European foods into WA. The Lake Street store, opened by John Re's son in 1936 when it was still hard to get Continental produce here, re-started importing foodstuffs. The Oxford Street store followed after the war. But though the Re Stores still get their stock from European Foods and do still feel very European, actually most of what they sell is Australian. There's always a choice; they never sell just one brand or variety of any item, not just because they want to be different, but to provide choice – one person's favourite kind of olive oil won't be to the liking of someone else.

Though both shops are big, with acres of floor space and very long counters, neither feels at all like a supermarket; rather, both have an old-fashioned, oddly small-shop kind of feel about them. This is deliberate. Anything displayed in these stores sells almost immediately (once, many years ago, they sold a container-full of Italian bicycles) and the range looks huge, but they limit the number and kind of products they sell. 'We can sell anything here,' says John Re's grandson Moreno, 'but if we did we'd no longer be the Re Store.' Come to either shop for any kind of cheese or cold meat or salami, cut to order and in beautiful condition; olive oils in big tins or little bottles; hundreds of different biscuits; colourful jars of pickled vegetables; jams and marmalades; sauces and dips; rice and pasta, fresh or dried; their own Braziliano brand coffee, roasted on the premises (plus many other brands); all sorts of teas, including T2; all the French fruit syrups; metres of chocolate of every kind; and not just one sort of mustard, but six or eight. It's like an Italian corner store on steroids.

THE RE STORE, LAKE STREET

72-74 Lake St
Northbridge WA 6003
9328 1877

Monday-Friday 8.00-5.30
Saturday 8.00-12.30 Closed Sundays and public holidays

This store, closer to the CBD, sells all of the above – we bought some roquefort cheese which was superb and some slices of their imported Parma ham which literally melted in the mouth, as good as it could be – but it also does a roaring trade in filled rolls for takeaway lunches. Lorenzo Berti makes all the fresh pasta here, both ribbon and filled. Because the flour here is not the same as in Italy, Lorenzo mixes his own. We bought some of his ravioli and a pot of basil and tomato sauce, and it was very good.

Aurora Berti, one of the four daughters of the founder (and mother of Lorenzo and Moreno) still comes in every Friday: 'I love it here, especially at Christmas. I just love it. It's in my blood.' The customers love it too. 'We've got regulars coming in from when my dad was here,' she says. 'If I'm bored at home, I just come in.'

As well as all the gourmet food, the Lake Street store carries a large stock of kitchenware.

THE RE STORE, OXFORD STREET

213 Oxford St
Leederville WA 6007
9444 9644

Monday-Friday 8.00-6.00
Saturday 8.00-4.00 Closed Sundays and public holidays

This branch is run by Lorenzo's brother, Moreno Berti, the fourth generation in the business. The main difference between this and the Lake Street store is that this branch has a very big range of fine wines, plus imported beers, spirits and liqueurs, and little or no kitchenware. Otherwise the shelves carry the same food lines as the Lake Street shop, and follow the same philosophy.

'We still have a small shop attitude in a big store,' says Moreno. Both shops have a clever system of indicating gluten-free foods: with a yellow label. Each shop makes its own fresh ribbon pasta. On Saturday mornings people queuing three or four deep for the deli counter may have to wait up to 40 minutes. 'But they don't seem to mind,' says Moreno, 'Our clients want freshly cut produce; they want their cheese cut from a big wheel. It's an experience; it's like a meeting place.'

TONY ALE & CO.

Lot 7, 84 Hammond Rd
Jandakot WA 6164
9414 8015

7 days 8.00–6.00
Closed public holidays
Ample car parking

Started as a small family business nearly 45 years ago, Tony Ale & Co. is now a big family business. Even so, every inch of the huge space in Jandakot which houses the wholesale and retail operation (and which now includes many products other than fruit and veg) feels as if it has his personal stamp of dedication very firmly all over it. 'Tony Ale is the best name in fruit and veg in Perth,' has been said to us several times during the course of our research.

The core business remains fruit and veg: there are long refrigerated shelves containing every conceivable kind of salad and gourmet leaves: the rocket, Swiss chard, salad leaves and baby spinach (which are sold washed) are all grown specially for him by growers who have been supplying him for 35 years. There are many different varieties of fruit in season: four kinds of plums, seven kinds of apples, the last of the figs, four grape varieties – and the most delicious Kensington Pride mangoes. 'Fresh, beautiful, tree-ripened in Baldivis,' he proudly boasts.

Next to the organic fridge, with its comprehensive range of fruit, vegetables and fruit juices, there is a cabinet of cut fruit and ready-to-go salads.

Supporting the fresh produce is a large cheese selection, including Borrello stracchino and La Vera pecorino. In the dairy section we found yoghurts, Bannister Downs milk and butter, the deli counter has Princi Italian sausages, Mondo D'oro salamis, homemade pies, olives, a selection of salads (Greek, rice, tomato and pepper etc) and a comprehensive selection of dried groceries. There's good bread from Bodhi's and Il Panino, and in the freezer you'll find gelati from Azzura, Il Gelato and La Cucina.

You could easily satisfy all your grocery needs here; it would be a very good place to stop and stock up at the beginning of a journey down south.

Also @ Tony Ale & Co.:

MARCO'S FUSSY MEATS
A modern busy butcher's shop owned and run by Chris Faulds in partnership with Marco's Fussy Meats in Applecross. Much of the meat has value-added. (See page 68.)

TEMPTATIONS BAKEHOUSE AND PATISSERIE
The full and varied range of Temptations bread, including Hans Sanders' signature German rye loaf. There is a large selection of cakes, tarts, biscuits and celebration cakes. (See page 41.)

FOOD-TO-GO

We are tremendously fortunate that food-to-go in Perth needn't mean a defrosted, reheated TV dinner. Some of the meals prepared by the people in this book for you to pop into the oven are, quite frankly, superb.

All of the meals we've considered are made by hand with real ingredients of the best quality – in the case of our butchers, always with the same meat they sell over the counter. One even makes her own rice wine vinegar for sushi, not trusting the bottled product, however good.

Often we've been told the chef (who may be the co-owner, aka the wife) has devised or adapted the recipe and then experimented with the dish at home, using her lucky family or the staff as guinea pigs, until it's perfected. So by the time the beef and burgundy pie, penne alla carbonara or Moroccan lamb shanks appear in the shop they are as good as, or better than, you could possibly make at home – and very useful when you're short of time.

The following butchers provide hot cooked food:

Crimea Quality Meats (see page 55)
Hadleys (see page 64)
Mondo di Carne (see page 71)
Peter's Butchers (see page 73)
The Meat Showcase (see page 86)
Weir's Butchers (see page 89)

ABSOLUTELY CHEZ UCHINO
622 Stirling Hwy
Mosman Park WA 6012
9385 2202
www.abcuchino.com.au

Monday and Saturday 4.30–9.00 Tuesday–Friday 12.00–9.00
Closed Sunday and public holidays
Parking behind, enter car park off Glyde Street

For 12 years, chef Osamu Uchino and wife Rico ran the highly acclaimed Chez Uchino restaurant, first in Cottesloe and, later, in Mosman Park. In 2002, they opened Absolutely Chez Uchino – an equally classy but less formal eatery on Stirling Highway, just opposite the Mosman Park train station.

Absolutely Chez Uchino offers a unique blend of Japanese/French food-to-go. It is perfect for a delicious, healthy take away, or BYO and have a simple meal in the small, relaxed dining area.

The extensive and delicious take-away menu includes made to order sushi and sashimi, Tataki beef with Ponzu sauce, udon noodle soups with grilled chicken or tofu, vegetable or fish tempura and a variety of spicy curries, all made using Liberty hormone-free chicken, Murry Williams hormone- and antibiotic-free beef and Amelia Park lamb.

There are soups – beetroot and orange, Thai pumpkin – and a selection of main meals – White Rocks Veal Marengo with brown rice and vegetables, chicken in miso and ginger sauce, risottos, beef Burgundy and grilled tuna teriyaki. And to finish off your meal; crème caramel, passionfruit or chocolate mousse, crepes with orange sauce or green tea ice cream.

Consulting with nutritionist, Jo Beer, Osamu and Rico have introduced a good range of healthy frozen meals.

If you are planning a dinner or cocktail party, Absolutely Chez Uchino can help you with their home catering service.

CHEZ FREDERIC GOURMET FOOD TO GO

16 North St (cnr Elizabeth St)
Cottesloe WA 6011
9286 2555

Monday–Saturday 5.00pm–8.30pm
Closed Sundays and public holidays
Parking on Elizabeth St

During the day, Chez Frederic sits quietly just back from the road, but when chef Frederic Poguet opens his doors at 5.00pm, it's to a rush of hungry people.

This much-loved local eatery, serving an extensive range of Mediterranean fare, is the perfect place to come when you don't feel like cooking, but do feel like eating something that is delicious and interesting and has a home-cooked feel.

There's something here for everyone, whether it's Mum, Dad and the kids, or busy 9–5ers driving home from work in search of tonight's dinner, or students on a budget or people dining alone.

The takeaway menu includes an array of fresh pastas (linguini marinara, duck ravioli or the classic carbonara), a good selection of vegetarian food (such as green gnocchi pesto), and a half dozen or so meat dishes. Every night there are daily blackboard specials, perhaps spinach and ricotta crêpes, or scallopini marsala, or osso bucco, or assorted meat and chicken curries and risotto.

The bestseller would have to be the deliciously sticky lamb shanks, but with such a varied menu, there's good food here to suit all tastes.

MARCO'S FUSSY MEATS

777 Canning Hwy
Applecross WA 6153
9364 3867

7 days 8.00–6.00
Cooked food: Monday–Friday 4.00pm–6.00pm
Closed public holidays
Ample car park and off-street parking round the back

During the day, Marco and his six butchers offer a full butcher's shop service with a large variety of meat, much of which has value added to it: Thai chicken, lamb shank pie, Victoria Bitter Swags, chicken many ways, beef swirls, to name but a few. There's also a good range of homemade sausages, made to Marco's own recipes: Italian, breakfast, barbecue and Cumberland.

Marco's two chefs prepare food for the cooked food counter. They sell a different roast dinner each day, with potatoes and vegetables, plus curries, stirfries, lasagne and spaghetti Bolognese.

Homemade pies to take away are also big sellers here: beef with red wine and mushroom, shepherd's pie, steak and kidney, beef with port wine or Guinness, chicken and veggies.

MOE SUSHI

Unit 3, 7 Station St
Cottesloe WA 6011
9286 1830

Monday-Saturday 10.30-2.30
Closed Sundays and public holidays
CASH only
Off-street parking

You'll see many familiar faces from sports, television and politics coming in here for the attractive and delicious sushi which Moses Maung – aka Moe – makes every day, throughout the day. 'It is my passion,' he says. 'I really love to create all the different sushi every time.' Burma-born Moe was trained in WA by a Japanese chef, Mr Keda, and has been established here for 6 years. He uses only the best ingredients, and the fresh produce is all from WA; the rice, seaweed and sauces are imported from Japan.

About ten different kinds of sushi are on offer each day, beautifully packaged and ready to go. Moe varies them according to which fresh fish is available. There are also some hot dishes, such as chicken or salmon teriyaki.

He will make specials to order and will also cater for parties.

Also @:

Shop 3A, Crossways Shopping Centre
180-184 Rokeby Rd
Subiaco WA 6008
9380 9911

Monday-Saturday 7.00-7.00
Closed Sundays and public holidays

MOTHER INDIA

23 Forrest St (cnr Wood St)
East Fremantle WA 6158
9430 4217

Wednesday, Thursday and Sunday 5.00pm–8.30pm
Friday–Saturday 5.00pm–9.00pm Closed Mondays and Tuesdays
CASH only
Ample parking in Forrest St
BYO for dine-in customers

Mother India, well loved by locals for 17 years under its previous name, Lal's, is now run by Sri Lanka-born Sathay Kan, and has an emphasis on healthy, locally sourced food which is chemical-free.

Using chickens from Farmgate, lamb cut to order from Morris Meat Market in Innaloo, local and WA seafood and fresh market vegetables, Sathay cooks to order here. The lamb is slow-cooked the day before to absorb the flavours, then reheated in sauces made daily. He makes his own bread and naan. 'I try to cook like my mother does at home,' he says – fresh, simple cooking.

Vindaloo and rogan josh remain popular, but it is his vegetarian delicacies – mattar paneer, palak paneer (cottage cheese with peas or spinach), vegetable jhal frazi, aloo baingan and palak – which are popular with his many new customers. His samosas, stuffed with spicy potato and vegetables, are crisp and not at all greasy. Butter chicken, in a mildly spiced tomato, cashew paste and butter sauce, could be cut with a spoon. The lamb in the lamb saag, which was in a slightly hotter sauce made from spinach, onions, cardamom and tomato, came in firm, meaty chunks.

This is a takeaway with a difference: healthy food-to-go. It can be eaten at home, or in the Horrie Long Reservation next door ... or you can dine in. Sathay now has half a dozen tables inside with waiter service. The poppadoms, which arrive with a carafe of water the moment you sit down, are excellent.

Party orders and catering are available including Value Packs – the Complete Indian meal for Two, Three or Four People. Delivery is free for orders of $50.00 or more.

NIPPON FARE

479 Hay St
Subiaco WA 6008
9388 2738

Monday–Friday 9.00–5.00
Saturday 9.00–3.00 Closed Sundays
CASH only
Car parks between Forrest and Barker Sts

Nippon Fare is a long-established Japanese takeaway and catering shop which has been offering authentic and affordable Japanese cuisine to its customers since 1992. It's owned and run by Noriko and Neville Gliddon. From this tiny shop, tucked away at the far end of Hay Street by the railway line, they produce beautiful food.

Their food-to-go menu has eight different Bento lunch boxes: beef teriyaki, chicken teriyaki, fish, beef curry and rice, tempura, chicken kushi, gyoza dumplings and beef sukiyaki. In the noodle department, there are two kinds of stirfry noodles – yaki soba and teriyaki udon – or vegetable tempura udon with soup.

Sushi rolls, in small boxes of five pieces or a large box of ten pieces, come in eleven different varieties, including chicken, octopus, tuna, salmon and prawn.

Noriko told us that they do lots of catering and special orders for summer parties, for cafés and restaurants, for hospital cafés and for doctors' morning teas.

Their biggest sellers are teriyaki – beef or chicken – and sushi rolls. Noriko's homemade teriyaki sauce is a firm favourite with the Subi regulars.

PEKO PEKO

1/172 St Brigids Tce
Doubleview WA 6018
9245 5077

Tuesday–Sunday 10.30–8.00 Closed Mondays
Car park at side of shop

Peko Peko, a modern, Euro-Japanese fusion-style café, takeaway and caterer, is the brainchild of Samantha and Tony Bottegal.

When Samantha returned to Australia after a decade in Japan, she was often 'peko peko' – a little bit hungry – for some sushi. Unable to find any she liked, she set up a Japanese cooking school, giving sushi-making classes. This in turn led her and Tony to open Peko Peko, with its cross-cultural flavours and bohemian feel.

Their Japanese chef makes teriyaki and prawn skewers, ricepaper rolls, nori maki sushi rolls and soup. Everything is handmade on the premises; they even make their own sushi vinegar rather than buying it in – it's simple, healthy, fresh food.

Students of the Japanese school down the road and Japanese housewives and their children frequent the café every day. There is a child-friendly area which Samantha says 'is accepted by both cultures'.

Lots of experimental work goes on, 'evolving tastes and recipes'. Using some organics and mainly WA produce – except for imported nori and some Japanese items – there is nothing artificial here. All the sushi is made daily and is not sliced until you have bought it, to ensure maximum freshness.

'We don't settle for mediocrity,' says Samantha. 'We're just determined to make the best sushi in Perth.'

Also @:

10/10 Scarborough Beach Rd
Scarborough WA 6019
9245 1144

Takeaway only: 7 days 10.00–10.00

SPICES

27 Hampden Rd
Nedlands WA 6009
9386 1691

7 days 7.00–8.00
Closed Christmas Day
Limited parking in Hampden Rd

People have been known to drive from all over Perth for the highlight of this local supermarket: their delicious Vietnamese fresh spring rolls.

One of Sony Tang's staff very deftly showed us how they are made: soaked rice paper, filled with crispy bean sprouts, fine softly cooked rice noodles, fresh, bright green mint leaves and either prawn, chicken or vegetables quickly rolled up into the familiar sausage shape. Then, says Sony, 'They should be eaten within two hours.' We, of course, ate ours immediately: the freshness was bursting out and they were heaven.

The dipping sauces, either hoi sin or a lemony fish sauce, are made by Sony's mother.

The Vietnamese rolls are only made for weekday lunchtimes – unfortunately, they're not available over the counter at weekends, unless you place a special order. There are some ready from 9am but they are often all gone by 2pm, so hurry along.

For special orders and party platters, phone and speak to Sony or his wife, Jenny.

Other foods to go are garden green salad, fresh fruit salad and freshly made sandwiches and rolls.

And while you're there, grab one of the many bags or buckets of seasonal fruit and vegetables from local growers – they are displayed on the footpath.

SWISH FISH 2 GO

Shop 5, 777 Canning Hwy
Applecross WA 6153
9364 7775

7 days 8.30–7.00
Closed public holidays
Off-street parking

Swish Fish 2 Go is just that: pre-prepared dishes such as fish parcels, fish cakes, fish kebabs and various marinated fish dishes, all looking fresh and tasty, ready to take-home and cook.

Other gourmet foods and salads are also on offer.

Some fresh local fish, including Freo sardines, saddletail cod and blue manna crabs, were available when we visited.

Outside catering and platters can be ordered.

This is an outlet of the Swish 'n Chips shop in Mt Lawley (see page 173).

THE SATAY SHOP

Shop 13, Chelsea Village
145 Stirling Hwy
Nedlands WA 6009
9389 8255

Monday-Friday 10.00-5.30
Saturday 10.00-1.00 Closed Sundays and public Holidays
CASH/CHEQUE only
Parking in Chelsea Village car park

Hidden away in among the fabric wholesalers and antique shops, the chiropractor and hairdressers in Chelsea Village is Mr Weezee, The Satay Shop. And what a find it is.

As the name says, it is a satay shop selling authentic beef and chicken satay in packs of twelve and 25, and the most delicious peanut satay sauce.

Victor Oee and Mr Weezee have recently added marinated chicken wings – called Tasty Angels' Wings – to the repertoire, and you can now also buy the beef and chicken prepared satay mix without the skewers, to use in stirfries.

Normally all the chicken and beef is sold frozen: it is only available as a fresh product on the day it is made. If you want to buy fresh satay, ring to check they have what you want – or place an order.

Also @:

Shop 6, 502 Marmion St
Booragoon WA 6154
9317 8586

Monday-Friday 10.00-5.30
Saturday 10.00-1.00
Closed Sundays and public Holidays

GOURMET CAFÉS AND BREAKFAST

This book is primarily about food shops and is not a restaurant guide. However, we thought that if we are encouraging you to explore new shopping areas, you might like to know about a nearby gourmet café where you may want to stop for coffee and a little something to keep up your strength.

And, in Perth, it seems that even people who hardly ever go out for dinner in restaurants do go out for breakfast. So for those reasons we have sought out a number of gourmet cafés, which all have distinct personalities. One thing they do have in common, though, is that they all serve very good coffee.

AUBERGINE GOURMET FOODS
Shop 1, 231 South Tce
South Fremantle WA 6162
9335 2115

7.00–4.00 365 days a year
CASH only
Ticket parking in South Tce and side streets

Aubergine's proprietor, Dave Cooney, says: 'It's a simple little business: we try to keep everything as simple as we can. We buy the best products we can find and do as little as possible to them.' And in this place, simple means beautiful. It has a comfortable feel about it – it's laidback, and there's a kind of organised chaos of the highest quality.

An easy-to-read blackboard on the wall tells you what's available, under the headings: Breakfast (All Day) and Other Stuff. Simplicity again with the drinks blackboard: Hot Drinks, Juices (eleven, all freshly squeezed) and Cold Drinks.

On a Monday morning at 9.30, Aubergine was buzzing. Their Breakfast Delight – Bircher muesli marinated overnight, served with yoghurt and berries, plus a portion of sliced fresh fruit, some fabulous thick organic fruit toast (from Abhi's across the road) plus two homemade ricotta hot cakes – was simply delicious. The All Day Breakfast menu goes from a simple coffee and croissant right through to the full catastrophe.

Under the guidance of head chef Paul Walters, the menu constantly evolves, but slowly and seasonally: more salads in summer; more soups in the winter. All the eggs are free-range and there is a strong leaning towards organic where possible.

The excellent coffee is from beans especially roasted for Aubergine each week in small batches by Mena Samios in Mt Lawley.

The staff here (nineteen in total, including six chefs) are very friendly and efficient: 'I hire an attitude, not a set of skills and the word NO is banned,' says Dave. It was all simply beautiful.

GOURMET CAFÉS AND BREAKFAST

BOUCLA CAFÉ

349 Rokeby Rd
Subiaco WA 6008
9381 2841

**Monday–Saturday 8.00–5.00 Closed Sundays
Parking on street**

When you come into this charming café, all trace of Perth disappears; to all intents and purposes you are in Greece. The furnishings, pictures, posters, carpets, pottery and glassware – some of which are for sale – all have a Mediterranean feel, and the atmosphere is like a very popular and busy taverna in Athens. Despina Tanner, the owner (and cake chef *par excellence*) presides over it all like a hostess at a family party. She appears to know everyone and pretty well everyone greets her by name.

This is a tremendously popular place, famous because of Despina's cakes. Those in the know come early and wait for them to come out of the oven. It's what she loves: 'Cakes are my palette for creativity,' she says. Her apple cake, made with twelve whole apples and lots of nuts, is most people's favourite, but we loved her soufra, a sweet filo tart with a soft, brûlee centre which took us back to our childhood's creamy bread and butter puddings. Despina no longer cooks from recipes or weighs out ingredients; she does it all instinctively, as more of an art than a craft. As well as the cakes and the baklava (made by an old family friend), the café menu features filo and spinach pies, Persian slippers (spicy pastry with beef, onion and garlic), chicken pies, soups and salads – all to eat in or to go. The excellent coffee is by Fiori.

Despina has a long history in food. She started the John St Café in Cottesloe in 1983 but came back to Subiaco, where her family lives and which is full of memories for her, out of sentiment. She started Boucla 3 years ago as an outlet for her creativity after a spell as a freelance caterer. Despina loves what she does and can't imagine stopping: 'While I can work like this, I will,' she says.

GOURMET CAFÉS AND BREAKFAST

BREAKFAST AT COTTESLOE BEACH

Come rain, hail or shine, Cottesloe Beach is always a beautiful place to start your day. With its beautiful sandy beach and stunning views across the ocean to Rottnest, just add family and friends, some good coffee and a hearty breakfast and you have the makings of a blissfully perfect day.

BARCHETTA

149 Marine Parade
9385 2411

Sunday-Tuesday 6.30-4.00
Wednesday-Saturday 6.30 am-8.00 pm
Breakfast served 6.30-11.00
No bookings on Sundays

If you come early you'll be sharing the place with those intrepid early-morning swimmers who start the day, summer and winter, with a dip in the Indian Ocean. A little later and it is young families and people on their way to work. On the site of the old North Cott kiosk, it is a modern building with an enclosed balcony overlooking the sea. Breakfasts range from the healthily organic, usually involving muesli (the toasted macadamia is recommended), to the cholesterol-charged catastrophe that is the Boaties' Breakfast. The coffee is the excellent Five Senses, blended specially for Barchetta; there are fresh smoothies and juices; and the daily papers are on hand. Dogs are welcome but must be left outside.

BEACHES CAFÉ

122 Marine Parade
9384 4412

Monday to Sunday 6.30 am–4.00 pm
CASH only

Come in your wet bathers, bring the dog; this is the most casual of the beach cafes. It is where the early-morning, Lycra-suited cyclists come for coffee. A little later you might see one or two suits, pausing on their way to work. Beaches is also popular with family groups – there is a children's playground just across the road and plenty of parking. It is a very customer-friendly, chatty sort of place serving excellent food and coffee – free-range eggs from Baldivis, bread from Lawley's and New Norcia, freshly squeezed juice and smoothies. Breakfast is served all day. Remember, it is cash only.

BLUE DUCK CAFÉ

151 Marine Parade
9385 2499

7 days 7.00–9.00
Breakfast served 7.30–11.30

Famous for its stunning views, this Cottesloe icon is where we bring our foreign visitors to show off – they're always impressed, and not just by the vista; the food is pretty good, too. We think of the Blue Duck as a little more formal than the other beach cafés. You'll usually see one or two business types having a working breakfast but it still has the relaxed feel that is essential to a beach-side café. The coffee is by Fiori; the breakfasts imaginative – buttermilk pancakes with a citrus and honey sauce, for example, and a vegetarian breakfast bruschetta – and, thrown in for nothing, one of the best views in the world.

JOHN STREET CAFÉ
37 John Street
9384 3390
7 days 7.00–5.00

A bright personality under the Norfolk Island pines, the Grecian-blue façade of this outstanding café is a welcoming sight. Tables and chairs spill out from the covered verandah onto the footpath, providing a beautiful place to sit and watch the world go by in a peaceful, relaxed atmosphere. The north-facing aspect makes this a good sitting-out place even in winter. It is very popular with beachgoers on their way home from a morning swim. Breakfast is served all day and all the food is cooked to order on the premises to accommodate personal preferences. They believe people are very particular about their breakfasts and that you have to get it right. The eggs are free-range and the toast organic. We love 'The Vegetarian Lot' with home-made hash browns and baked beans and they serve a really good breakfast bagel with bacon, avocado, snowpea sprouts and cream cheese. They have delicious muffins and a huge selection of home-made cakes, some gluten-free.

CAFÉ 55

55 High St
Fremantle WA 6160
9336 2604

Monday–Friday 7.00–3.00
Saturday 9.00–3.00
CASH only
Ticket parking on the High St

Thanh Johnson, an ex-commercial banker, and her husband Wayne, an ex-engineer, founded Café 55 5 years ago, and what a wonderful place they have created. This small, narrow café opening onto High Street positively buzzes with energy. There are good things to eat in, take out or take home.

A fairly traditional breakfast menu kicks off the day: rolls, croissants, and toasted sandwiches, or a cooked breakfast with eggs, bacon and tomato. And the very best coffee. They use a Silvana blend and it's superbly made by Alexandra, described to us as 'more of an asset than an employee'. There is also a good variety of leaf tea available.

By mid-morning Café 55 has put on its other hat, and the traditional Vietnamese and Asian lunch menu takes the stage. There's a choice of twelve dishes ranging from pho (beef soup with rice noodles) to laksa lemak (coconut curry soups) to nyonya curries.

Their rice paper rolls (chicken, prawn or vegetarian), sold in packs of two with dipping sauce and peanuts, are a big seller with their regular clientele, about 65 per cent of whom are women, wanting a healthy, low-fat, low-sugar lunch.

Freshly made sandwiches and home-baked filled rolls are here too, along with a large display cabinet of sushi, rice and noodles, pastries, cakes and biscuits. Café 55 sells over 400 homemade pasties and pies a week. If you want beautiful handmade homemade food, sourced from the best local ingredients and coupled with excellent service, this is the place to come.

GOURMET CAFÉS AND BREAKFAST

CIMBALINO

105 Waratah Ave
Dalkeith WA 6009
9386 9009

7 days 7.00–5.00
Open public holidays
CASH only
Parking on Waratah Ave; angle parking opposite by Genesta Park

Cimbalino might only be few years old but it has the relaxed feel and ease of an old-timer. This is a café that really cherishes its customers. The names of the regulars are painted on the walls, hundreds and hundreds of them, with their favourite choice of coffee (cap. lat. skfw, lb, sb etc) painted alongside. But even if you're not a regular, the service is very attentive. We went for breakfast on an autumn Friday morning, and the friendly staff checked two or three times to see that we had everything we wanted.

Four of us shared perfect scrambled eggs, mushrooms, grilled tomatoes, carefully poached eggs, very crispy bacon and beautiful toast. It was all excellent: the portions are generous and the coffee – proprietor Steve Kenyon's own blend, which he has roasted to order – is first class.

There are lots of free newspapers available to read, even the *Financial Review* for business types pausing for breakfast on their way to the office.

There's a steady flow of regulars throughout the day; this seems to be the place where the locals meet. You can sit outside at tables on the pavement, or in two big rooms inside, or in a courtyard out the back.

The croissants and baguette at Cimbalino are made for them by Eric Masure, who you can find at Subi Station Markets every Friday, Saturday and Sunday as La Galette de France, and now also at La Galette de France South Perth (see page 104).

COODE STREET CAFÉ

24 Coode St (cnr 3rd Ave)
Mt Lawley WA 6050
9371 9900

Monday-Saturday 7.00-6.00
Sunday 8.00-6.00
Parking in Coode St
BYO

Coode Street Café is definitely a destinational food stop. It's on the corner of a quiet, suburban leafy crossroads – two of which are dead-ends – between Beaufort Street and the Perth–Guildford railway line. If you are in the area and prefer not to sit among the fumes and hurly burly of the Mt Lawley strip, this is the place for you.

Terry Burgon has been serving up 'generous home-style food rather than restaurant-style food' for the last 15 years. He must have been doing something right, as he seems to have been rewarded with many regular clients. 'We get lots of return business,' he says. 'We have some clients who come twice a day.'

At the weekends, breakfast is busy: on a typical Sunday they will serve as many as 200 customers: their WNL? (Who Needs Lunch?) – bacon, eggs, chipolata, tomato and mushroom with New Norcia toast – and their eggs Benedict are firm favourites.

The full breakfast menu is served every day of the week: coffee, by Fiori, is served eight ways. There are also freshly squeezed fruit juices, fruit combos, vegetable combos, smoothies, lassis, milkshakes and frappes all available, as are plunger teas (five ways), iced or hot chocolate and soft drinks.

At lunchtime there are daily seasonal specials: always a soup, a bagel, a pasta and a sandwich special. The main lunch menu offers homemade pies, quiche, tarts, club sandwiches, bruschetta and salads Niçoise, Caesar or warm chicken. Some of the food is available as food-to-go.

GOURMET CAFÉS AND BREAKFAST

GEORGES

Shop 13, The Boulevard Shopping Centre
31 Gayton Rd
City Beach WA 6015
9285 0240
www.georgescatering.com

Monday–Friday 7.00–6.00
Saturday and Sunday 7.00–5.00
Open all public holidays except Christmas Day and Good Friday
Ample parking in car park

George Hombert and his wife, Sandrine, have created a wonderfully eclectic food business up here near City Beach. Everything is cooked on the premises by George and his team of four chefs. If you eat in (or sit outside on the terrace), you can have a full breakfast menu, a light lunch, snacks and drinks. There is also a range of food-to-go and a full outside catering service.

On the breakfast menu, there are the usual breakfast things, as well as one or two interesting variations, including a traditional French breakfast consisting of baguette, jam, butter and a big bowl of coffee. They are famous for their savoury muffins.

Throughout the day, there is homemade quiche and cake, tart and tourte, frittata and flans, baguettes and burgers.

In the display cabinets, as food-to-go, there are duck rillettes, chicken liver parfait, a selection of seven different salads, pies, pastries and some French cheese. Main courses on offer include chicken chasseur, stroganoff, duck confit and five different savoury crepes. There are also warming soups for winter, to eat in or to go.

A full catering service is available for dinner parties, buffets, cocktail parties, weddings, corporate events and any family occasion.

Sandrine jokes that Georges would prefer to not have a menu but just cook 'the best range of food using the best produce available'. Regardless, they're building a very regular clientele: 'We see them all every day.'

HUBBLE'S YARD

50 George St
East Fremantle WA 6158
9339 5850

Tuesday–Saturday 7.30–3.00
Closed Sundays, Mondays and public holidays
CASH only
Parking on George St, Hubble St

Beautifully made fresh coffee and nine different leaf teas, plus iced tea, fresh juice and fresh lemon and bitters are on the menu at this child-friendly gourmet café – which has become a favourite haunt of many in the neighbourhood since its opening last year.

Delicious muffins, baked daily on the premises, toast made from New Norcia bread or sourdough, pastries, pies, savoury tarts, risotto cake, some gluten-free cakes (including orange and almond), and fruit salad are all on offer. The menu is constantly changing: earlier this year they began their cooked breakfast menu.

The need to have a 'guaranteed good coffee close to home' was the inspiration behind Samantha and Grant Mooney's decision to buy and renovate the Hubble's yard building, for which they have won a heritage award.

There's a playroom for toddlers off the main seating area, and seats outside where you can watch the world go up and down George Street.

The whole ambience is casual and relaxed; it's stylish yet homely, with friendly, happy-looking staff. And terrific coffee.

It's a good place to come to if you're visiting Wine Liaisons (see page 28) or George Street Merchants (see page 143).

LEMON ESPRESSO

2 St Quentin Ave
Claremont WA 6010
9383 2373

Monday–Saturday 7.00–4.30
Sunday 7.00–2.00 Closed Christmas Day
CASH only
Parking under Coles

There's an energetic buzz about Lemon Espresso. If the number of people who pass through the doors of this hip, busy little café in St Quentin Ave is any indication of quality, then Lemon Espresso must be doing something right. And that 'something right' is that they serve one of the best coffees around.

Owner Mark Coulson was the coffee-maker at the famous and ground-breaking Oriel Café in its heyday. He founded Lemon Espresso a couple of years ago because he felt the area 'needed a good place selling the best coffee ... the best of everything. We go for quality over speed, and our customers seem to be happy with that.'

So you can have coffee nine different ways, freshly squeezed juice six ways, smoothies five ways, milkshakes six ways ... and that's just the drinks blackboard.

Many regulars drop in for coffee, snacks and lunch, but on the food front, we think it's at breakfast time that Lemon Espresso really comes into its own. Everything is cooked to order – so your food may take a little longer to arrive than at some other places – but the results are superlative and well worth the wait. Mark says, 'It's not so much a different menu; it's just better.' But actually, we thought it *was* a bit different. There are a few lovely, rather unusual dishes: balsamic mushrooms, feta, spinach and herbs on toast, slow-roasted tomatoes with goats' cheese, rocket and pesto, and oven-roasted bacon and egg toastie with caramelised onion and chutney – all are well worth a try.

But the nicest thing of all at Lemon Espresso is that they respect that many people are very *particular* about breakfast. Here they will always do 'free-range eggs, as you like' with whatever extras you want. We love that attitude.

Lemon Lane – Mark Coulson's latest venture – is scheduled to open in the spring of 2007. It is located in Maude Jackson Lane, next to the liquor store on Bayview Terrace, Claremont.

MILKD

32 Angove St
North Perth WA 6006
9228 8867
www.milkd.com.au

7 days 7.00–7.00
CASH only
Parking in Angove St

There's a unique feel about Milkd: we think something a bit special is going on here.

Opened just over 2 years ago by Lorena Tati, Milkd has had a strong personality of its own from the beginning. It's a personality which is very inclusive of its customers; there's a vibrant yet relaxed, inviting and warm atmosphere and the staff are terrific.

There's more than a whiff and a sniff of high quality about the place, the coffee and the menu: locally sourced, organic where possible, always fresh, always the best. The Arabica coffee, Essenza, is roasted daily for them by the master roaster Mena Samios; meat and chorizo come from Mondo; New Norcia provide the bread; cupcakes are from Baby Cakes.

The innovative all-day menu, which changes seasonally, is a real temptation – delicious, simple breakfasts (but with sufficient choice for almost anyone), a trio of salads (Italian sausage plus vegies, blue cheese, pear and walnut, and smoked salmon), lightly toasted sandwiches, bruschetta, or Milkd salsiccia or Milkd mezze. There is absolutely nothing over-complicated about the food – thank goodness.

You can sit inside and hear some great music, or at the pavement tables and watch the world go by.

This part of Angove Street has become a small but beautiful shopping destination, with The Ginger Pig just up the road and Ici et La, the eclectic French shop next door – and Milkd is right at the heart of the action.

NEW NORCIA CAFÉ

Mt Hawthorn Café and Bakery
163 Scarborough Beach Rd
Mt Hawthorn WA 6016
9443 4114

7 days 7.00–6.00
Car park at rear in Anvil Lane

Despite the name, it was here in Mt Hawthorn, in the wood-fired oven in the basement of this café, that all the New Norcia bread was baked for almost a decade, between 1996 and 2005. (Breadmaking in the wood-fired oven of the New Norcia Monastery was discontinued after the first 3 years; since then it is used only for the famous New Norcia nutcake and biscotti.)

This huge, magnificent oven has recently been refurbished and is once again in use, baking traditional, hand-crafted loaves for the café and the Subiaco shop. Ask and you may be allowed to watch beautiful bread being made.

The café, which has an appropriately Spanish feel (the Benedictine Monastery at New Norcia was founded in 1846 by two Spanish monks, Bishop Rosendo Salvado and Dom Joseph Serra), is very popular. On Saturday morning, the queue spills onto the street.

Part-owner Kingsley Sullivan, an important figure in the WA food world, is often found in the kitchen. When we went, he had made that day's potato and leek soup himself. The café menu is simpler now than it used to be – 'we've pulled the menu back to its roots' – and is primarily focused on baking: good sandwiches, good toast, croissants, brioche, muffins, four varieties of pie, savoury flans, sweet tarts and cake. It's café food: simple, delicious breakfasts and light lunches that showcase just what the owners are about.

For newcomers, the café is next to the shop: the menu asks you to 'feast your eyes on the freshly baked breads and pastry in the bakery before ordering. If you want to try something different, the full range of sourdough bread is available to café customers.' So be adventurous and taste a bread you haven't had before.

No. 44 KING STREET PURVEYORS OF FINE FOOD, COFFEE AND WINE

44 King St
Perth WA 6000
9321 4476

7 days 7.00–late
Car parks Murray St, King St, Hay St

No. 44 King Street, a former carpet warehouse a few steps from His Majesty's Theatre, still has a slightly cavernous industrial feel about it. It was very much at the cutting edge of the Perth food scene when it first opened some 15 years ago, and it is still offering interesting and innovative food at breakfast, lunch, morning and afternoon coffee time, plus dinner and post-theatre supper. The breakfast menu includes a tomato, prosciutto, egg and caramelised onion breakfast pizza.

All the daily papers are in racks on the wall if you want to catch up with the news while you eat your breakfast. The lunch and dinner menus are seasonal – they change every week. Appropriate wines are recommended to accompany each dish.

They bake their own hand-moulded bread from unbleached flours in brick-floored bakers' ovens, and you can buy the loaves from wooden racks by the till. There's Etruscan (with cornmeal and honey), sourdough, olive, Turkish flatbread, Parisian baguette and ficelle, ciabatta and fruit breads: this is one of the few places in Perth where they are still making free-form, handmade bread, without additives or preservatives, on a daily basis.

You can see everything being baked at the back of the establishment: as well as the bread, all the cakes and pastries are available as take out.

No. 44 King Street's own espresso coffee is available to take home. Although the huge roaster, which used to be part of the attraction, is still there, it is no longer in use – the coffee beans are roasted elsewhere.

RIKI BLAKE'S CAFÉ

4A Blake St
North Perth WA 6006
9443 9494

Tuesday-Friday 8.30-5.30 breakfast, lunch, coffee and cake
Saturday -Sunday 8.00-5.30 breakfast, lunch, coffee and cake
Friday-Saturday 6.00-late: dine, jazz on Saturday (or coffee and cake after dinner)

The atmosphere here, like the food, has elements of France, North Africa and the Middle East. It is dark and warm, slightly earthy, serving food that feels traditional and authentic but with an original twist.

Riki Kaspi, the chef who owns the café with her jazz saxophonist husband Heni, was born in Israel into a house and a multicultural environment that revolved around food. Food was the main topic of conversation and the frequent excuse to have company. While still young she tasted the true flavours of the dishes of Turkey, Romania, Greece and Morocco ... and learned to make them. There were no recipe books; recipes had always been handed down orally. Travelling with Heni, Riki worked in restaurants in France, cooking and designing dishes, and in other European countries, and so her repertoire grew. The pair then travelled through Asia, picking up more ideas, before settling in Perth in 1996. Riki trained here formally as a chef, and in 2002 took over an existing café and transformed it.

'We were steeped in fine dining at a young age and good food became a major interest. Japanese and Asian food added new exotic flavours and ideas to our range of foods,' says Heni. Riki has clear ideas about her goals: 'My first priority is the taste of each dish. I won't compromise on that. If it's French, Moroccan or Israeli it must have its own special, distinctive flavour.'

We particularly liked harayme, a fish dish with tomato, capsicum and Moroccan spices. Other dishes popular with the customers include Moroccan chicken, slow-cooked with preserved lemons, and Algerian couscous with three meats and aromatic vegetables. Breakfast ranges from shak shuka, a North African dish of eggs poached in a rich sauce made from fresh tomatoes cooked for hours with garlic and spices and served with dill butter and fresh baguette – to a large, homemade French brioche still warm from the oven.

On Saturday nights Heni, on sax or clarinet, joins an acoustic guitar player to provide mellow background music in a traditional jazz style.

Riki has devised a wonderful Mediterranean to-go menu, including main courses, soups and salads, dips, spreads and pickles: it's healthy food, freshly cooked, using fine ingredients – much more than a takeaway.

The main courses – Bukhara beef stew, chicken in fig sauce, lamb meatball, harayme, chicken tagine, goat in fig sauce, lamb stew, Moroccan chicken or coq au vin – all come in medium packs (for one to two people) and family packs (for three to four). Aromatic couscous, majadara (green rice, cooked with lentils, lemon and herbs), red or yellow rice, mashed potato or potato gratin are available in the same size packs. A dish of the day and daily specials supplement this food-to-go menu.

We took home babaganoush, the harayme, lamb meatballs with yellow rice, Moroccan carrot and madbuha (tomato and capsicum slow-cooked with herbs and spices). It was all delicious, and some of the very best food-to-go we have tasted.

Riki Blake's café, during the day, Riki Blake's restaurant on Fridays and Saturdays, and Riki Blake's food-to-go – all three elements of this establishment have a unique and very distinctive feel and taste, with a personality all their own.

SENSATIONS EN ARDROSS

Shop 43a Ardross St
Applecross WA 6153
9364 8806

7 days 7.30–5.30
+ Wednesday–Friday 5.30–late
Parking in Ardross St and car park at side

Sensations en Ardross has become a day-long meeting place for the Applecross Village locals. The regulars come for the breakfast – the Big Sensation Breakfast, the no-carb breakfast or just a coffee – and from mid-morning through lunchtime and until evening there's a steady stream of customers, enjoying shaded alfresco dining under the jacaranda trees or at the scrubbed pine tables indoors.

All the food here is made from local, seasonal produce and there's a big emphasis on gluten-free food. So it's great free-range eggs from York, chickens from Bindoon and sensational Five Senses coffee.

The menu usually has a minimum of five savoury and five sweet dishes, ranging from pasta, crêpes, salads and roulades to rhubarb friand cake.

They also stock and sell a small range of gourmet groceries, all of which are used in their prepared dishes.

On Wednesday, Thursday and Friday they are open till late, with a short blackboard menu to choose from.

'For a small business to grow and develop from nothing, you have to have a passion – you have to love it,' says owner Suzanne Evans. Her passion means that Sensations en Ardross is a very popular meeting place.

Office breakfasts, finger food catering and some corporate work are also available. Ring Suzanne for more information.

GOURMET CAFÉS AND BREAKFAST

SODA

21 West Coast Drive
North Beach WA 6020
9448 7472
www.sodacafe.com.au

Monday–Tuesday 7.00–5.00 Wednesday–Sunday 7.00–late evening
Closed Christmas Day, Boxing Day, Good Friday
Car park at rear

When we walked into Soda, we knew we were somewhere special. There's a light, modern, fresh feel about the place; the staff looked genuinely pleased to see us. We knew we were going to have a very happy experience ... and we did.

At breakfast time, part-owner and head chef Ben Andrijasevich and his wife, Bridget LeGrove, who runs front of house, focus on simplicity and consistency: 'We want to keep it simple. We concentrate on what we do and keep it right.'

The breakfast menu *is* simple: fresh fruit, Greek yoghurt, today's house-baked muffin, New Norcia toast (white, multigrain or fruit) and preserves, pancakes and lemon butter, bacon and eggs (scrambled, fried, poached), eggs Benedict or Florentine, or Soda Works: eggs, bacon, chipolatas, tomato and hash browns.

Coffee (from Grinders) comes six ways; tea (from Tea For Me in Subiaco) comes seven ways. Orange or mixed fruit juice is freshly squeezed to order: banana smoothie, ditto.

For lunch and dinner, Soda offers something very different. Constantly searching for the 'absolutely best product we can find', they're not playing safe. The seared scallops on char siu pork with an apple, chilli and cress salad was excellent. When we asked if there was something special we should try, Bridget said 'Look, it's all pretty good: we aim very high here.'

Wonderfully innovative, great-tasting food served by terrific staff; an excellent wine list, good beers, and a 180° view of the ocean – that's what you get at Soda.

THE GLOBE COFFEE HOUSE

672 Beaufort St
Mt Lawley WA 6050
9271 3408

Sunday–Monday 6.00am–9.00pm
Tuesday–Thursday 6.00am–11.00pm
Friday–Saturday 6.00am–midnight
CASH only
Ample parking in car parks by Post Office and across the road

Last year The Globe moved across the road to this new location; it's the breakfast and coffee destination of choice for some of Mt Lawley's trendiest young businessmen, and the regulars (of whom there are many) report business as usual.

The permanent menu is divided into Globe Breakfast, Globe Favourites, Globe Crepes (savoury and sweet) and Globe Lunch, but most of the menu is available all day and evening.

Globe Breakfast offers all the usual suspects but, aided and abetted by the Specials Blackboard, it also tempts with an excellent choice of interesting and different dishes, many of them vegetarian: Norwegian eggs (with smoked salmon); potato, mint and feta pancakes with smoked salmon, poached eggs, sour cream and chives; bruschetta with pesto, roast capsicum, pumpkin and feta; and a vegetarian version of the full catastrophe – stuffed mushrooms, grilled tomatoes, corn fritters (a house speciality), eggs and toast.

Globe Favourites are bircher muesli and fruit compote, eggs Benedict or Florentine, corn fritters and potato pancakes. Globe Crepes are savoury (bacon, salsa and Jarlsberg) or sweet. Globe Lunch is salads (Cajun chicken, Caesar or baby spinach), savoury tarts and an open rye sandwich.

Freshly made sandwiches, with a large choice of fillings, are available on white, wholegrain or rye bread, bagels or focaccia.

Everything is cooked to order, and at the moment, all the tarts, biscuits, cakes and pastry are made on the premises.

VAN'S

1 Napoleon St
Cottesloe WA 6011
9384 0696

364 days a year 7.00–late
Closed Christmas Day
Free car park at the railway

The food at Van's all feels very familiar … but subtly different. Irishman Kevin McCabe, co-owner and very hands-on manager, is aiming to recapture the kinds of tastes everyone remembers fondly from their childhood, but presented in a modern way. On the menu when we were last there was that old staple, corned beef and cabbage with carrots and mustard sauce – but this was corned wagyu beef, the cabbage was prawn Colcannon, the carrots baby and the mustard sauce, Hollandaise. It is so popular they can hardly make enough of it. From time to time Kevin and his head chef, Leigh Nash, revive an old classic dish like this which has lapsed into cliché elsewhere, give it a new twist and pop it on the menu.

All the dishes are ingredient-driven, and though well presented, are not fussy. To ensure freshness and to keep up with demand, vegetables, salads and fruit are delivered twice daily. Everything is local and seasonal. 'As soon as the local asparagus comes in, we put it on the menu. If it's from Thailand, we send it back.'

The clientele comes in waves throughout the day, starting with breakfast, for which Van's is famous. But they are, understandably, keen to be known for more than that: mothers come in for a post-school run coffee; at lunchtime it's business people and ladies who lunch; and the afternoon tea crowd merges into the busy, buzzy dinner scene. And what a terrific success it has all become; we unashamedly admit to it being one of our favourite haunts.

Breakfast is everything you would expect (including a generous array of help-yourself jams and preserves – no nasty, little, hard-to-open plastic sachets here), but they are quite happy to depart from the menu. 'If you want one mushroom on half a piece of toast, you can have that,' says Kevin. For lunch and dinner many dishes come in two sizes: you can choose to have a light meal or a more substantial one of the same dish; there are also vegetarian dishes and two or three gluten-free options. And there's always a selection of seasonal dishes of the day which the young, smart and helpful staff gallantly try to recite without looking down to their cheat sheets. We've always been greeted with a welcoming smile.

Kevin trained as a chef in Dublin and London but got his love of food and cooking from his Italian grandmother, Rosa. His co-owner is Dave Cooney.

Van's has a small but interesting wine list – every wine is available by the glass – but you can BYO if you prefer.

X-WRAY

Lot 4, 3-13 Essex St
Fremantle WA 6160
9430 9399

Sunday-Wednesday 7.00-6.00
Thursday-Saturday 7.00-late
Ticket parking in Essex and Norfolk Sts
Live music Friday and Saturday evenings

The X-Wray café, owned and run by Greg and Sue Leaver, tucked away in the courtyard outside Luna on Essex cinema, began in September 2005, the day after their lease ran out on the much-loved Wray Café and Bookshop. They had no idea so many customers would move with them – about 90 per cent. A few regulars hardly bother to order: the staff see them coming and start cooking.

Much of the produce comes from small local suppliers: bread from Abhi's; Turkish bread delivered daily from nearby Turkish restaurant, Istanbul; meat from Frank's; and seafood from Worldwide Seafoods. 'If it's not in season, we give them something that is,' Greg says.

The breakfast, toasted muesli (homemade and 100 per cent fat free) is served with yoghurt and/or fruit, including, when in season, rhubarb – which is home grown and home stewed by Greg's mother, Jo. His parents also provide many of their cakes and biscuits. Another breakfast favourite is their toasted organic bread with either vegemite or avocado and a lemon wedge, and there is a good selection of croissants, both sweet and savoury. Cooked breakfasts include free-range eggs any style with toast, or scrambled with basil and feta, pancakes with berries, and poached pears with cinnamon ricotta on grilled sultana and polenta toast.

This is a friendly, relaxed place, catering for locals and using the best quality produce that manager Tim Grey-Smith can find.

On Thursday, Friday and Saturday nights, visiting chef Robert Malcolm is given creative freedom to produce a small eclectic tapas menu using seasonal produce.

GREENGROCERS

In Perth, all year round, we have fruit and vegetables to nourish and delight us: leafy greens, the refreshing crunch of salads... new asparagus freshly steamed and lightly drizzled with butter – that's the colour and taste of spring ... fruity richness of ripe figs, a rose-tinted papaya (paw paw) with a squeeze of lime – could there be a better breakfast on a hot day? ... plums bursting with sweet, sticky juice ... a tomato, sun-ripened on the vine, sliced on a plate with cracked pepper and Dandaragan olive oil – these spell summer ... creamy mashed potato ... the earthy taste of mushrooms ... the tartness of rhubarb cutting through a creamy custard ... the mouth-watering smell of frying onions drifting out on an autumn evening ... the warm, comforting solidity of winter vegetables bubbling in a rich soup or casserole.

We are blessed in Western Australia with very good produce – there's no reason to buy asparagus from Thailand or garlic from China. Nutrients decay rapidly after picking. For instance, broccoli will lose up to one-third of its vitamin C after one week in the fridge and spinach will lose up to one-half.

We are also blessed with people: growers and sellers who are passionate about the Earth's bounty. They understand it, care about it and know what's in season and at its best. A surprising number of people we talked to have told us the same thing: 'If I wouldn't buy it, I wouldn't sell it.'

This book lists some of the best greengrocers in the Perth area.

At the back of the book you will find a WA Seasonal Fresh Produce Guide (see pages 348 and 349).

The following places have excellent greengrocery sections:

Absolutely Organic, Gwelup (see page 319)
Boatshed Fresh Food, Cottesloe (see page 186)
Brighton Road Food Market, Scarborough (see page 189)
City Farm Organic Growers' Market (see page 307)
Claremont Fresh, Claremont (see page 195)
Edgecombe Brothers, Swan Valley (see page 309)
Fresh Provisions: Bicton, Claremont & Mt Lawley (see page 202)
Herdsman Fresh Essentials (see page 205)
Hype @ The Boulevard, City Beach (see page 321)
Manna Wholefoods, South Fremantle (see page 324)
Mt Lawley Wholefoods, Inglewood (see page 326)
Peaches Organic, South Fremantle (see page 328)
Scutti – A Taste of Europe, South Perth (see page 219)
Subi Fresh @ Crossways Shopping Centre, Subiaco (see page 199)
Swansea Street Fresh Markets (see page 221)
Tony Ale & Co., Jandakot (see page 230)

APPLE FRESH

Shop 5, 37 Ardross St
Applecross WA 6153
9316 3317

7 days 7.00–7.00
7.00–5.00 public holidays Closed Christmas Day
Ample parking

This is the fruit and vegetable shop, opened 2 years ago by Toan To and his mother, in the very attractive Applecross Village.

When we went he had wonderful displays of in-season stone fruit (nectarines, peaches and plums) outside the shop, and the Bartlett and new-season Bosc pears had just come in. About 70 per cent of his sales are fruit but there's also plenty of good quality vegetables, lettuces and washed salad leaves.

Toan finds that there is a demand here for vegetables for stirfries, so there's a good range of suitable fresh ingredients which he backs up with a cabinet full of Asian sauces and noodles. He also stocks hydroponic Roma tomatoes and the newly fashionable, sweet little Momoko tomatoes.

There is a small but beautifully fresh selection of cut flowers on sale.

Toan told us that about 80 per cent of his customers are regulars, and are locals.

BROADWAY FRESH

Broadway Fair Shopping Centre
88 Broadway
Nedlands WA 6009
9389 8054

7 days 8.00–7.00
Closed Christmas Day, New Year's Day, Good Friday, Easter Monday
Parking in shopping centre car park

There's no passing trade here, so the large loyal band of customers and the excellent reputation that John and Maria Terzanidis have built up over the years are no accident – they are well earned.

John is passionate about his produce – its quality, provenance and freshness – and the service he provides. All the fruit and vegies are from WA, except sugar snap and snow peas. 'I avoid overseas produce: I will go without rather than use imported,' he says. 'The young ones need a lot of educating about seasonal fruit and vegetables,' he adds, so it's house policy here to cut up a piece of fruit for the customer to try, so that 'when you get it home, you know what you have bought'.

On our first visit, the smell of the ripe guavas which filled the shop was divine.

David Coomer, proprietor and chef at the award-winning Star Anise restaurant told us: 'John selects for me on flavour and merit rather than on looks. I go into that shop every day to pick up my fruit and vegetables for the restaurant. They're like a terribly good, old-fashioned, Greek greengrocer; they are really genuine lovely people who are honest about what they do.'

BURRENDAH FRESH GOURMET

Shop 2, 61 Apsley Rd
Willetton WA 6155
9457 4357

Monday-Thuesday 7.00-7.30
Friday-Sunday 7.00-7.00
Ample parking

Peter Liu and his wife, Isabel Wang, opened this fruit and vegetable shop with adjoining deli 3 years ago. Focusing on quality fruit and vegies, there is a good range of in-season produce and salads, with a small section of organic fresh food and groceries, including organic butter and tea bags.

In the deli section there's New Norcia bread, Casa yoghurt, pre-packed olives, nuts, butter, cheese and eggs, along with a range of cooking sauces.

There is also a large freezer stocking locally caught and imported frozen fish fillets and seafood.

If you're buying your meat at Hadley's, on the same block (see page 64), this is a good and useful shop for those other things.

CRIMEA GROWERS MARKET

Cnr Morley Dr and Crimea St
Morley WA 6062
9276 8042

Monday-Friday 8.00-6.00
Saturday 8.00-1.00 Sunday 8.00-12.00
Off-street parking

This smallish fresh market, run by Peter Stillitano and his son-in-law Craig Gaske, epitomises what this book is about: it's a small, honest, unpretentious, local greengrocer selling high quality, spanking-fresh seasonal WA produce, punching far above its weight for the demographics of the area and obviating the need for anyone in the neighbourhood ever to set foot in a mass-market supermarket again. As the sign on his wall has it: 'Good fruit isn't cheap and cheap fruit isn't good.'

On a winter's day when we were there they had lovely pumpkins, the best carrots from Spearwood, pristine cauliflowers all white and green and crunchy, delicious-looking crisp salad leaves and freshly picked herbs, bright red cherry tomatoes, ripe avocados, English spinach and salad mix. The fresh fruit in stock included several kinds of new season apples, Gingin navel oranges and mandarins, Packham and Bosc pears.

There was also a small but classy cheese section, a few olives and antipasto and a small, but good, range of continental groceries. They are situated next door to the excellent Crimea Quality Meats (see page 55), so you can buy everything you need for dinner right here.

LIMES FRESH FRUIT & VEG. CO.

Melville Central
Marshall St (cnr Leach Hwy and North Lake Rd)
Myaree WA 6154
9330 2251

7 days 7.00–7.00
Closed Good Friday, Easter Sunday, Christmas Day
Parking in adjoining car parks

Since taking over in October 2005, Paul Harry and Jim Neville – aka Limes Fresh Fruit & Veg. Co. – have injected much-welcomed new life into the fruit and veg section of Melville Central.

Taking full advantage of this huge space has enabled them to offer four distinctive displays of fruit and vegetables. First, the top quality, pick-of-the-bunch produce is displayed in refrigerated cabinets down the whole of the left-hand side. This is beautifully arranged, very fresh seasonal and obviously carefully selected produce, including several varieties of picked and washed loose salad leaves and an excellent selection of fresh herbs. There is also a small refrigerated cabinet of certified organic produce.

Opposite them is the middle range – 'more family priced' – but still looking very good. The third section is the buckets: usually in-season fresh fruit which is smaller (but not inferior grade) and excellent value. The fourth, a small section, is very clearly labelled 'Reduced to clear' and you take this as you find it.

Much of the produce comes direct from WA growers, some of whom deliver themselves: we saw Kipfler potatoes, many different melons, delicious-looking stone fruit in season, many varieties of new season's apples and pears, vine-ripened Momoko tomatoes, a Japanese variety of very sweet but small tomatoes from Baldivis, and Kensington Pride mangoes from Gingin.

They have a variety of made-up salads, including a very colourful Greek salad with cherry tomatoes. Juice is freshly squeezed to order: a popular one is apple, pear, lemon zest, beetroot (for colour) and fresh ginger.

MIDLAND JUNCTION FRESH MARKETS

380 Great Eastern Hwy
Midland WA 6056
9250 1205

7 days 7.00–7.00
Closed Christmas Day
Parking in car park

The fast turnover of locally sourced produce is the secret of freshness – and freshness is what Scott Brice guarantees to deliver. The secret, he explained to us, is not to overstock and 'to keep it moving'. By buying fresh fruit and vegetables three times a week and running down the previous lot before restocking, Scott ensures that nothing has been sitting on the shelves for more than a couple of days: 'My goal is that anything you buy here should last at least a week in your fridge because it has not been long in ours. If it comes in on Monday, it is sold by Wednesday; Wednesday's new stock is sold by Friday; Friday's by Sunday. There's no need to stockpile here.'

Scott buys as much produce locally as he can (he's very near the great salad bowl of Wanneroo and the Swan Valley, after all), and only if he can't get something here does he buy it in from the eastern states, and only with the greatest reluctance does he buy from overseas. Garlic from China and asparagus from Peru are, he believes, necessary evils because the customers want them, but he wishes we would all learn to love food in its season.

The big growth area here at the moment is organic, but Scott says: 'It is very hard to find enough genuinely organic produce, of sufficiently good quality, to keep up with the demand.'

As well as the fresh produce, Midland Junction carries an extensive range of high quality packaged groceries and a small selection of everyday essentials, but it does not try to replicate the goods to be found in a supermarket. 'If we're offered something that is already in a supermarket, we refuse it. We can't compete and don't want to.'

The staff here – six full-time and about another 30 part-timers – are particularly friendly and sufficiently knowledgeable about the produce to be helpful. 'We are very staff-oriented; happy staff equals happy customers. The checkout lady is the last person the customer sees, and her attitude is what sticks in the memory.' We often shop here and can attest to the quality of the produce and the helpfulness of the staff.

We can also say that, good though it has always been, we think that there has been a marked improvement in the last couple of years. Scott is aiming high and moving into the premier league of independent fresh food providores.

MOSMAN PARK FRESH

Shop 5, Mosman Park Shopping Centre
Monument St
Mosman Park WA 6012
9384 4232

Monday-Saturday 8.00-6.00
Thursday 8.00-7.00 Sunday 8.00-5.00
Closed Christmas Day; check on public holidays by telephoning

The Vietnamese family who run this popular shop are extremely friendly and obliging, and the quality and range of their fruit and veg is high. We have both shopped here often and never been disappointed.

Recently the broccoli looked particularly beautiful; they also had early asparagus from Carnarvon, a good selection of very fresh, green herbs and salad leaves, lovely scarlet rhubarb, long, pale leeks and some winter organics. The locally grown silverbeet we had for Sunday lunch with lamb from Pronto Gourmet Butcher across the way (see page 78) was delicious and extremely fresh.

Most of their produce is from WA, sourced from Wanneroo growers and Canning Vale Market. They do import sugar snaps, baby corn and navel oranges when they are not in season here.

There's also a large range of packaged nuts and a few groceries on offer.

MR FRESH GROWERS MARKET

Shop 12, Carine Glades Shopping Centre
473 Beach Rd
Duncraig WA 6023
9477 4066

364 days a year 8.00-8.00
Parking in car parks

When the Cucel family – Kim, his perfectionist wife Lyn and their sons Joel and Ryan – came here 4 years ago from Cottesloe, they 'inherited' Sac Meechamnan, their buyer. And what a happy and fortuitous inheritance that has turned out to be.

When you walk into this beautifully clean shop, you sense very strongly that not much happens here by accident. It's the way it is because a great deal of care and attention to detail goes into every aspect of the business, from the buying to the storage, to the display and to the service.

'We just go for the quality,' says Kim. 'People seem to be getting more and more health-conscious.' Ninety per cent of their sales are of fruit and vegetables. The aim is that everything looks as good at the end of the day as it does at the beginning – this is often talked about, but rarely achieved, in our opinion, but they are managing to do just that. All the produce looks great and in excellent condition.

Particularly beautiful new season's Pink Lady apples, local mandarins and local broccoli were all superb.

The enlarged and improved fresh-cut section looked a picture and 'is going really well'. The dairy section had Bannister Downs milk, Athena yoghurt, Berrywise frozen fruit and some food-to-go – Malay chicken curry and prepared salads.

Mr Fresh won the Retailer of the Year again in 2007. Richly deserved, we'd say. It is an absolute pleasure to shop here.

MR ORGANIC
Stalls 119/120
Fremantle Markets
Cnr Henderson St and South Tce
Fremantle WA 6160

Market hours
CASH only
Parking in surrounding car parks: Henderson St, Parry St

Mr Organic — aka Gerry Drenthe — still firmly believes what he has always believed: 'that the strength of the market is the freshness'.

Freshness has always been his main criteria — and that means mostly local and WA sources, and a fast turnover: 'I wouldn't sell a Californian orange if you paid me.' So, go early if you can: Friday is better than Sunday, although he does have an on-site coolroom.

Organic food is sometimes a little more expensive to buy, but Gerry maintains that it is often cheaper in the long run because there is less waste. 'If a punnet of my organic strawberries gets pushed to the back of the fridge and you find them there a week later, they'll still be good to eat. Supermarket strawberries will have turned to water by then.'

The Gala apples, from Kirup, were sweet and crunchy, the Nashi pears were small and delicious, and the fine green beans looked as if each one had been made in heaven — real beans, not has-beens. Everything here is of the highest quality and, as Gerry says, 'Quality always sells.' They also stock organic free-range eggs.

A 30-year veteran of Fremantle Markets, Gerry was the first organic retailer in WA selling fruit and vegetables grown by organic pioneers like the Bombaras of Pierce Brook and the Cavallaro family of Kirup. He and his wife Titia are in the market each week with his son Richard and daughter-in-law Renae. Many of their customers are now second generation: 'Our customers have become our friends.'

O2H

Unit 3, 23 Carrington St
Nedlands WA 6009
0408 313 036
www.o2h.com.au
6389 2030 fax

Tuesday, Thursday and Friday 8.30–5.00
Saturday 8.30–13.00
CASH and cheque only at the shop; online banking for online orders
Car parking in front of shop

O2H means from orchard to home. Fresh fruit and vegetables, much of it from Loretta Lade's family's own orchards in the hills south of Perth, can be delivered to your home, or you can pick it out yourself from her shop, which is tucked away behind Karakatta Cemetery at the end of Government Road.

If you want it delivered, order by phone or fax, email or online. Loretta and her team will simply pack you a box of what you order, to a specified price. Most clients choose what they want online; some clients ask Loretta to select for them, taking into account their particular likes and dislikes. In our experience, the service they provide here at O2H – however you choose to order – is very personal, individual and spot-on.

The produce always looks great, but more importantly, it's always seasonal, fresh and in perfect condition – the locally grown broccoli we had from O2H was the best we'd ever had from anywhere. The emphasis here is on buying direct from growers and family, wherever possible.

What started as a small family business in 2004 has grown into something bigger now, without losing the family affair feel. Loretta's cousin still grows the carrots, onions and parsnips, her brother has an orchard in Dwellingup, she makes the relishes herself; their own-label, award-winning jams are made for them by Mandy Hall.

O2H has unearthed a new supplier of biodynamic vegetables: cauliflower, broccoli, pumpkin, silverbeet, bok choy: 'Whatever is in season,' says Loretta. 'All spray-free and absolutely beautiful.'

Your box of goodies can also contain products from Maggie Edmonds in Gingin – think fresh passionfruit juice and olive oil – as well as Borrello cheeses, Bannister Downs milk, Five Senses coffee and a small selection of groceries, mainly from local WA suppliers. A chemical-free, very small dairy in Billawarra is making handmade yoghurts, fromage frais and haloumi cheese for them.

Corporate boxes of fruit for offices and schools are despatched on Mondays.

Deliveries are to within the radius of Wembley Downs to the north, East Perth, and North Fremantle to the south.

Many busy people are already using the wonderful service provided by O2H. This is also a great way to shop if you are elderly, have been ill or are house-bound – it would be a really useful gift to a young mother at home with a new baby.

SCOTTY'S
Stalls 114/115
Fremantle Markets
Cnr Henderson St and South Tce
Fremantle WA 6160

Market hours
CASH only
Parking in surrounding car parks: Henderson St, Parry St

Scotty's is Mark Scott, an engaging former professional cricketer who has run his outstanding fruit and vegetable stall in the market for more than 20 years (he previously worked for 6 years in the Wellington Street Market in Perth); his knowledge of and enthusiasm for the produce he sells are huge.

He sources most of his fruit and vegetables direct from WA growers, so it's asparagus from Denmark, beans and strawberries from Albany, fruit from Dwellingup and Manjimup. What he looks for is fresh, high quality, seasonal produce: most of his fruit is naturally ripened on the tree, and local – about 98 per cent – and he insists that taste is more important than appearance. 'Better that it eats well than that it looks good,' he says. However, if it tastes better than it looks, it should be sensational, because all the produce on his stall looks drop-dead gorgeous. Everything is labelled, in Scotty's beautiful calligraphy, with its place of origin.

What you get from Scotty is very personal, friendly service from an expert purveyor of fruit and vegetables who knows the provenance of everything he sells and cares passionately about it.

His Italian wife is a wine merchant and they spend their European holidays going round farmers' markets.

THE FRUIT BASKET

76 Cranford Ave
Mt Pleasant WA 6153
9364 3417

7 days 7.00–7.00
Closed Christmas Day and Easter Sunday
Parking in front of parade of shops

Brothers Tony and Sam Pizzata have owned and run The Fruit Basket for the last 4 years, and what a pleasant surprise it was to find them.

There's a very good selection of high quality fresh, seasonal local produce here. Tomatoes, new season's apples, Teagan Blue plums and some excellent mangoes were almost fighting each other for front place; the mixed, washed salad leaves were competitively priced, and the fresh herbs looked beautiful.

The organic section had fresh fruit and vegetables, including bananas and tomatoes. There were also free-range organic eggs, some dried fruit and muesli, some cheese and milk.

Elsewhere in the shop there's a good selection of flowers, and there's a cabinet of cut fruit and prepared salads.

In the fridges you'll find pre-packed cold meats (from Mondo and Princi), cheeses (from Blue Cow and Borrello), Avon Valley milk and fruit juices.

ICE CREAM AND GELATI

A quiet revolution, akin to the one that took place among coffee shops more than 30 years ago, is taking place among WA's growing band of ice cream shops.

Hand-made ice creams, sorbets and gelatos, many of them freshly-made daily from high-quality local ingredients by men and women passionate about their product are displacing the old factory-made ices that could be weeks or even months old by the time you ate them.

We visited lots of gelaterie, including one that was using a customer's fresh figs from the fig tree in his garden and making them into something closely resembling true heaven. But these are the new boys.

The old boys – Nick Odorisio at Azzura Gelati, Oreste Collodel at Collodel's in Kalamunda and Darcy McKay at The Junction Ice-Creamery at Midland Junction are all still making beautiful, hand-made ice cream in the old-fashioned way.

AMANO – THE GELATO COMPANY
6 South Tce
Fremantle WA 6160
9336 1695

7 days 6.00-midnight (summer) 7 days 6.00-10.30/11.00 (winter)
CASH only
Fremantle car parks and off-street

'A mano' means 'by hand', and through a window in the back of the shop you can see the *laboratorio*, with the fruit being cut up and the gelato being handmade.

Two varieties of gelato are made here: Amano Frutto, a fruit-based ice, like a sorbet but not as hard, made with real fruit, and Amano Crema, made from full-cream Harvey milk, repasteurised (cooked) on the premises, then simultaneously frozen and stirred in a machine called a *manticatore* (imported from Italy).

Michael Della Penna, who runs Amano with partners Andrea Rossi (his cousin) and Stefano Del Dosso, says: 'Why would you eat factory-made ice cream that may be 6 months old when you can get it freshly made every day?' Why, indeed? They also make a fruttini, like a brightly coloured and very intensely flavoured ice-lolly in a sort of shot glass on a stick, which was intended for children but has been enthusiastically taken up by adults. Among the gelati, Amano's Freo Delight (coffee, pine nuts and vanilla) is very popular, and their pistachio has won Gold both here and in Italy. The day we visited they were attempting to perfect a tomato sorbet. You can buy their gelati to take home in 500ml, 750ml or 1 litre insulated tubs which will keep it frozen for one hour, if you can wait that long.

Locals can bring their own fruit (lemons, figs, mangoes etc) and have it made into gelati on the premises. But please ring and speak to Maria before arriving on the Strip with 30kg of figs.

Other AMANO outlets @:
Gateway, Cockurn; Galleria, Morley; Garden City, Booragoon; Karrinyup

AZZURA GELATI

7 Zeta Cres
O'Connor WA 6163
9314 1656

Thursday-Friday 1.00-4.00 Saturday 9.30-12 noon
CASH only
Plenty of off-street parking by factory

Chef Nick Odorisio and his wife Rey founded Azzura Gelati in 1985. No one else in WA makes this kind of designer dessert, and few in Australia make such a big variety.

Most readers will have seen their very realistic-looking gelati-filled confectionery fruits at parties or restaurants. The range includes: Green Pears (fresh pear gelato in tinted white chocolate with a chocolate fudge centre), Apple Sensation (apple gelato covered in milk chocolate with a chocolate fudge centre), and Peach Fantasia (yellow peach fruit gelato with a chocolate nut centre and a peach-tinted chocolate casing). They are made with real fruit, bought by the tonne in season from WA growers, processed and then kept throughout the year in cold stores so the quality remains consistent. Bananas and mangoes come from Carnarvon and Gingin, apples and pears from Donnybrook, strawberries from Albany and the north, and passionfruit from the Moore River.

Nick is extremely particular about the quality of the fruit he buys. It is this, plus his great attention to detail, which Rey thinks provides the consistency that is one of the distinguishing characteristics of Azzura.

Azzura's wholesale-to-the-public range is available on Thursday and Friday afternoons and Saturday mornings.

Wholesale to the public also @:

EVEREST FOOD SERVICE
146 Carrington St
O'Connor WA 6163
Monday-Friday 9.00-5.00
Saturday 9.30-12.00

COLLODEL ICE CREAM AND SORBET

30 Haynes St
Kalamunda WA
6293 1463

Tuesday–Sunday 10.00–6.00 Closed Mondays
Closed all of July
CASH only
Street parking in Haynes St; car parks in Canning Rd, Mead St, Barber St.

The ice cream counter of Mary and Oreste Collodel's tiny shop in the centre of Kalamunda opens directly onto the pavement, revealing a colourful array of delicious-looking ice creams and sorbets. These are the real thing and well worth a special journey in their own right.

Oreste came to Australia after selling his ice cream shop in Rheinberg, Germany in the early 1990s. He makes all the ice cream on the premises, fresh every day, using a traditional artisan method, in old-fashioned manual batch freezers which, though labour intensive – he has to scrape out the ice cream by hand with a wooden spatula – produce the most superb ice cream, full of character and flavour.

He uses only free-range eggs from a farm in nearby Bickley and milk and cream from Harvey Fresh. All stone fruits, peaches, plums, nectarines and apricots come from local orchards in the Perth Hills: the strawberries are local; mangoes, when available in March, come, tree-ripened, from a grower in Kalamunda. Vanilla beans, not extract, are used for the vanilla ice cream. Other ice cream flavourings – syrups, hazelnuts, chocolate, frozen fruit products – are imported from France and Italy.

All the ice creams we have tried are excellent. The hazelnut is unique – you have to taste it to believe it. The Collodels sell two types of full-cream ice cream: one with eggs, called yellow base, which is pasteurised, and one without eggs, cold base, which is not. They make about 20 different flavours. The sorbets, all dairy-free of course, are only ever made from fresh fruit and consequently particular flavours are only available when that fruit is in season here. They also make and sell frozen yoghurt and, in the winter, crepes.

This is some of the best ice cream we have ever tasted. The secret must be in the freshness: the freshness of the base products, the freshness in the making and the freshness in the eating.

And before you go home, pop across the road to Sebastian butchers (see page 82) and discover another great reason to come to Kalamunda.

IL GELATO

81 Rokeby Rd
Subiaco WA 6008
9382 2600
www.ilgelato.com.au

Sunday–Thursday 11.30–10.00
Friday–Saturday 11.30–11.30
CASH only
Car parks between Forrest St and Barker St behind shop; some short-term parking on Rokeby Rd

Il Gelato was in at the start of the present boom in the new-style gelateria, and when their first gelato parlour opened here in March 2003 its fresh (six times a week), handmade gelati and ice cream was an instant success. The second shop, in Cottesloe, and a third, in Northbridge, followed in 2004. There are now three more – in Carillon City, Fremantle and Leederville – and five more are planned.

All the ice creams and gelati are made from Harvey milk and fresh produce from local growers in their *laboratorio*/factory in Osborne Park (every day except Sunday), to ensure total quality control in all the shops.

This award-winning gelato is available in sixteen different flavours. They have a flavour of the month each month (when we went it was Piña Colada), and the takeaway tubs are particularly to be recommended. They also make a speciality of ice cream cakes made to order in four designs, three sizes and three flavours from the 22 on offer. For special occasions they will write a message on the cake for you.

Founder Lucca Naldoni was a chef in Italy but found, when he came to Perth, that chefs were not as highly esteemed here as there, so he decided to see if the gelato habit, just about universal in Italy, would catch on here. Now teamed up with Tony Calabro and expanding fast, he seems to have guessed right.

Also @:

MKI Carillon Arcade
Perth WA 6000
9324 3844

88 Marine Parade
Cottesloe WA 6011
9286 2800

11 South Tce
Fremantle WA 6160
9433 6611

115 Oxford St
Leederville WA 6007
9444 8844

89 James St
Northbridge WA 6003
9228 2400

THE JUNCTION ICE CREAMERY

Shop 3, 380 Great Eastern Hwy (cnr Morrison Rd)
Midland WA 6056
9274 1013

Summer: Sunday–Wednesday 9.00–6.00; Thursday–Saturday
9.00–9.00 Winter: 7 days 9.00–6.00
CASH only
Off-street parking

The many prizes awarded to this family-run ice cream maker – including Golds and Silvers from the Perth Royal Show, Sydney Royal Show and Australian Dairy Industry Association for, among many others, their English Toffee, Cookie Dough, Vanilla, Chocolate and Honeycomb Crunch ice creams – are one measure of the quality of their product. Another, even more reliable one, is the happy looks on customers' faces, nearly all of whom are regulars and provide valuable feedback and suggestions for new flavours.

The Junction Ice Creamery also make and sell 97 per cent fat-free soya ice cream, sorbets, frozen yoghurt and will make ice cream cakes to order (they need a minimum of 3 days' notice). You can watch the ice cream being made in the front of the shop; that's part of the attraction. Darcy McKay, plus his mother, father, sister and wife, are all involved in the business: 'Dad is a great mentor for me,' says Darcy. 'We're in it for the long haul.'

The ice cream is made from the best ingredients – Harvey milk, fresh fruit (customers bring in lemons from their backyard trees) and raw sugar – but Darcy also has another ingredient: 'We put a lot of tender, loving care into it.'

The family have been in the ice cream business for 26 years, 21 in this shop, and Darcy loves it: 'I have ice cream in my blood.' You can buy the ice cream in cones or tubs of 500ml, 750ml, 1.5 or 2 litres. We usually – no, always – have one in the freezer at home.

There's a small dine-in café where they sell coffee and tea, milkshakes and smoothies, cakes, Florentines and tarts, waffles, pancakes, sandwiches and rolls, sundaes – and just ice cream.

KITCHENWARE

Perth has more than its share of excellent kitchenware and equipment shops. There's the traditional, older-style specialist shop, which is very professional and up-market, offering superb service, knowledge and a carefully-chosen range of the world's best products. And there's the newer, bigger kind of place, which stocks a huge range of every conceivable gadget and product, ranging from everyday to top quality. Browsing in these places is fun, they are full of culinary toys, gadgets we don't really need but love the idea of, like mechanical apple-peelers-and-corers or knife-sharpeners that look as though you'd need an operator's licence to use.

We believe that buying good, solid, well-made equipment – whether it is a pan, a cast-iron casserole or a wonderful knife – is as important as buying good food. And, as with food, the higher the quality, the less of it you need.

As a matter of interest, kitchen appliances made by the big names – Magimix, Kitchen Aid and Bamix – are all sold in Australia at a fixed price. So don't think that buying these expensive items from a small specialist shop is going to cost more than they would from a much bigger store. Go to whoever offers you the type of *service* you prefer: the product, and the price, are the same wherever.

AMANO COOKING SCHOOL AND KITCHENWARE

12 Station St
Cottesloe WA 6011
9384 0378
www.amano.com.au

Monday-Friday 9.30-5.30
Saturday 9.30-4.00
Free angle parking outside shop

This is the shop to come to if you are a serious vacational or vocational cook or chef looking to buy very high quality kitchen- and cookware from knowledgeable, experienced and friendly staff.

For Bev Sprague, Amano is a passion rather than a career – a passion for food and fine equipment which she has turned into a business. Everything here is beautiful, practical, carefully chosen and singing above top C.

There's Demeyere cookware from Belgium, copper tarte tatin dishes from France; china from Pillivuyt, knives from Wüsthof. 'If you only have two very good knives and a wonderful Benriner mandolin, you can survive,' Bev believes, but who would want to just survive when there is this standard and range of products to choose from?

The shop is two large rooms, full of most things you could ever imagine wanting but by no means overcrowded. Behind these is the Amano Cooking School and Kitchenware Specialist (see page 133). They have a beautiful demonstration kitchen in which they hold evening classes, lectures and talks, demonstrations and private corporate special events.

CUT IT OUT

413 Murray Street
Perth WA 6000
9321 9539
www.cutitout.com.au

Monday–Friday 9.00–5.30
Saturday 9.00–3.00
Car parks on Murray Street

Cut it Out is a haven for the professional chef or anyone who loves cooking. Since 1979 they have been supplying knives, kitchenware and locally manufactured chef's uniforms to professionals and cooking enthusiasts. They stock the largest range of knives in WA, maybe even the Southern Hemisphere; Wusthof, Trident, Mundial, Global and an excellent range of super-sharp Japanese knives. 'Everyone needs a great chef's knife,' says owner Andrea Coffey who took over the business in 2001. Alongside the rows of gleaming knives, you will find an extensive range of cookware – Le Chasseur, Berndes, Studio and Professional, a wide selection of bakeware including the silicon Wonderflex moulds, and just about any kitchen utensil imaginable. They also stock a fabulous collection of cookbooks.

Cut it Out is staffed by industry trained people – mostly ex-chefs – who are all very knowledgeable about cooking and the products they stock. Their aim is to help both domestic and trade customers choose the right tool for any cooking task and make the best decision to satisfy individual needs. 'Buy only what you need and the best quality that you can afford,' says Andrea. If Cut it Out don't stock what you are looking for, they will make every effort to find it for you.

'Our market continues to grow each year due to the increasing awareness and interest in the preparation of good quality, healthy food and produce. Cooking has re-emerged as the central focus of homes for the pleasure of family and friends,' says Andrea. They offer a professional sharpening service every Wednesday and Friday.

EPICURIOUS

Shop 8, Subiaco Village
531 Hay St
Subiaco WA 6008
9380 4799
www.epicurious.com.au

Monday–Saturday 10.00–5.00
Car parks between Forrest and Barker Sts

Epicurious is a fascinating shop, a mix of quality kitchenware, gadgets and utensils, fine food and unusual ingredients and culinary and wine books. Mother and daughter partnership Marilyn Trevor and Jane Mills have been here for 5 years now, supplying catering products for retail customers. Their clients range from chefs to passionate home cooks to beginners. Jane says: 'The one thing they have in common is that they are all serious about food.'

The kitchenware and gadget section has a professional feel about it and is all top of the range: Kitchen Aid, Pullivuyt French white china, Essence, and the French-made Jamie Oliver Tefal range of pans. Their top-selling item is an electric, stone-based benchtop pizza oven called The Pizza Maker, which makes authentic Italian crispy pizzas in 5 minutes.

But it's in the food range that this shop's nature shines through – and in Jane's love of sourcing the many unusual ingredients which customers find hard to get elsewhere. Gelatine leaves, non-melting icing sugar, the big-selling frozen pizza dough, Persian fairyfloss, Little Dipper ice cream cones, ten different olive oils, savoury canapé cases, couverture chocolate, sugar flowers and cake decorations are just some of the items which come from their 350 different suppliers, many of whom supply only one product. In the fridge and freezer are John and Connie Zito's Nutpatch (hazelnut) nougat from Tasmania, beautiful fresh stock, specially made pizza sauces and, of course, the frozen pizza dough.

This is a great shop for browsing, particularly among the well-stocked bookshelves.

KITCHEN WAREHOUSE

Shop 10, 381 Scarborough Beach Rd
Osborne Park WA 6017
9444 7244
www.kitchenwarehouse.com.au

Monday–Wednesday, Friday 9.00–5.30 Thursday 9.00–9.00
Saturday 9.00–5.00 Sunday 11.00–4.00
Plenty of parking

This family-owned chain runs some of the largest kitchenware stores in Australia, each with a very comprehensive range of kitchen equipment, tools and appliances, including all the well-known brands. There are literally thousands of lines; there is nothing you couldn't get here.

Each of these big shops has a wood–fired pizza oven, and all offer regular cooking classes and demonstrations by experienced chefs. They have a regular newsletter, and you can order online.

Also @:

Shop 102
Westfield Carousel
Cannington WA 6107
9358 27777

Melville Home Town
276 Leach Hwy
Booragoon WA 6154
9333 5400

KITCHEN WITCH

500 Hay St
Subiaco WA 6008
9380 4788

Monday–Wednesday, Friday 9.00–5.30 Thursday 9.00–9.00
Saturday 9.00–5.00

Alain Lapelerie, a lanky Frenchman from New Caledonia, loves good quality products that do what the manufacturer says they will do and that don't wear out in 5 minutes. He likes things built to last. Everything is tested at home: 'I put new items through their paces.' Then his staff test them too, so they can speak confidently and answer customers' questions knowledgeably. 'It lends credibility to what our staff say if they know how to use the product themselves. We really try to inform and educate our customers rather than exaggerating our way through a sale,' he says.

His current favourite is a really good knife-sharpening tool called The Warthog, from South Africa: 'It looks like a mediaeval instrument of torture, but it works really well.' His products are smart but workmanlike rather than trendy.

Kitchen Witch carries many good brands, including Fissler from Germany, Swiss Diamond, Kitchen Aid, Magimix and Bamix, Le Creuset, Simac Italian electrical ice cream makers, Marcato manual Italian-made pasta machines, Mundial knives made in Brazil from German steel, and the full range of Cashmere white china from Maxwell Williams.

Also @:

82/93 Joondalup Dr
Edgewater WA 6027
9301 5222

Harvey Norman Centre
9/9 Gordon Rd
Mandurah WA 6210
9581 9799

LADY KITCHENER

Shop 50, The Bayview Centre
Old Theatre Lane
Claremont WA 6010
9383 1055

Monday-Wednesday, Friday 9.00-5.30 Thursday 9.00-9.00
Saturday 9.00-5.00 Closed Sundays and public holidays
Open Sundays around Christmas-time
Parking in Leura Ave car parks

Tucked away down Old Theatre Lane, Lady Kitchener has been very much her own woman for over a quarter of a century. She's a delight: quite smart in front, but homely, in a Mrs Tiggywinkle-ish sort of way, at the back. She's living proof that an established, traditional, old-fashioned institution can also be fun and fascinating.

Michelle Otway-Melvin and her husband Wes took over Lady Kitchener 6 years ago from his parents. It's still run as a small family business and there's a strong sense of continuity. The service here, dished out by friendly staff – many of them mature, country women with life experience – is just that what you would expect: personal, genuine and helpful. When they say: 'If it's not right, bring it back,' they really mean it. 'You don't get that kind of service if you shop on the internet,' Michelle laughs.

There's a terrific stock of all sorts of kitchen, oven and tableware, some of which you won't find easily elsewhere. One area where Lady Kitchener really excels is its very large range of high quality polycarbonate plastic glasses, cups, bowls, dinner plates, dishes and trays suitable (and safe) for boats or by swimming pools. Most are completely indistinguishable from fine glass and china except that they are lighter and won't break if dropped. The Strahl range of glasses is particularly attractive and you can put them in your dishwasher – unlike acrylic glasses, they won't go dull or get crazed with tiny cracks. The square, white serving platters made by JAB Design in several sizes are elegant, light and almost impossible to tell from real china.

Among the conventional items are many tins for flans, tarts, cakes, loaves and cupcakes, plain or non-stick, and of every shape and size (and lots of pretty cupcake papers, too); there are also many different patterns of cookie-cutters, old-fashioned jelly moulds, enamel pie dishes and numerous non-stick baking trays and tins.

They carry a comprehensive range of Le Creuset ovenware. There are cabinets full of every kind of knife a cook could ever use, including Wusthof Trident and shelves of the Magimix, Kitchen Aid and Bamix machines. There are eight or ten different kinds of Thermos flasks.

There's a lovely selection of good quality cotton and linen tablecloths, napkins, aprons and tea-towels.

Overall, the range is too big to do more here than hint at, but we would be surprised if you had to look elsewhere for anything but the most esoteric piece of equipment.

KITCHENWARE

MA CUISINE

8 Napoleon St
Cottesloe WA
9384 3400

Monday-Wednesday, Friday 9.00-5.30
Thursday 9.00-7.00
Saturday 9.00-5.00
Closed Sundays and public holidays
Parking in Railway and Napoleon Sts

During the 20 years Jill Braslin has owned and run Ma Cuisine, the emphasis may have moved away from kitchenware, but this Napoleon Street favourite is a must. Jill now also carries a beautiful (and wide) range of imported homewares, including baby clothes, luxury bedding and linen. The kitchen and dining ware she does stock is all of excellent quality.

Kitchen Aid blenders and mixers, Alessi products, knives from Global and WMF, Le Chasseur casseroles, all shapes and sizes of Brabantia wastebins, white Primo tableware, the Scanpan range, Bodum whiteware, Danish Design House and digital weighing scales from Salter and Terrallion can all be found here.

Jill's many regular and longstanding clients love what she does best. As she says, 'We're not over the top, but I do look for the best product at the best price.'

MATTERS OF TASTE

103 Harris Rd
Cnr Pembroke St
Bicton WA 6157
08 9319 1097
www.mattersoftaste.com.au

Monday–Saturday 9.00–5.00
Closed Sunday, public holidays and from 25 December to end of first week in January
Plenty of off-street parking outside the shop

There is a very welcoming and inclusive feel about this beautiful shop, which sells a small but excellent range of kitchenware alongside selected fine grocery items.

All of the kitchen equipment on sale – whether it's a large electrical product or a fabulous *Cuisiproi* grater – has been thoroughly tested and utilised in demonstrations in the adjoining cooking school. They are sold to you by staff who are extremely familiar with the product they are selling.

And it's the same with the grocery items: most of the ingredients have been included in class demonstrations and there are always free recipes available to you when you purchase produce. There is a priority to stock food items that are 'hand-made in small batches, preferably locally'. They only source from the eastern states and overseas if it cannot be found here in WA.

Tracey Cotterell has created a shop with a terrific ambience which completely reflects her own passion and love of good food and cooking and her desire to educate and involve us all.

PRESSURE COOKER CENTRE

337 Rokeby Rd
Subiaco WA 6008
9388 7797
Toll free 1800 266 069
www.pressurecooker.com.au

Monday-Friday 10.00-5.00
Saturday 10.00-2.00
Closed Sundays
Parking in Rokeby and Heytesbury Rds

This is the most amazing shop, right next door to Jean-Claude's Patisserie on Rokeby Road. As the name indicates, they specialise in … guess what? Pressure cookers. It's the only outlet in Australia to carry the full range of every pressure cooker available in Australia, and also the only place that supplies spare parts and servicing for virtually every brand of pressure cooker currently or previously sold in Australia. So if you have a problem with yours, this is the place to come for expert professional advice and help.

Chantal Roger, the proprietor, also sells some traditional cookware, woks, steamers, double-boilers and a few kitchen gadgets, but the raison d'etre of this shop is pressure cookers: be it a new one, servicing an old one, spare parts, cookbooks about pressure cooking or cooking classes.

THE HOME PROVEDORE KITCHEN ESSENTIALS

44 Bayview Tce
Claremont WA 6010
9286 1331

Monday–Friday 9.00–5.30

Saturday 9.00–5.00
Sunday 10.00–5.00
Bunning's car park at rear

The new branch of The Home Provedore Kitchen Essentials has opened on the site of the old Claremont Drapers. It's a large floor space: the range of stock is similar but not identical to the Fremantle shop (see next entry), with some additions, including more giftware and some Alessi and Ritzenhoff products.

Kathy is running cooking demonstrations in the Claremont store once a fortnight: daytimes are 10.00–12.00 and evenings are 6.00–8.00. As well as the demonstration, the session price includes eats, drinks and a recipe pack.

THE HOME PROVEDORE KITCHEN ESSENTIALS

39 Market St
Fremantle WA 6160
9336 3331

Monday-Friday 9.00-5.30
Saturday 9.00-5.00 Sunday 10.00-5.00
Ticket parking on Market St, High St, railway station car park

The Home Provedore has been a Fremantle destination for locals and visitors (many come by train, as the station is just up the road) for 12 years, and is now under new ownership. Kathy Smith came to work here several years ago and liked it so much she bought the business. The biggest change Kathy has made is to take over the shop on the next corner, which is now The Home Provedore Baking Essentials (see page 92). This new space houses a now enlarged bakeware section – it was previously squeezed into the back room of the original shop.

The now de-cluttered Home Provedore Kitchen Essentials carries an excellent selection of some high quality ranges of cookware such as Le Creuset and Chasseur enamelled cast iron, Scanpan, Mauviel, bright shiny copper pots and stainless steel pans, cooking knives (Victorinox, Global and Wusthof), kitchen machines (Kitchen Aid, Magimix), many different coffee and tea makers, ice cream makers, frypans, kettles (including Alessi), Dutch ovens, china (including Portmeirion), tagines, woks, glassware, stemware, selection of cookbooks – and much, much more. Chefs shop here, so there's a good range of professional gear.

The staff are cheerful, helpful and very motivated. And for any food items you might need, the wonderful Kakulas Sister (see page 209) is almost next door.

THE KITCHEN STORE
Unit 13, Centro Galleria Shopping Centre
Cnr Lloyd and Clayton Sts
Midland WA 6056
9274 4582
www.kitchenstore.com.au

Monday – Friday 9.00–5.30
Saturday 9.00 – 5.00
Off-street parking

This big shop, the newest branch of Chris Murphy's expanding chain, is what a Master of Business Administration – which Chris is, as well as being a trained chef – would call 'vertically integrated'.

The Kitchen Store has a cooking corner with a pizza oven where visiting chefs hold cooking classes, and sells a smallish amount of mostly packaged food items – along with a huge range of high quality cooking equipment and tableware. Where the vertical integration comes in is that the classes use produce from the food section and equipment from the shop floor. If you buy a hamper containing Five Senses coffee, Rochelle Adonis nougat and a Sophisticake panforte from Lake Grace, it might also contain a La Cafetiere coffee maker and a couple of Maxwell & Williams' mugs. And after you've watched Dale Sniffen making fresh pasta, you can buy a bag of Italian OO flour, a pasta roller and a jar of Peter Watson's pasta sauce, then go home and do it yourself.

As far as kitchen equipment goes, there is everything you could possibly want from some of the best makers – Bamix, Magimix, Scanpan, Estelle, Mauviel, Kitchen Aid, Le Creuset, Le Chasseur, Wusthof, Victorinox. There are Riedel glasses and decanters and Maxwell & Williams tableware. There's a cookbook section and shelves and racks of knives, peelers, sieves and gadgets.

Also, you can hire speciality cake tins; this is a great idea, as you're not likely to want to make the same novelty cake for your child's birthday two years in a row – you may as well hire the tin you make it in rather than buy it.

WHEEL & BARROW

Shop F123, Karrinyup Shopping Centre
200 Karrinyup Rd
Karrinyup WA 6018
9445 2004

Monday–Saturday 9.00–5.30

We have more than a soft spot for Wheel & Barrow. Everything they stock seems to have a well-designed, contemporary feel about it; there are good basics, good white china, good glassware, lots of cookware, baking dishes and trays, tableware, electric mixers, blenders or food processors, knives and other kitchen tools, and an excellent range of serving dishes.

They're a bit seasonal, too, so expect something Christmassy at Christmas time and a display with an Easter feel at Easter time.

Wheel & Barrow also stock a few things you don't find elsewhere, such as the German-made Silex grill press – which is fantastic, and ideal for boats.

They also sell a few food items – olive oil, coffee and syrups (including the very popular Wild Hibiscus flowers in syrup) – and a few cookbooks.

Helpful, friendly and informed staff complete the picture.

Also @:

**Shop 134
Garden City Shopping Centre
125 Risely St
Booragoon WA 6154
9315 1874**

MARKETS

This book is mainly about the small retail shops, usually family owned, in Perth that are striving to bring the best fresh, local, seasonal produce to their customers.

But before shops, there were markets. Open-air food markets are the oldest form of shopping. The bustling Arab *souk*, noisy and vibrant and full of tantalising smells, is still where shoppers in the Middle East get their produce. On holiday in France and Italy we love browsing in the growers' markets with their stalls piled high with colourful food.

Perth and the surrounding area has its markets, too, and there is good reason to patronise them. The produce, fruit and vegetables in particular, is almost certain to be locally grown and in season. Market stallholders rarely have the facilities to stockpile out of season produce. Similarly, if it is local and seasonal it is sure to be fresh and will often have been picked only hours before the grower sets off for market.

Very often the fruit and veg will have been grown by the stallholder and his or her family on something less than the industrial scale of the big commercial producers. This means that even if the produce is not actually certified organic (and some is), at least it will usually have had less exposure to chemicals than the goods on the shelves of your local supermarket.

And markets are fun, too. As well as the food stalls, where you'll find homemade cakes, biscuits, honey, nuts, jams and preserves, farmhouse cheeses and delicious crusty bread, there are usually stalls selling handicrafts of one kind or another to a mixture of regular customers and curious tourists. Here, very briefly, we list a few.

CITY FARM ORGANIC GROWERS' MARKET

City Farm Place
Lime Street, off Royal Street
East Perth WA 6004
08 9325 7229
www.cityfarmperth.org.au

Saturday only: 8.00 to 12 noon
CASH only
No plastic bags supplied; bring your own bags.
There's plenty of parking but if you don't want to drive you can take the train to Claisebrook Station which is right next door. The yellow, free CAT bus stops just a few metres away.

The market, in an old engineering workshop on the reclaimed City Farm, is the main outlet for the organic farm itself but also provides space for ten or twelve other stalls. Most stallholders are selling their own organic and/or bio-dynamic foodstuffs – grower-direct; other stallholders sell bought-in organic produce and a few other products. Most of the stall holders are small, niche, or boutique producers. This is still the only solely organic growers' market in WA.

The farm is a community-based project, run by a small staff and volunteers, all of whom are very friendly and hospitable and very committed to and knowledgeable about organic farming and produce.

Not every stallholder is here every Saturday; some come only when their produce is in season; others come twice a month. For example, Sid and Edith de Burgh of 'Baramba' near Gingin are here on the first and third Saturday of each month. They sell biodynamic beef and hogget from the stall, frozen, in serves of two or you can order the beef fresh in bulk between October and February. All their Shorthorn/Devon cross cattle and Merino sheep are raised without the use of artificial fertilizers, chemicals, steroids, hormones or antibiotics. Bill and Fay Tannock of Just Herbs, who also sell good bread – we bought the spelt loaf, which was excellent – also come on the first and third Saturdays.

Gabrielle Kervella who makes the famous Kervella goats'-milk cheese at her farm in Gidegannup is here in person manning her stall just inside the door every fortnight. If you haven't tried chevre really fresh, as it is here, then you must. It is a revelation.

All the food here is very fresh. The fruit and vegetables on the stalls on Saturday mornings were only picked the day before: 'This produce is grown by people who have a passion for the land. You can taste the freshness,' says Thom Scott, a long-standing member of the City Farm community.

We liked the organic hummus and babaganoush made by Harry and Sona Toutikian from Gidgegannup; they also sell jams and preserves plus biodynamic fruit and vegetables. Jean and Cliff Brockway have an organic orchard – 'Llanelly' – in Roleystone. They were selling delicious home-made pies, tarts, dried fruit and honey and were doing a good trade in freshly-squeezed fruit juices. Suong and Hoa Lam are here every Saturday with their organic fruit and vegetables.

The City Farm's own stall sells the oranges, lemons, spinach and honey, poultry and eggs they have raised themselves and which you can see just out the back door. They also sell fresh organic dairy products: milk, yoghurt, cream and cheeses. We also bought some Eagle Hill Farm organic rye flour there for bread-making.

More than 90% of what is sold at City Farm is food of one kind or another but as they try to move towards being a one-stop-shop for their customers, there are now non-food items on offer – environmentally-friendly cleaning materials, face, body and baby products.

Cleaning up this heavily polluted former oil-storage depot has been a huge task (they replaced the polluted soil with 300,000 wheelbarrow loads of organic compost) but they are creating a fruitful garden out of a wasteland: 'This is a huge labour of love by a lot of people,' Thom told us over a cup of organic coffee.

EDGECOMBE BROTHERS
12130 West Swan Rd
Cnr Gnangara and West Swan Rds
Belhus WA 6069
9296 4307

7 days 9.00-6.00

We have bought asparagus here which was picked at dawn, graded, sorted and in the farm fridge by the time we arrived at 9 am. You could imagine it still had the dew on it. When steamed a few hours later, the taste was out of this world – so much better than asparagus picked a week earlier and imported from Peru that you could hardly compare them. And it's not just the taste as asparagus is a vegetable that loses nutrients rapidly. In any case, we think asparagus is very much a seasonal delicacy – in the Swan Valley that can be from as early as August until December – and our enjoyment is the greater if that's when we have it. We look forward to the first asparagus of the season with as much enthusiasm as we used to look forward to Christmas as children.

The original Edgecombe brothers, Don and Frank, founded the business as a vineyard in 1925, and today some ten of their descendants are involved. They have diversified into fruit and veg – melons, pumpkins, broad beans, all grown in season and picked and sold in the farm shop the same day – and table grapes fresh or dried as sultanas or currants. The family farm all of their 70 or so acres (around 28 hectares). The asparagus was the idea of Walter Edgecombe, who had always grown some in the garden, and that's still his department. They grow green and purple asparagus, thick, medium and thin, and have just started experimenting with white.

There is a lovely café with tables inside and under the shady vines, and regular wine tastings. 'We are a small family-run company selling seasonal produce from our own land,' says Alfred Edgecombe.

Edgecombe Brothers are on the Swan Valley food and wine tourist trail and are definitely worth a visit if you are out this way. You won't taste fresher asparagus than theirs.

FREMANTLE MARKETS

Cnr Henderson St and South Tce
Fremantle WA 6160
9335 2515
www.fremantlemarkets.com.au

Friday 9.00–9.00 Saturday 9.00–5.00
Sunday 10.00–5.00 Monday public holidays 10.00–5.00
Closed Good Friday
CASH only
Parking in surrounding car parks: Henderson St, Parry St

Founded in 1897, there are over 300 stalls here, including 20 in the fruit and vegetable market, selling a huge variety of fresh, seasonal, locally grown produce.

ANNIE'S BREAD SHOP
Stall 88

A wide variety of excellent bread, sourced from 18 different bakeries, now under the ownership of Abhi's Bread (see page 32).

LAWLEY'S BREAD SHOP
Stall 110

A newcomer to the market, situated at the back of the fruit and veg. Many of the Lawley fourteen Daily Breads, flatbreads, rolls, bagels, pies, rolls, quiches, pastries, cakes and petits fours are here. (See Lawley's Bakery and Café page 37.)

MR ORGANIC
Stall 119

An excellent, wide selection of high quality organic fruit and vegetables. (See page 278).

SCOTTY'S
Stalls 114/115

Fresh, seasonal, naturally ripened high quality fruit and vegetables direct from the growers. (See page 281.)

SUNNY WHOLEFOODS
Stall 8

Bulk dried wholefoods, dried fruit and nuts, organic eggs, milk, butter, cream, yoghurt, plus freshly made hummus and peanut butter. (See page 329.)

THE COFFEE CONNECTION
Stall 89

Specialising in flavoured coffee beans and some coffee-making equipment. (See page 341.)

THE FREMANTLE FISH MARKET
Stalls 11/12

Good selection of fresh local fish, prawns, oysters and marinated sardines and octopus. (See page 174.)

the herb+spice+tea shop
Stalls 92/93

Dried herbs, spices and herbal and remedial teas, some organic, plus freshly ground dukka. (See page 342.)

THE MOUSETRAP
Stall 95

Long-established cheese stall, now under new ownership: over 50 different varieties of cheese and half a dozen varieties of herbed olives, plus crispbreads and biscuits.

GINGIN SUNDAY MARKET
Eliza's on Granville Tearooms
Cnr Granville and Weld Sts
Gingin WA

Sundays: 8.00-11.00

There are three to five stalls selling locally grown, seasonal fruit and vegetables, jams, preserves and other products. The stalls are situated in the car park outside Eliza's on Granville, the pretty tearooms in the middle of Gingin.

Maggie Edmonds (Gingin Heritage Estate and The Get Stuffed Olive Company: 9575 1107) is here every week, selling her olive oil, passionfruit spread, Membrillo, Lake salt with herbs, rosemary and chilli. She usually has some bread from the Bindoon bakery, salad from the local Loose Leaf Lettuce Co., local free-range eggs, apples from Vergone Farms in Dwellingup and locally grown proteas. You can also get Maggie Edmonds' products at Fresh Provisions, O2H, Wine Liaisons, the Boatshed and other shops in Perth and from Edgecombe Brothers in the Swan Valley.

A very regular grower-direct stallholder is Wayne Brock and his wife Margaret (9571 0044) who sell their bio-dynamic Demeter certified produce from their smallholding down the Great Northern Highway in Muchea. All the seasonal produce on the stall looked beautiful. We ate their broccoli that night and it was superb. Everything is in wonderful condition: it is picked the night before and kept in a mobile refrigerated trailer attached to their vehicle. The Brocks' produce can be bought at Absolutely Organic, O2H, Midland Fresh and Mt Lawley Wholefoods.

If you want to sell your home-grown produce here, call Maggie Edmonds (9575 1107) and enquire about a stall. This Sunday morning market is very small at the moment but it is hoping to grow and it would be wonderful if it did.

KALAMUNDA

Town Square and Gardens
Cnr Haynes St and Central St
Kalamunda WA 6076
9257 2266

First Saturday in the month; morning is best

This is not a food market (it has about 150 stalls selling mainly arts and crafts), but it does have a few outstanding food stalls (though not every stallholder is here every week), including Smashing Platters (homemade preserves), The Homemade Collection (jams and chutneys), Cookies Galore (biscuits and cookies), The Mason Farmyard (condiments). There is also a good cheese stall and two fruit and veg stalls, one of which is organic, and Little Miss Cupcake has a very pretty stall selling her beautiful cupcakes.

There are usually musicians busking; it is quite a fun place ... and you can always go over the road to Collodel's for one of their wonderful ice creams.

SUBIACO STATION STREET MARKETS

41 Station St
Subiaco WA 6008
9382 2832

Friday, Saturday, Sunday and public holiday Mondays 9.00–5.30
Parking in Station St car parks

ANGRY ALMOND

This continental grocer specialises in olives, olive oil, antipasto, coffee, cheese, pasta, vinegar, jams and tomato products. They also stock Paradise Beach Purveyors' produce, Kangaroo Island yoghurt, Meredith Dairy yoghurt, Rose Valley cheese and some Maggie Beer products. (See page 183.)

GROWERS LANE

This area has three large fruit and vegetable stalls, which almost merge into one another.

GOLDEN CHOICE

This is the middle of the three stalls: it's always busy here, and there are lots of seasonal bargains.

TR & TR GROWER DIRECT

This is a great fruit and vegetable stall owned and run by the Tran family. Much of the produce comes direct from the growers in Wanneroo. They have very fresh herbs, including wonderful mint and basil. The Trans grow their own silverbeet and broccoli.

YEN'S FRUIT AND VEG

Seasonal and imported fruit and veg.

LA GALETTE DE FRANCE

A tiny stall making very traditional French produce: crêpes, galettes, biscuits, croissants and pastries. Eric Masure and his team make *everything* themselves: he gave us an almond croissant, which had just come out of the oven, to taste. It was out of this world. (See page 104.)

THE FLOWER GUYS SUBIACO
This lovely flower stall at the entrance to the market sells seasonal cut flowers, hand ties, and posies. Most of the flowers come direct from the growers. There is also a great range of plants and bulbs in pots, depending on the season: roses, orchids, cyclamen, iris, daffodils and tulips.

THE FRESH YOGHURT PLACE
Freshly squeezed orange juice and creamy Athena yoghurt, plain or with fruit topping, are on sale here.

TRADITIONAL GOZLEME
This stall sells freshly baked traditional Turkish gozleme. These are made with a dough made of only flour, water and salt (no yeast and no egg). The balls of dough are rolled out, almost like a pizza base, and then filled with spiced mince and vegetables, chicken, cheese and spinach or vegetables with feta and spinach. The dough is then folded over in half but not sealed down at the edges. This is then cooked on a hot griddle. And very delicious they are too.

OTHER MARKETS

CANNING VALE
Bannister Rd
Canning Vale WA 6155
9455 1389

Sunday 7.00-2.00
CASH only

During the week this is West Australia's main wholesale fruit and vegetable market but on Sundays it becomes the pitch for some 400 stallholders selling a very diverse selection of goods including food and attracting up to 7,000 visitors a day.

GOSNELLS RAILWAY MARKETS
Cnr Albany Hwy and Fremantle Rd
Gosnells WA 6110

Thursday-Sunday and public holidays
Fruit and veg growers selling their own produce in season.

MALAGA MARKETS
Cnr Beach Rd and Alexander Dr
Malaga WA 6090
9249 9970

Friday-Sunday 9.00-6.00

More than 100 stalls selling fresh produce at bargain prices.

MIDLAND FARMERS' MARKET
Old Great Northern Hwy
Midland WA 6056

Sunday mornings

Grower-owned stalls selling their fresh fruit and vegetables in season right in the middle of Midland.

MONDO DI CARNE

824 Beaufort St, cnr Sixth Ave
Inglewood WA 6052

Saturday mornings from September until Christmas 8-12.30

This is a small market of over 20 stalls selling their own WA produce in a courtyard behind the newly extended Mondo Di Carne butcher (see page 71).

WANNEROO MARKETS

33 Prindiville Dr (off Wanneroo Rd)
Wangara WA 6065
9409 8397

**Friday 7.00-5.00 (fresh produce only)
Saturday-Sunday and public holiday Mondays 9.00-5.30**

WA's biggest retail market, with over 180 stalls and shops under cover, including ten selling fresh produce. There is also a bakery and a fish market, and snack food is available.

ORGANIC AND HEALTH FOOD

Organic food is gaining a big following here. Locally grown organic food is certainly good for you and can taste wonderful – the slower, natural growth rate of fruit and vegetables that have not been artificially fertilised concentrates the flavour. Local supply, however, is not always up to the demand – there are no organic carrots grown in WA for example – so a lot have to be imported.

Butchers, too, have difficulty getting enough organic meat and, as far as we know, there are no butchers in WA who are wholly or solely organic. Most tackle the problem by having a small organic section alongside more conventionally grown or reared produce.

However, there are some shops that do make a point of selling only certified organic food and usually a few other organic products.

Apart from the following entries see:

Boatshed Quality Meats (page 47)

City Farm Organic Growers' Market (page 307)

Mr Organic (page 278)

ABSOLUTELY ORGANIC WA

782 North Beach Rd
Gwelup WA 6018
9242 7711

Monday-Friday 10.00-6.00
Saturday 10.00-4.00 Closed Sundays
Off-street parking by shop

Rick and Annie Dunn started as organic growers nearby 15 years ago, and began selling everything they grew from a tin shed on their property. So when they moved here, to a proper shop, 5 years ago, they already had a customer base. Since then they have expanded from a staff of five to a staff of 22 (aged from fourteen to 84). They now buy produce from a number of sources, including directly from local growers, but the demand for certified organic food is now too great to be satisfied completely in that way, so they have had to diversify into wholesale markets here and interstate.

Organic fruit and vegetables are not often as good to look at as those on display here (the mandarins from Victoria that had come in the day we visited looked particularly good, and they were very pleased with the lettuce, from Keysbrook, which had been in short supply). Annie says this is because she selects the best of what comes in and passes the rest on to other outlets. 'We are fussy, so we pass on the stuff that doesn't look so good,' she told us.

Absolutely Organic IS absolutely organic, by the way, and people travel long distances to shop here, but Annie says it takes constant detective work by daughter Debbie, checking labels and suppliers, to make sure this remains so: 'Our customers trust us, so we have to trust our suppliers. But we have to be vigilant.' All the labels in the shop include the growers' names and where the produce comes from, and Annie encourages shoppers to read them: 'We encourage people to notice who the grower is. Just because it is organic doesn't mean it is always the best.'

As well as the fresh organic produce there are shelves of

packaged produce, including Holle baby foods, and there are fifteen to twenty bins of organic pulses, grains, flours, seeds and nuts from which you can help yourself. They buy in organic meat from Peter Griffiths at Boatshed Quality Meats (see page 47), freeze it and sell it frozen. If you want to buy fresh meat from them before it is frozen, phone and speak to Debbie Hayward or Annie Dunn.

They carry some organic products which are not food, and while they recognise that they need to supply a fairly good range, including all the basics, Annie says they don't want to stock too much. But you'll find most of what you want here.

No chemicals are used even in keeping the place clean; they improvise with things like vinegar and bicarbonate of soda as recommended in that most unlikely of bestsellers, *Spotless*, by Shannon Lush and Jennifer Fleming.

ORGANIC AND HEALTH FOOD

HYPE

The Boulevard Shopping Centre
31 Gayton Rd
City Beach WA 6015
9285 2565

Tuesday–Saturday 8.00–4.00
Closed Sundays and Mondays
Ample parking in car park

Just around the corner from Georges (see page 252), his wife, Sandrine, has opened a new organic shop and café.

This is a completely organic, largely gluten-free and dairy-free place, selling organic fruit and vegetables – oranges, mangoes, pears, melons, tomatoes, avocados, ginger, potatoes, sweet potatoes, onions, carrots. They will juice any of the fruit for you.

There is also a good range of tinned groceries – sweetcorn, tomatoes, peas, lentils – plus gluten-free pasta, eggs and yoghurt. Abhi's bread, Five Senses coffee and many different kinds of Toby's Estate teas can be found on the shelves here.

Angela Bunyan oversees the kitchen, which is producing a good selection of vegetarian salads and other vegetarian dishes. All the cakes are gluten-free; soups and risottos are available to eat in or to go.

ORGANIC AND HEALTH FOOD

LOOSE PRODUCE

2 Hobbs Ave
Como WA 6152
9474 9100
www.looseproduce.com
keryn@looseproduce.com

**Monday–Friday 9.00–5.00
Saturday 9.00–4.00 Closed Sundays
Parking outside shop**

The challenge here is to find something Keryn Rose and Nikki White *don't* have among the more than 1000 food items they stock, many of which are in bins, sacks or drums from which you help yourself. You are encouraged to bring your own containers. The idea is that you buy a little at a time and pay only for what you need: 'By the teaspoon or the truckload,' says Keryn. The bulk items include lots of whole and rolled grains, pulses, flours – including spelt – and nuts, seeds, spices, dried fruits and oils. Many customers buy the raw materials and make up muesli to their own recipes. 'Breakfast is the most important meal of the day, so look forward to it,' Keryn advises.

Loose Produce is not exactly a health food shop, nor wholly organic, but it does sell a lot of healthy food ingredients: there are some organic, some gluten-free and some wheat-free ingredients and products. As well as the bulk produce there are island shelves of packaged goods and glass-fronted fridges of perishables, including some organic meat. They try to buy local, WA-produced food wherever possible: they have a small range of certified organic, seasonal fresh produce.

From Asian food to baking products, bread, coffee, dairy and fruit and veg, it all looked very wholesome and inviting, but what you can buy on the shop floor is by no means all that is going on here. There are evening cooking classes by chefs such as Ann Meyer ('Brunch', the 'Flavour of Tuscany') and Zarin Miller ('Japanese Nori Rolls'); there are also cooking classes for the boys, classes for kids in the school holidays, and free demos, tastings and talks on Saturday mornings. There's a monthly newsletter which you can get by email.

We didn't know about Loose Produce until recently, and we think that they're something more than rather a good find. The place has a comfortable feel about it; there is a children's playroom at the back of the shop and the staff are friendly and helpful. This is their sixth year in business so they – and we – reckon they're doing something right.

If you've done your shopping here and want a quick coffee, go around the corner to Raspberry Fields (2 Birdwood Ave, 9368 2000). It's a pretty gift shop which also sells coffee. The cupcakes and gluten-free orange and almond slice come from Sugar Cube and the biscuits come from Simply Beautiful Biscuits. They also carry a small stock of packaged gourmet food products.

MANNA WHOLEFOODS AND CAFÉ

274 South Tce
South Fremantle WA 6162
9335 7995
mannawholefoods@iinet.net.au

Monday–Friday 8.00–6.00
Saturday 8.30–3.00 Closed Sundays
Parking in South Tce and side streets

Manna, an old, established wholefood shop, has been a worthy Fremantle institution for the last 15 years, but under its new owner, Myra Thomas (who is a registered naturopath and herbalist), and her daughter Virginia Ivory, it has acquired a real buzz and a much more lively atmosphere.

Ths shop carries a good range of certified organic fruit and vegetables, nearly all from WA, plus wholefoods and groceries, and biodynamic, macrobiotic, gluten-free and vegan products. There is a similar amount of non-organic fresh produce.

There is a good range of bulk foods, including many kinds of specialist flour (some are gluten-free) – wheat, spelt, buckwheat, potato, soy, coconut and rice – and pulses and rice in big tubs from which you help yourself into brown paper bags.

They stock a limited range of organic beef, lamb, chicken and pork. There's free-range organic eggs, of course, and you can even get non-homogenised milk with a thick layer of cream on top sold in glass bottles which you can bring back to be refilled. Shelves are full of jars of organic jams and relishes; they make their own chutneys and Virginia's homemade hummus is famous in Freo.

To one side of the big main room is a busy café (all food cooked on the premises by Sasha and her team) serving mainly organic dishes (including sausage rolls, tuna patties, Brazil nut patties). Many, but not all, are vegetarian (spinach and filo parcels) and some are vegan. Seasonal homemade soups are the winter mainstay; delicious salads do the job in the warmer months.

There is even a gluten-free, vegan lasagne made without cheese; it sounds impossible but is said to be delicious.

Manna can be used as a normal neighbourhood grocer, but it is also especially good for people who have particular food requirements (those on macrobiotic diets, or those who are coeliac, for instance): 'Our aim is to provide the Fremantle community with good organic choices, decent wholefood, real food – and to cater for people with special dietary needs,' says Myra.

Requests from customers are encouraged and special orders are taken.

There is a natural skin care and cosmetic section, and a small selection of specialist cookbooks. Naturopaths are available for consultations.

ORGANIC AND HEALTH FOOD

MT LAWLEY WHOLE FOODS

Unit 3, 885 Beaufort St
Cnr 9th Ave
Inglewood WA 6052
9371 6408
www.mtlawleywholefoods.com.au

**Monday–Friday 9.00–5.45
Saturday 9.00–3.00
Closed Sundays
Car park at side of shop and opposite**

Mt Lawley Whole Foods stocks a large and comprehensive range of fresh certified organic fruit and vegetables alongside bulk foods, grains, flours, nuts, dried fruit and seeds and dried groceries (including Fair Trade coffee, tea and chocolate).

In the fruit section we saw quality melons, avocados, grapes, plums, pears, apples, kiwi fruit and peaches; among the vegetables were red cabbage, cauliflower and spinach, zucchini, potatoes, sweet potatoes and spinach.

There's a large range of gluten- and wheat-free produce here as well as unprocessed honey, free-range eggs and Lawley's bread. In the fridges you'll find biodynamic dairy produce, unhomogenised full-cream milk, organic butter and goats' milk. In the freezer section there are free-range chickens which are antibiotic- and hormone-free, certified organic beef, lamb and pork (sausages, chops and bacon) and a small selection of organic ice cream.

Allen Robinson, the proprietor, is a qualified herbalist: he gives reasonably priced hour-long consultations by appointment.

Metro and WA country deliveries are available.

There's a new-ish vegetarian café within the shop, called Tempting Thyme, selling dairy-free, egg-free and gluten-free prepared produce: there is an appetising collection of fresh salads, quiches, spinach and ricotta rolls, patties, smoothies, freshly squeezed juice and organic tea and coffee. Dine in or take away (contact Dylan Weiner on 0413 753 290).

ORGANIC AND HEALTH FOOD

NATURE'S HARVEST
20 Napoleon St
Cottesloe WA 6011
9384 8900

Monday–Friday 8.30–5.30
Saturday 9.00–4.00 Closed Sundays
Very limited parking on street but free parking by railway line

This is really an organic grocer, with a very comprehensive range of products. A health-conscious vegetarian allergic to cows' milk, sensitive to washing powder and with a baby suffering from nappy rash could shop here and never have to go anywhere else.

In this one shop you can buy pretty well every organic product that is available: not just food, but also such diverse and improbable items as nappies and cleaning materials – even shaving cream. Some of the products (brown risotto rice or wholemeal couscous, for example), which new owners Juliette Smith and Graham Saltmer say they tracked down only with difficulty, would be hard to find anywhere else. They also make a point of catering for people with particular dietary requirements, so many products are wheat-free, gluten-free, dairy-free, sugar-free and Fair Trade.

The huge floor space and storage areas allow them to carry a bigger range than most health shops, but because they believe passionately in freshness they aim for a high turnover in fruit and vegetables. They buy direct from WA organic growers and offer a boxed service which is becoming increasingly popular. They give the grower some idea of the customer's likes and dislikes and every Tuesday, a box of seasonal fruit and vegetables arrives, which the customer can pick up on Wednesday.

They also have a huge range of bulk food, some of which is organic, in over 100 clear plastic-fronted boxes from which you help yourself with a scoop.

Juliette's daughters, Grace and Sophie make the peanut butter. Nature's Harvest has been here for years, but since Graham and Juliette took it over in early 2007 they have transformed it.

PEACHES ORGANIC

Shop 1, 195 Hampton Rd
South Fremantle WA 6162

9430 5025
7 days 8.00–7.00
Plenty of parking

Cross over the green line on the floor into the new extension of Peaches and you are in the organic section, where *everything* is certified organic.

Added in late 2006 in response to rising customer demand, a very wide range of organic produce is now available: fruit and vegetables, dry groceries, dairy produce, eggs, tea, coffee, pasta and rice, bread (including Abhi's panini), frozen chicken, chocolate, soaps, shampoos and baby products.

In the greengrocery fridges, a good seasonal selection of rockmelons and watermelons, silverbeet, corn, new season apples, cabbages, celery and grapes were the order of the day when we visited. Robert Di Tullio told me they always try to have a good stock of fresh organic lettuce available. On special offer were large pineapples, and beautiful tomatoes sold in 1kg bags.

In the fridges, their new Pitango organic soups stood alongside another selection of delicious-looking soups from FitKitchen; there were also pizza bases, tofu and a wide range of yoghurts, milk, cream, butter and spreads.

In the freezer we saw frozen certified organic chickens, some frozen fish and the Gigi organic ice cream range.

The advantage for shoppers of everything being under one roof, although sold at different ends of the same shop, is that if an item is not available in the organic section, a high quality non-organic option is available a few steps away (see page 216).

ORGANIC AND HEALTH FOOD

SUNNY WHOLEFOODS

Shop 8, Fremantle Markets
Cnr Henderson St and South Tce
Fremantle WA 6160
9335 8355

Friday 9.00–9.00
Saturday 9.00–5.00 Sunday 10.00–5.00
Monday public holidays 10.00–5.00 Closed Good Friday
CASH only
Parking in surrounding car parks: Henderson St, Parry St

Bulk dried wholefoods, both organic and non-organic, dried fruit and nuts, free-range organic eggs, a fridge full of Margaret River organic milk, butter and cream, Paris Creek organic yoghurt, goats' milk and yoghurt ... this may be a small shop, but there's lots here.

Owner Googie Rummer makes fresh hummus each week and her own freshly ground peanut butter daily. The chickpea patties, made by the same supplier for the last 15 years, are famous.

The sugar-free, wheat-free slices are exclusive to Sunny's.

TEA AND COFFEE

We have chosen for this book only small, independent coffee merchants who roast and blend their own coffee in WA. As roasting and blending are as much art as science and as coffee is a crop subject to the vagaries of climate, smelling and tasting are the only ways to decide which is best for you.

All the coffee merchants we met are keen for you to taste and try their coffee and all will advise you how to best store the coffee, when to grind it and how to make the perfect cup.

Many believe that Tea is the New Coffee and tea merchants are also very pleased to be consulted. They are all absolutely in love with their product and are full of interesting information.

Every tea merchant and coffee roaster we met in the course of researching this book is passionate about what they are doing. The whole food scene in WA is much, much more than Butcher, Baker, Chocolate maker. Tea merchants and coffee roasters are right up there with the most passionate of food retailers.

If you would like to learn more about coffee and techniques of making good coffee, the Western Australian Barista Academy is the place to go. They are at 135 Lake Street, Northbridge and can be contacted on 9328 7675. Or go their website at www.baristaacademy.com.au

BREW-HA
Shops 3-4, 162 Rokeby Rd
Subiaco WA 6008
9388 7272
www.brew-ha.com.au

7 days 6.30-6.00
Shopping centre car park

Peter Barile roasts coffee here every day, sometimes mixing different green coffee beans together before roasting and sometimes roasting the individual types of bean separately and mixing a blend later. Each of the twelve standard blends is available by the cup or to take away by the bag. This is where you come to in Subiaco if you want very freshly roasted coffee beans.

Brew-Ha also sells 40–50 different blends of premium quality loose leaf teas, including Ceylon organic tea.

Over the last 18 months, Brew-Ha, an Australian-owned small family business, has been increasing its wholesale output, and from July 2007, the coffee roasting for export and wholesale customers has moved to their new factory in Wangara. Coffee for the café is still, thank heavens, being roasted on the premises here.

This is also a fine place to come and rest after some vigorous food shopping at Sas's (see page 145), to enjoy a cup of beautifully made fresh coffee. The place has a welcoming feel about it and there seemed to be many regular clients when we visited.

FIORI

9 Douglas St
West Perth WA 6005
9328 4988
fioricoffee@bigpond.com
www.fioricoffee.com

Back in WA after 7 years roasting coffee in Sydney, Kamran Nowduschani and his partner Louise Gordon are causing quite a stir with their Fiori coffee.

The beans Kamran blends and roasts are all estate grown, single-origin Arabica, but because they come from all over the world they have different characteristics, which he manipulates to achieve the qualities he's after: some for body, others for acidity, some for sweetness, others for floral highlights. 'Because coffee's a natural product, it's never exactly the same, but we try for consistency and to give people a fantastic experience,' says Kamran. 'I roast to a recipe, but also I go with my feeling for it, as well depending on factors like the weather and the newness of the crop.' Kamran uses no exact measures so there is no absolute consistency, but this is very good coffee indeed.

You can buy Fiori coffee by contacting them directly, or by mail order, or at good food stores such as Fresh Provisions or The Grocer. You can taste it at gourmet cafés such as Boucla in Subiaco or the Blue Duck in Cottesloe.

You can also sign on for a couple of short courses in the art of coffee: one explaining the history, origins, science of blending and how to taste; the other on how to make the perfect cup.

'We love what we do, and our efforts are fuelled by our obsession to create the ultimate cup of coffee,' they say.

FIVE SENSES COFFEE

3 Arkwright St
Rockingham WA 6168
9528 6200
www.fivesensescoffee.com.au

Monday–Friday 8.00–5.00
Closed Saturdays, Sundays, all public holidays and between Christmas and New Year
Ample parking

Dean Gallagher and the Five Senses team are going to extraordinary lengths to fulfil his ambition that everyone in Australia has the opportunity to drink a cup of really good coffee. 'Life's too short to drink bad coffee,' he says.

If there isn't a shop near you which stocks Five Senses, you don't have to drive all the way to the wonderful-smelling small retail shop, attached to the factory near Rockingham: just hop onto their website and place your order overnight. Whatever you've chosen – their AM blend, their 24/7 blend or the coffee of the week – will be delivered by courier within 24 hours if you live in the metropolitan area or by Australia Post overnight. This fast delivery system ensures that their coffee can be enjoyed by anyone at its peak of freshness.

Firmly believing that roasting coffee is a culinary art, Dean and the Five Senses roasters may spend many days, weeks or even months adapting a blend for a particular café or restaurant owner. 'A good roaster is someone who can manipulate the product, tweak it and improve it,' he says. You don't have to be a large wholesale customer to enjoy this service: they will roast small quantitites to order for Friday collection or delivery.

Dean started Five Senses in 2000, very much as a one-man band, after returning from a remote part of Papua New Guinea where he had lived and worked for 3 years as a Principal of an International School. It was while he was in PNG that he discovered an exceptionally beautiful coffee bean. He was determined to make it more widely accessible ... and Five Senses was born.

Dean and the team are incredibly passionate about their coffee. If you are in the Rockingham area, Five Senses are very well worth a visit. They may even give you a sample of beautiful coffee to drink. Some of the places around Perth where you can enjoy Five Senses coffee are: Epic in West Perth, Mooba in Wembley, Velvet in King Street Perth, Lemon Espresso in Clarement, Long Macc in Fremantle and The Beaufort Street Merchant.

LEAF

29 Napoleon St
Cottesloe WA 6011
9284 3830
www.leafteamerchants.com.

Monday–Saturday 8.00–6.30
Sunday 9.00–6.00
Parking in railway car park

Is tea the new coffee? That's what Philip May, a coffee roaster by trade who started The Dome coffee houses here, and his partner, Sri Lankan tea guru Hilary White, think. They backed their judgment by opening this cool, contemporary tea house 4 years ago and its slightly larger sister shop in Mt Lawley 2 years later. It's a long narrow room, ochre and burnt umber – think clean, fresh, different – with banquettes down one side and little tables and chairs on the other, occupied (when we went) mainly by mums who'd just dropped their children at school and were sharing a reviving infusion and catching up with the news.

'We wanted to give a contemporary expression of the venerable and ancient art of tea drinking,' says Philip. And what has been created here *is* very different – and delightful.

They have about 50 different teas to choose from – black teas such as Ceylon, Darjeeling, Assam, Earl Grey, English and Irish Breakfast, and some flavoured with fruits or spices; green and China teas such as Lapsang Souchong, Oolong and Gunpowder; many different herbal, fruit and berry infusions; plus the caffeine-free and healthy Rooibos from the mountains of Southern Africa. They can all be sipped there or taken away in paper sacks.

There are beautiful biscuits and little cakes, many gluten-free, all baked on the premises to maintain control of the quality, and using local and seasonal ingredients … and the best scones in WA, according to Janie-Lee, the cook that day.

But the owners, and area manager Lhani Davies, don't want this to be just a place where you drop in for a cup of tea (and definitely not a 'cuppa'); they want everything to be an 'event'. Hence Parisian Rose Morning Tea, an exotic experience to share with friends, consisting of a selection of baby quiche, smoked salmon bites, tiny sandwiches and cakes and Parisian rose tea (every morning till midday); or High Tea on Sunday afternoons, with an even larger selection of tea-time treats. Light meals and afternoon Tiffin are available every day. There are pretty little teapots and cups for sale – they'd make nice house-warming gifts along with a packet of special tea.

Also @:

60 Walcott St
Mt Lawley WA 6050
9471 1105
Monday-Saturday 9.00-5.30
Sunday 9.00-6.00

ROASTED

Shop 1, 36 South Tce
Fremantle WA 6160
9433 4334

Sunday-Thursday 7.00-6.00
Friday-Saturday 7.00-10.00
Numerous car parks; ticket street parking
Licensed

Dave Gagiero's passion is coffee. He roasts and grinds best quality Arabica beans every day to order, in small quanities to ensure consistency, at the back of this glass-fronted shop and coffee bar.

Dave stocks six kinds of coffee bean: Colombian Dark, Kenyan AA, Certified Organic Fair Trade, Organic Rainforest Alliance and Organic Decaf. His house blend, Passion, is made up of Rainforest Alliance plus Bukit Marante and Tiger Mountain: it's an espresso blend and recommended for domestic espresso machines.

He sells whole beans wholesale to other cafés and either whole beans or ground to individual customers.

The Tea Leaf Menu includes classic black teas (English Breakfast, Earl Grey, Darjeeling), Chai, green teas (Chinese Gunpowder, Japanese Sencha, Jasmine and Chai Sencha) and a choice of six herbal teas.

Dave believes that the best advertising in the world is word of mouth: 'Just let the product and the service speak for themselves.'

This small family business is also a gourmet café, serving breakfast and light lunches. His philosophy is to be seasonal, and where possible to use organic and locally sourced produce. His chef Mick catches and fillets his own whiting; meat comes from Frank's; fruit and vegetables from Scotty in the market; bread and Zen toasted muesli and pastries from Abhi's; shortbreads and biscuits from Cindy Cunningham near Rockingham. 'The food we eat shouldn't travel 5000km to get to us,' he believes.

RUBRA

1800 119 755
allan@rubracoffee.com.au
www.rubracoffee.com.au

After 12 years in the coffee business Allan McMurray began roasting his own coffee only in order to maintain control of the quality of the coffee he sold. He imported a roaster from Germany, took a few lessons from friends in the industry and almost immediately started winning prizes – four at the 2006 Sydney Royal Show alone: 'I thought, this can't be that hard – but it *was* a bit of a journey.'

He says roasting coffee is a blend of art and science. He roasts to a profile of blend, time and temperature (that's the science) tempered with art (the sight of the roasting beans, their colour, and the sound of crackling, which tells how the moisture is reacting).

Beans, both Arabica and Robusta come from Costa Rica, Guatemala, Brazil, Colombia, Papua New Guinea, India and Kenya.

Rubra coffee is available at Liquorice Gourmet Foods and Herdsman Fresh Essentials (see pages 211 and 205).

TEA FOR ME – GOURMET TEA

Shop 3, 94 Rokeby Rd
Subiaco WA 6008
9380 9377

Monday-Friday 9.30-5.00:
Saturday 9.30-4.00 Closed Sundays
Car parks and short-term street parking

This charming shop feels just right for an emporium selling tea, with its ceiling-high dark wooden shelves stacked with colourful packets of tea, antique tea pots and ceramics. Tea For Me is owned and run by Barry and Ding Dawson, who stock 85 different flavoured teas and up to 40 seasonally specific single-garden teas, about 90 per cent of which come from Sri Lanka.

It was in Sri Lanka that Barry became a tea merchant ... almost by accident. He ordered tea in the Colombo Hilton, where he was negotiating its redecoration, but repeatedly sent it back either because the pot was cold or the tea was too thin. Watching this was a Sri Lankan tea merchant called Anselm Perera, who eventually intervened and told the staff how to make the tea properly. He and Barry became friends, and in the course of many friendly visits to Anselm's factory and much tasting of tea, Barry eventually became a tea expert, too.

In 2000, when he and Ding returned to live in Australia from their home in Singapore, Barry's new-found expertise gave them the perfect opportunity to start their business.

Barry returns to Sri Lanka several times each year to taste and buy teas, often from individual growers. Ding travels regularly to China and Vietnam to buy tea and ceramics. Both believe it is essential to do the buying personally: 'To keep the quality, you have to go and build up a relationship with the individual grower. That way, we are sure to get what we order.' In many cases, Tea For Me is the only outlet for the small growers they deal with.

Barry resolved for us that old question about whether you should put the milk in first, as they do in England, or last, as seems more sensible. Barry puts it in last and says the milk-in-first custom only arose because pouring hot tea into fine bone china cups could crack them. So unless you have fine bone china cups, it is OK to put the milk in after you've poured the tea. We thought you'd like to know that.

Apart from their regular retail customers, Ding and Barry sell to many of the leading hotels, restaurants and cafés in Perth.

If you like tea, or want to experiment and try something different, do go along and see what Ding has on offer for you to taste. If you're in a hurry, Ding prefers you to take home some samples and try them at your leisure before you buy a new tea.

Also @:

Shop 20, London Court
Perth WA 6000
9221 7175

THE COFFEE CONNECTION

Stall 89, Fremantle Markets
Cnr South Tce and Henderson St
Fremantle WA 6160
9336 3163

Market hours
Parking in surrounding car parks: Henderson St, Parry St

The Coffee Connection sells 35 different kinds of coffee sourced from eleven different countries, all bought under the Fair Trade scheme. The Arabica beans are freshly roasted locally and flavoured each week for Gabby and her brother Justin Paris, who is the Coffee Connection parent and wholesaler. Sacks of pure Colombian, Mocha, Blue Mountain, Java, Australian Wombah, Kenyan and Guatemalan, plus her own house blend, a Brazilian mix are open on the counter. But it's the flavoured coffee beans that set her apart from others. There are 24 different natural flavours, including liqueur flavoured (Amaretto, Grand Marnier and Jamaican Rum), and another selection flavoured like desserts (Blackforest, Caramel Fudge, Chocolate Macadamia and Vanilla Nut). Some flavours are available decaffeinated.

To help you have coffee at home the way you have it in a café or restaurant, there are starter packs available and a good selection of accessories: percolators, plungers, milk frothing jugs, coffee mills and electric grinders.

Gabby stocks 35 different loose teas, including strawberry, mango, vanilla, blackcurrant, lemon peel and cinnamon as well as the more familiar blends from Ceylon, India and China.

Their new big seller is chocolate-coated coffee beans (available in milk or dark chocolate or mixed bags) and a selection of chocolate-coated nuts and confectionery: almonds, hazelnut, nougat, ginger and liquorice.

the herb+spice+teashop

Fremantle Markets
Cnr South Tce and Henderson St
Fremantle WA 6160

Friday 9.00–9.00 Saturday 9.00–5.00 Sunday 10.00–5.00
Monday public holidays 10.00–5.00 Closed Good Friday
CASH only
Parking in surrounding car parks: Henderson St, Parry St

Donna Harper has been in the market for over 20 years at the herb+spice+teashop, and has more than 150 big glass jars of dried herbs and spices, including some usually hard-to-get items such as blade mace, and many whose use was unknown to us ... but not to Donna, who can explain them all.

She also stocks many different kinds of herbal tea, including bush teas and green teas, plus big sacks of nuts, preserves and chutneys from Lizzie's Preserves and Ooh la la, and tubs of lemon myrtle, mountain pepper and bush tomatoes.

She also carries a big range of Healthy brand remedial teas, said to be good for headaches, sinus problems, colds and flu.

Donna blends her own dukka freshly each week.

WINE STORES AND COURSES

There are a lot of wines out there to choose from. While most wine stores stock many of the same wines, there are some independent wine retailers in Perth that are the exception, offering a more specialised selection. They specialise in carrying wines from small boutique producers, European-direct imports, Australian and European back vintage wines, classics and limited release wines. Some have extensive cellared selections to browse.

These wine merchants are knowledgeable about their stock and will advise you on the appropriate wine for what you are planning to cook. Matching the perfect wine with the perfect food can be really exciting, and often the heart of great culinary moments. And if you're planning a curry night, there's even a beer shop for you to visit.

For one of the best selections of Italian wine, you can't go past The Re Store, Leederville (see page 229).

If wine is a passion and you would like to learn more, The Wine Education Centre is the educational arm of the Wine Industry Association of WA and offers excellent wine appreciation courses to suit all ages and levels of experience. Contact them at 22 Prowse Street West Perth, telephone 9226 1188 or visit their website www.winewa.asn.au

CHATEAU GUILDFORD
124 Swan Street
Guildford WA 6055
9377 3311

INTERNATIONAL BEER SHOP
69 McCourt Street
West Leederville WA 6007
9381 1202
www.internationalbeershop.com.au

LA VIGNA
302 Walcott Street
Mt Lawley WA 6050
9271 1179
www.lavigna.com.au

LIQUOR BARONS MT LAWLEY
654 Beaufort Street
Mt Lawley WA 6050
9271 0866

OLD BRIDGE CELLARS
221 Queen Victoria Street
North Fremantle WA 6159
9335 2702

STEPHEN MCHENRY WINE MERCHANTS
171 Broadway
Nedlands WA 6009
9389 0107
www.steves.com.au

SWANBOURNE CELLARS
103 Claremont Cres
Swanbourne WA 6010
9384 2111

THE WINE STORE
48 George Street
East Fremantle WA 6158
6424 9500
www.thewinestore.com.au

VINTAGE CELLARS SHENTON PARK
95 Nicholson Road
Shenton Park WA 6008
9381 6555

USEFUL INFORMATION

MEAT STANDARDS AUSTRALIA

Meat Standards Australia™ (MSA) is a beef- and sheep-meat eating quality program that labels beef and sheepmeat with a guaranteed grade and recommended cooking method to identify eating quality according to consumer perceptions.

Guaranteeing eating quality MSA has established eating quality standards based on over 520,000 consumer taste tests.

A wide range of cattle and sheep management practices, processing systems, cuts, ageing periods and cooking methods have been researched to determine the impact each has on eating quality.

This information is taken from the Meat Livestock Australia website.

SEASONAL FOOD CHARTS

WA SEASONAL SEAFOOD GUIDE

SPECIES	SEASON
Dhufish	Feb–Nov
Gummy Shark	Feb–Aug
Herring	Aug–May
Mangrove Jack	Dec–Sep
Mullet	Jul–Apr
Mulloway	Apr–Oct
Nanygai	Mar–Oct
Pearl Perch	Dec–Sep
Pink Snapper	Oct–Jul
Rankin Cod	Dec–Sep
Red Emperor	Dec–Sep
Redthroat Emperor	May–Oct
Scarlet Seaperch	Dec–Sep
Silver Bream	Oct–Jul
Silver Trevally	Dec–Sep
Spanish Mackeral	Feb–Sep
Tailor	Jul–Apr
Whiting	Mar–Nov
Fresh Exmouth prawns	Mar–Nov
Swan River crabs	Jan–Jun
Mussels	Apr–Jan
Crayfish	15 Nov–30 Jun
Scallops	Jan–Jun

Kindly supplied by Seafresh Innaloo 9445 2451

WA seasonal fresh produce guide

Season's Best: Summer

VEGETABLES
Capsicum
Chillis
Cucumbers
Eggplant
Herbs
Lettuce
Mushrooms – Flats
Onions
Peas
Potatoes – Royal Blue
Radish
Runner Beans
Snow Peas
Spring Onions
Stringless Beans
Sweet Corn

FRUIT
Apricots
Bartlett Pears
Cherries
Figs
Grapes
Honeydew Melons
Mangoes
Nectarines
Peaches
Plums
Rockmelon
Royal Gala Apples
Tomatoes
Watermelons

Season's Best: Autumn

VEGETABLES
Asian Vegetables
Courgettes
English Spinach
Mushrooms – Cups
Onions
Parsnips
Potatoes – Ruby Lou
Pumpkins
Rhubarb
Swedes
Turnips

FRUIT
Carambola
Chestnuts
Fuji Apples
Fuyu Persimons
Golden Delicious Apples
Granny Smith Apples
Hi Early and Red Delicious Apples
Kiwifruit
Limes
Nashi Fruit
Olives
Packham Pears
Quinces
Red Grapefruit
Tamarillos
White Grapefruit

Season's Best: Winter

VEGETABLES
Broccoli
Brussels Sprouts
Capsicum
Cabbage
Cauliflower
Chillies
Eggplant NW
Leeks
Mushrooms – Portobello
Potatoes – Delaware
Pumpkins NW
Runner Beans NW
Stringless Beans NW
Squash NW
Sweet Corn NW
Zucchini

FRUIT
Fuerte Avocados
Honeydew NW
Lady Williams Apples
Lemons
Limes NW
Mandarins
Navel Oranges
Pink Lady Apples
Sundowner Apples
Watermelon NW

Season's Best: Spring

VEGETABLES
Asparagus
Beetroot
Broad Beans
Carrots
Celery
English Spinach
Fennel
Garlic
Globe Artichokes
Lettuce
Mushrooms – Button
Potatoes – Mondial
Salad Onions
Silver Beet
Sweet Potatoes

FRUIT
Bananas
Berries
Early stone fruit
Hass Avocados
Mangoes
Papaya
Passionfruit
Strawberries

Kindly supplied by Fresh Finesse 9388 277 www.freshf.com.au

ACKNOWLEDGEMENTS

Many people have helped make this book possible and we would like to thank them *all* wholeheartedly:

Martin Woollacott, former foreign editor, *The Guardian*, thought Perth needed a food lovers' guide and suggested we write it; Karen McDonald encouraged us and introduced us to Clive Newman at Fremantle Press; and John Patterson at The Human Interface – our database guru.

At Fremantle Press: Clive Newman gave us the opportunity to write this book; Margaret Whiskin, with her sound judgement and sense of humour, has been a most patient and enthusiastic publisher with whom we have loved working; Tracey Gibbs designed the book cover and map; and Sarah Shrubb, our copy editor.

Within the food industry, many people have given us advice and guidance and been very generous with their time: in particular Louis Lynch, Noelene Swain, Carla Hummel, Steve Perry, Jamie Kronborg, Carol Gaby and Pauline Lynch.

Our friend, nutritionist Jo Beer BSc. (Hons) checked our nutritional information. After reading the manuscript, Janet Holmes à Court very kindly wrote the Foreword.

We are indebted to our many friends and acquaintances who shared their food shopping secrets with us and to the shopkeepers and suppliers who appear in this book, who have patiently answered our endless questions. We have learned a great deal from them.

Our thanks also to our understanding families who, throughout this project, have had less than our full attention, particularly Hunter, India and Scarlett.

And finally, we would like to thank our husbands, Nelson and Fraser, to whom this book is dedicated. Each of them has willed us both to succeed: we could not have written it without their help, encouragement and love. Thank you.

Julie and Lisa

BUSINESS NAME INDEX

A

Abhi's Bread: *Bread*, 30

Absolute Flowers: *Florists*, 179

Absolutely Chez Uchino: *Food-to-go*, 233

Absolutely Organic WA: *Organic and Health Food*, 319

Amano – The Gelato Company: *Ice Cream and Gelati*, 284

Amano Cooking School and Kitchenware Specialist: *Books for Cooks*, 27

Amano Cooking School and Kitchenware Specialist: *Cooking Schools*, 133

Amano Cooking School and Kitchenware Specialist *Kitchenware*, 292

Angry Almond: *Food Stores and Grocers*, 183

Annie's Bread Shop: *Bread*, 32

Antonio's Fresh Continental Store: *Food Stores and Grocers*, 184

Apple Fresh: *Greengrocers*, 269

Ararat Kebabs: Broadway Fair Shopping Centre, 191

Atlantic Seafoods: *Asian Food*, 11

Aubergine Gourmet Foods: *Gourmet Cafés and Breakfast*, 244

Azzura Gelati: *Ice Cream and Gelati*, 285

B

Barchetta: *Gourmet Cafés and Breakfast*, 246

Barleyfield Meats: *Butchers*, 46

Barrett's Bread: *Bread*, 33

Bayview Bakery: *Bread*, 34

Bayview Flowers: *Florists*, 179

Beaches Café: *Gourmet Cafés and Breakfast*, 247

Bean There Café: Carine Glades Shopping Centre, 194

Beaufort Street Merchant, see The Beaufort Street Merchant: *Food Stores and Grocers*, 222

Beaumonde Catering: *Caterers*, 118

Bloom By Design: *Florists*, 179

Blue Duck Café: *Gourmet Cafés and Breakfast*, 247

Boatshed Fish Co.: *Fishmongers*, 155

Boatshed Flowers: *Florists*, 179

Boatshed Fresh Food: *Food Stores and Grocers*, 186

Boatshed Quality Meats: *Butchers*, 47

Boffins Bookshop: *Books for Cooks*, 27

Bookcaffe: *Books for Cooks*, 27

Borrello Cheese: *Delicatessens and Cheese Shops*, 140

Boucla Café: *Gourmet Cafés and Breakfast*, 245

Boulevard Shopping Centre, see The Boulevard Shopping Centre: *Food Stores and Grocers*, 223

Bread Craft: Melville Central, 213

Breakfast at Cottesloe Beach: *Gourmet Cafés and Breakfast*, 246

Brew-Ha: *Tea and Coffee*, 331

Brighton Meat Supply: *Butchers*, 49

Brighton Road Food Market: *Food Stores and Grocers*, 189

Broadway Fair Health Foods: Broadway Fair Shopping Centre, 191

Broadway Fair Shopping Centre: *Food Stores and Grocers*, 190

BUSINESS NAME INDEX

Broadway Fresh: *Greengrocers*, 270

Brumby's Bread: Herdsman Fresh Essentials, 207

Brush Fork + Pencil: *Caterers*, 118

Burrendah Fresh Gourmet: *Greengrocers*, 271

By Word of Mouth Catering: *Caterers*, 119

C

C. LoPresti & Son: *Food Stores and Grocers*, 197

Café 55: *Gourmet Cafés and Breakfast*, 249

Café Mozart: *Asian Food*, 11

Cakes Delight: *Cakes and Patisserie*, 94

Canning Vale: *Markets*, 316

Carine Cuisine Gourmet Foods: Carine Glades Shopping Centre, 194

Carine Glades Shopping Centre: *Food Stores and Grocers*, 192

Carl Torre and Sons: *Butchers*, 50

Centurion Seafood: *Asian Food*, 12

Chan Brothers Oriental Supermarket: Melville Central, 213

Chateau Guildford: *Wine Stores and Courses*, 344

Chez Frederic Gourmet Food To Go: *Food-to-go*, 234

Chez Jean-Claude Patisserie: *Cakes and Patisserie*, 95

Chocolate Factory, see The Chocolate Factory: *Chocolates and Confectionery*, 131

Choux: *Cakes and Patisserie*, 97

Cimbalino: *Gourmet Cafés and Breakfast*, 250

City Farm Organic Growers' Market: *Markets*, 307

Claremont Fresh: *Food Stores and Grocers*, 195

Claytons Quality Meats: *Butchers*, 52

Coffee Connection, see The Coffee Connection, 341

Collodel Ice Cream and Sorbet: *Ice Cream and Gelati*, 286

Continental Meat Supply: *Butchers*, 53

Coode Street Café: *Gourmet Cafés and Breakfast*, 251

Coral Seafood: *Fishmongers*, 156

Corica: *Cakes and Patisserie*, 98

Creative Meats: *Butchers*, 54

Crimea Growers Market: *Greengrocers*, 272

Crimea Quality Meats: *Butchers*, 55

Crossways Shopping Centre: *Food Stores and Grocers*, 198

Cut It Out: *Books for Cooks*, 27

Cut It Out: *Kitchenware*, 293

D

Daily Supermarket: *Asian Food*, 21

Dat Thanh Butcher: *Asian Food*, 12

David Jones Food Hall: *Food Stores and Grocers*, 200

Deli di Mondo: *Delicatessens and Cheese Shops*, 141

Dolce & Salato: *Cakes and Patisserie*, 99

Dragon Seafood Chinese Restaurant: *Asian Food*, 12

Dragon Tea House: *Asian Food*, 13

Dubrovnik Butchers: *Butchers*, 57

Dymocks: *Books for Cooks*, 27

E

Edgecombe Brothers: *Markets*, 309

Elmar's Smallgoods: *Butchers*, 58

Emma's Seafood and Dim Sum Restaurant: *Asian Food*, 13

BUSINESS NAME INDEX

Emma's Seafood Yong Tofu: *Asian Food*, 13

Epicurious: *Books for Cooks*, 28

Epicurious: *Kitchenware*, 294

Essential Blooms: *Florists*, 179

Eufloria: *Florists*, 179

F

Festival Fish: *Fishmongers*, 157

Fig Jam: *Delicatessens and Cheese Shops*, 142

Finesse Butchery (City Beach): *Butchers*, 60

Finesse Butchery (Dalkeith): *Butchers*, 61

Fiori: *Tea and Coffee*, 332

Fishermen's Basket: *Fishmongers*, 158

Five Senses Coffee: *Tea and Coffee*, 333

Fleurtatious: *Florists*, 180

Flower Guys, see The Flower Guys: Subiaco Station Street Markets, 315

Flowers and Unique Designs: *Florists*, 180

For the Coffee Table: *Cakes and Patisserie*, 101

Forno Wood Fired Ovens: *Caterers*, 120

François: *Cakes and Patisserie*, 102

Frank's Gourmet Meats: *Butchers*, 62

Fremantle Fish Market, see The Fremantle Fish Market: *Fishmongers*, 174

Fremantle Markets: *Markets*, 310

Fremantle Mini Mart: *Asian Food*, 22

Fresh 'n Crusty: *Bread*, 35

Fresh Provisions (Bicton): *Food Stores and Grocers*, 202

Fresh Provisions (Claremont): *Food Stores and Grocers*, 203

Fresh Provisions (Mt Lawley): *Food Stores and Grocers*, 204

Fresh Yoghurt Place, see The Fresh Yoghurt Place: Subiaco Station Street Markets, 315

Freshocean: *Fishmongers*, 159

Fruit Basket, see The Fruit Basket: *Greengrocers*, 282

Funky Bunches: *Florists*, 180

G

George Street Merchants: *Delicatessens and Cheese Shops*, 143

Georges: *Caterers*, 121

Georges: *Gourmet Cafés and Breakfast*, 252

Ginger Pig, see The Ginger Pig: *Delicatessens and Cheese Shops*, 147

Gingin Sunday Market: *Markets*, 312

Globe Coffee House, see The Globe Coffee House: *Gourmet Cafés and Breakfast*, 263

Golden Choice, Growers Lane: Subiaco Station Street Markets, 314

Good Fortune Roast Duck House: *Asian Food*, 14

Good Mood Food: *Caterers*, 121

Good Store, see The Good Store: *Eclectic Shops*, 152

Gosnells Railway Markets: *Markets*, 316

Gourmet Centro: Melville Central, 213

Gourmet Deli, see The Gourmet Deli: *Delicatessens and Cheese Shops*, 149

Great Northern Meat Supply: *Butchers*, 63

Grocer, see The Grocer: *Food Stores and Grocers*, 224

Groper and His Wife, see The Groper and His Wife: *Fishmongers*, 175

Growers Lane: Subiaco Station Street Markets, 314

H

Hadley's: *Butchers*, 64

Hela Continental Smallgoods: *Butchers*, 65

herb+spice+teashop, see the herb+spice+teashop: *Tea and Coffee*, 342

Herdsman Fresh Essentials: *Food Stores and Grocers*, 205

Heyder & Shears: *Caterers*, 122

Home Provedore Baking Essentials, see The Home Provedore Baking Essentials: *Cake Decorating Supplies and Services*, 92

Home Provedore Kitchen Essentials (Claremont), see The Home Provedore Kitchen Essentials (Claremont): *Kitchenware*, 302

Home Provedore Kitchen Essentials (Fremantle), see The Home Provedore Kitchen Essentials (Fremantle): *Kitchenware*, 303

Hubble's Yard: *Gourmet Cafés and Breakfast*, 253

Hype: *Organic and Health Food*, 321

I

Icey Ice: *Asian Food*, 14

Il Gelato: *Ice Cream and Gelati*, 288

Il Paiolo Wood Fired Oven Catering: *Caterers*, 123

Il Panino Bakery: *Bread*, 36

International Beer Shop: *Wine Stores and Courses*, 344

J

J. & A. Marchesani: *Butchers*, 66

Jeremy's Exclusive Butchery: *Butchers*, 67

John Street Café: *Gourmet Cafés and Breakfast*, 248

John Walker Chocolatier: *Chocolates and Confectionery*, 129

Junction Ice Creamery, see The Junction Ice Creamery: *Ice Cream and Gelati*, 290

K

Kailis Bros: *Fishmongers*, 160

Kakulas Brothers: *Food Stores and Grocers*, 208

Kakulas Sister: *Food Stores and Grocers*, 209

Kalamunda: *Markets*, 313

Kitchen Store, see The Kitchen Store: *Kitchenware*, 304

Kitchen Warehouse: *Kitchenware*, 295

Kitchen Witch: *Kitchenware*, 296

Kong's Oriental Supermart: *Asian Food*, 23

Kongs Trading: *Asian Food*, 15

Kosher Food Centre, see The Kosher Food Centre: *Food Stores and Grocers*, 225

L

La Galette de France South Perth: *Cakes and Patisserie*, 104

La Vigna: *Wine Stores and Courses*, 344

Lady Kitchener: *Kitchenware*, 297

Lane Bookshop, see The Lane Bookshop: *Books for Cooks*, 28

Larner's Oyster Supply: *Fishmongers*, 161

Lawless Cooking: *Caterers*, 124

Lawless Cooking: *Cooking Schools*, 134

Lawley's Bakery and Café: *Bread*, 37

Leaf: *Tea and Coffee*, 335

BUSINESS NAME INDEX

Lemon Espresso: *Gourmet Cafés and Breakfast*, 254

Leonidas – les Prlines Belge: *Chocolates and Confectionery*, 130

Lime Flowers: *Florists*, 180

Limes Fresh Fruit & Veg. Co.: *Greengrocers*, 273

Liquor Barrons Mt Lawley: *Wine Stores and Courses*, 344

Liquorice Gourmet Foods: *Food Stores and Grocers*, 211

Little Home Bakery: *Bread*, 38

Loose Produce: *Organic and Health Food*, 322

Lucky Import and Export: *Asian Food*, 15

M

M. & M. Princi Butchers: *Butchers*, 74

Ma Cuisine: *Kitchenware*, 299

Mad Butcher, see The Mad Butcher: *Butchers*, 84

Magnolias of Central Park: *Florists*, 180

Major Cakes: *Cake Decorating Supplies and Services*, 91

Malaga Markets: *Markets*, 316

Manic Botanic: *Florists*, 181

Manna Wholefoods and Café: *Organic and Health Food*, 324

Marco's Fussy Meats (Applecross): *Food-to-go*, 235

Marco's Fussy Meats (Yangebup): *Butchers*, 68

Matters of Taste: *Cooking Schools*, 135

Matters of Taste: *Kitchenware*, 300

Meat Direct: *Butchers*, 69

Meat Lovers' Paradise: *Butchers*, 70

Meat Safe, see The Meat Safe: *Butchers*, 85

Meat Showcase, see The Meat Showcase: *Butchers*, 86

Mediterranean Woodfired Ovens: *Caterers*, 125

Mela Indian Sweets & Eats: *Asian Food*, 16

Melville Central: *Food Stores and Grocers*, 212

Melville Seafoods: *Fishmongers*, 162

Michael's Gourmet: Broadway Fair Shopping Centre, 191

Midland Farmers' Market: *Markets*, 316

Midland Junction Food Store: *Food Stores and Grocers*, 214

Midland Junction Fresh Markets: *Greengrocers*, 274

Milkd: *Gourmet Cafés and Breakfast*, 256

Millpoint Caffe Bookshop: *Books for Cooks*, 28

Miss Minnie's Garden: *Florists*, 181

Moe Sushi: *Food-to-go*, 236

Mondo di Carne: *Butchers*, 71

Mondo di Carne: *Markets*, 317

Mosman Park Fresh: *Greengrocers*, 276

Mother India: *Food-to-go*, 237

Mousetrap, see The Mousetrap: Fremantle Markets, 311

Mr Fresh Growers Market: *Greengrocers*, 277

Mr Organic: *Greengrocers*, 278

Mt Lawley Whole Foods: *Organic and Health Food*, 326

My Little Fish Shop: *Fishmongers*, 163

N

Nature's Harvest: *Organic and Health Food*, 327

New Edition Bookshop: *Books for Cooks*, 28

New Life Bakery: *Asian Food*, 16

BUSINESS NAME INDEX

New Norcia Bakeries: *Bread*, 39

New Norcia Café: *Gourmet Cafés and Breakfast*, 257

Nippon Fare: *Food-to-go*, 238

Nippon Food Supplies: *Asian Food*, 24

No. 44 King Street Pruveyors of Fine Food, Coffee and Wine: *Gourmet Cafés and Breakfast*, 258

O

O2H: *Greengrocers*, 279

Old Bridge Cellars: *Wine Stores and Courses*, 344

Oliver's Fine Foods: *Delicatessens and Cheese Shops*, 144

P

Pansini Seafoods: *Fishmongers*, 164

Partridges: *Fishmongers*, 165

Patisserie la Vespa: *Cakes and Patisserie,* 105

Peaches Organic: *Organic and Health Food*, 328

Peaches: *Food Stores and Grocers*, 216

Pearl of Highgate, see The Pearl of Highgate: *Cakes and Patisserie*, 115

Peko Peko: *Food-to-go*, 239

Peter's Butchers: *Butchers*, 73

Picobello Patisserie: *Cakes and Patisserie*, 106

Poppy's Flowers: *Florists*, 181

Pressure Cooker Centre: *Kitchenware*, 301

Prime Products: *Asian Food*, 17

Princi Butchers: *Butchers*, 76

Princi's at Romanos: *Food Stores and Grocers*, 218

Prinz of Vienna: *Cakes and Patisserie*, 107

Pronto Gourmet Butcher: *Butchers*, 78

Pusey's Puffs: *Cakes and Patisserie*, 108

R

Rainforest, see The Rainforest: *Florists*, 181

Re Store, Lake Street, see The Re Store, Lake Street: *Food Stores and Grocers*, 228

Re Store, Oxford Street, see The Re Store, Oxford Street: *Food Stores and Grocers*, 229

Red Teapot, see The Red Teapot: *Asian Food*, 17

Reid's Meats and Delicatessen: *Butchers*, 79

Riki Blakes Café: *Gourmet Cafés and Breakfast*, 259

Roasted: *Tea and Coffee*, 337

Roasting Duck, see The Roasting Duck: *Asian Food*, 18

Rochelle Adonis: *Cakes and Patisserie*, 109

Room for Dessert: *Cakes and Patisserie*, 110

Rossmoyne Family Meats: *Butchers*, 80

Rubra: *Tea and Coffee*, 338

Ruby's Patisserie: *Cakes and Patisserie*, 111

S

Sas's: *Delicatessens and Cheese Shops*, 145

Satay Shop, see The Satay Shop: *Food-to-go*, 242

Scarfo's Meating Place: *Butchers*, 81

Scotty's: *Greengrocers*, 281

Scutti – A Taste of Europe: *Food Stores and Grocers*, 219

Seafood Secrets: *Fishmongers*, 166

Seafresh Claremont: *Fishmongers*, 167

Seafresh Innaloo: *Fishmongers*, 168

BUSINESS NAME INDEX

Sealanes: *Fishmongers*, 170

Sebastian Butchers: *Butchers*, 82

Sensations en Ardross: *Gourmet Cafés and Breakfast*, 261

Simon Johnson: *Food Stores and Grocers*, 220

Simply Beautiful Biscuits: *Cakes and Patisserie*, 112

Soda: *Gourmet Cafés and Breakfast*, 262

Sorelle Deli: *Delicatessens and Cheese Shops*, 146

South Perth Seafoods: *Fishmongers*, 171

Spices: *Food-to-go*, 240

Splash's Fish House: *Fishmongers*, 172

Stephen McHenry Wine Merchants: *Wine Stores and Courses*, 344

Subi Fresh: Crossways Shopping Centre, 199

Subiaco Station Street Markets: *Markets*, 314

Sugar Cube: *Cakes and Patisserie*, 113

Sunny Wholefoods: *Organic and Health Food*, 329

Swanbourne Cellars: *Wine Stores and Courses*, 344

Swansea Street Fresh Markets: *Food Stores and Grocers*, 221

Sweet Violets Florist: *Florists*, 181

Sweets of London: *Eclectic Shops*, 151

Swish 'n' Chips: *Fishmongers*, 173

Swish Fish 2 Go: *Food-to-go*, 241

T

Tea for Me – Gourmet Tea: *Tea and Coffee*, 339

Temptations Bakehouse and Patisserie: *Bread*, 41

The Beaufort Street Merchant: *Food Stores and Grocers*, 222

The Boulevard Shopping Centre: *Food Stores and Grocers*, 223

The Chocolate Factory, Fremantle: *Chocolates and Confectionery*, 131

The Coffee Connection: *Tea and Coffee*, 341

The Flower Guys Subiaco: Subiaco Station Street Markets, 315

The Fremantle Fish Market: *Fishmongers*, 174

The Fresh Yoghurt Place: Subiaco Station Street Markets, 315

The Fruit Basket: *Greengrocers*, 282

The Ginger Pig: *Delicatessens and Cheese Shops*, 147

The Globe Coffee House: *Gourmet Cafés and Breakfast*, 263

The Good Store: *Eclectic Shops*, 152

The Gourmet Deli: *Delicatessens and Cheese Shops*, 149

The Grocer: *Food Stores and Grocers*, 224

The Groper and His Wife: *Fishmongers*, 175

the herb+spice+teashop: *Tea and Coffee*, 342

The Home Provedore Baking Essentials: *Cake Decorating Supplies and Services*, 92

The Home Provedore Kitchen Essentials (Claremont): *Kitchenware*, 302

The Home Provedore Kitchen Essentials (Fremantle): *Kitchenware*, 303

The Junction Ice Creamery: *Ice Cream and Gelati*, 290

The Kitchen Store: *Kitchenware*, 304

The Kosher Food Centre: *Food Stores and Grocers*, 225

The Lane Bookshop: *Books for Cooks*, 28

BUSINESS NAME INDEX

The Mad Butcher: *Butchers*, 84

The Meat Safe: *Butchers*, 85

The Meat Showcase: *Butchers*, 86

The Mousetrap: *Fremantle Markets*, 311

The Pearl of Highgate: *Cakes and Patisserie*, 115

The Rainforest: *Florists*, 181

The Re Store, Lake Street: *Food Stores and Grocers*, 228

The Re Store, Oxford Street: *Food Stores and Grocers*, 229

The Red Teapot: *Asian Food*, 17

The Roasting Duck: *Asian Food*, 18

The Satay Shop: *Food-to-go*, 242

The Urban Pantry: *Caterers*, 126

The Wine Education Centre: *Wine Stores and Courses*, 343

The Wine Store: *Wine Stores and Courses*, 344

Tony Ale & Co.: *Food Stores and Grocers*, 230

Tony's House of Tender Meats: *Butchers*, 87

Torre & Mordini Gourmet Meats: *Butchers*, 88

TR and TR Grower Direct, Growers Lane: *Subiaco Station Street Markets*, 314

Traditional Gozleme: *Subiaco Station Street Markets*, 315

Tramps Food, Tastes & Trends: *Caterers*, 127

Tran's Emporioum: *Asian Food*, 18

U

Ultimo Catering: *Caterers*, 127

United Bakery: *Bread*, 43

Upper Crust Cooking Classes: *Cooking Schools*, 136

Urban Pantry see, The Urban Pantry: *Caterers*, 126

Urban Provider, Cooking Passions: *Cooking Schools*, 137

V

Van's: *Gourmet Cafés and Breakfast*, 264

Vegetal: *Florists*, 181

VHT Perth: *Asian Food*, 19

Vintage Cellars Shenton Park: *Wine Stores and Courses*, 344

W

WA Seasonal Freah Produce Guide: *Useful Information*, 348

WA Seasonal Seafood Guide: *Useful Information*, 347

Walson Foods: *Asian Food*, 19

Wandering Wok Tours: *Asian Food*, 20

Wanneroo Markets: *Markets*, 317

Weir's Butchers: *Butchers*, 89

Wheel & Barrow: *Kitchenware*, 305

Whole Food Cooking: *Cooking Schools*, 138

Wine Liaisons: *Books for Cooks*, 28

Wine Liaisons: *Eclectic Shops*, 153

Wine Store, see The Wine Store: *Wine Stores and Courses*, 344

Wing Hong Butcher: *Asian Food*, 20

Worldwide Seafoods: *Fishmongers*, 176

X

X-Wray: *Gourmet Cafés and Breakfast*, 266

Y

Yee Seng Oriental SuperMarket: *Asian Food*, 25

Yen's Fruit and Veg, Growers Lane: *Subiaco Station Street Markets*, 315

LOCALITY INDEX

APPLECROSS
Apple Fresh: *Greengrocers*, 269

Freshocean: *Fishmongers*, 159

Marco's Fussy Meats: *Food-to-go*, 235

Reid's Meats and Delicatessen: *Butchers*, 79

Sensations en Ardross: *Gourmet Cafés and Breakfast*, 261

Sugar Cube: *Cakes and Patisserie*, 113

Swish Fish 2 Go: *Food-to-go*, 241

ATTADALE
Deli di Mondo: *Delicatessens and Cheese Shops*, 141

Prinz of Vienna: *Cakes and Patisserie*, 107

BASSENDEAN
Beaumonde Catering: *Caterers*, 118

BEACONSFIELD
Princi Butchers: *Butchers*, 76

Princi's at Romanos: *Food Stores and Grocers*, 218

BELHUS
Edgecombe Brothers: *Markets*, 309

BICTON
Fresh Provisions: *Food Stores and Grocers*, 202

Matters of Taste: *Cooking Schools*, 135

Matters of Taste: *Kitchenware*, 300

My Little Fish Shop: *Fishmongers*, 163

Picobello Patisserie: *Cakes and Patisserie*, 106

BOORAGOON
John Walker Chocolatier: *Chocolates and Confectionery*, 129

Kitchen Warehouse: *Kitchenware*, 295

Seafood Secrets: *Fishmongers*, 166

The Satay Shop: *Food-to-go*, 242

Wheel & Barrow: *Kitchenware*, 305

BURSWOOD
Ultimo Catering: *Caterers*, 127

CANNING VALE
Canning Vale: *Markets*, 316

CANNINGTON
Kitchen Warehouse: *Kitchenware*, 295

CARINE
Rainforest, see The Rainforest: *Florists*, 181

The Rainforest: *Florists*, 181

CHURCHLANDS
Brumby's Bread: Herdsman Fresh Essentials, 207

Creative Meats: *Butchers*, 54

Essential Blooms: *Florists*, 179

Festival Fish: *Fishmongers*, 157

Herdsman Fresh Essentials: *Food Stores and Grocers*, 205

CITY BEACH
Boulevard Shopping Centre, see The Boulevard Shopping Centre: *Food Stores and Grocers*, 223

Finesse Butchery: *Butchers*, 60

359

LOCALITY INDEX

Georges: *Caterers*, 121

Georges: *Gourmet Cafés and Breakfast*, 252

Groper and His Wife, see The Groper and His Wife: *Fishmongers*, 175

Hype: *Organic and Health Food*, 321

The Boulevard Shopping Centre: *Food Stores and Grocers*, 223

The Groper and His Wife: *Fishmongers*, 175

CLAREMONT

Bayview Bakery: *Bread*, 34

Bayview Flowers: *Florists*, 179

Claremont Fresh: *Food Stores and Grocers*, 195

Fresh Provisions: *Food Stores and Grocers*, 203

Home Provedore Kitchen Essentials, see The Home Provedore Kitchen Essentials: *Kitchenware*, 302

Lady Kitchener: *Kitchenware*, 297

Lane Bookshop, see The Lane Bookshop: *Books for Cooks*, 28

Lemon Espresso: *Gourmet Cafés and Breakfast*, 254

Meat Showcase, see The Meat Showcase: *Butchers*, 86

Peter's Butchers: *Butchers*, 73

Seafresh Claremont: *Fishmongers*, 167

The Home Provedore Kitchen Essentials: *Kitchenware*, 302

The Lane Bookshop: *Books for Cooks*, 28

The Meat Showcase: *Butchers*, 86

COMO

Funky Bunches: *Florists*, 180

Loose Produce: *Organic and Health Food*, 322

COTTESLOE

Amano Cooking School and Kitchenware Specialist: *Books for Cooks*, 27

Amano Cooking School and Kitchenware Specialist: *Cooking Schools*, 133

Cooking School and Kitchenware Specialist: *Kitchenware*, 292

Barchetta: *Gourmet Cafés and Breakfast*, 246

Beaches Café: *Gourmet Cafés and Breakfast*, 247

Blue Duck Café: *Gourmet Cafés and Breakfast*, 247

Boatshed Fish Co.: *Fishmongers*, 155

Boatshed Flowers: *Florists*, 179

Boatshed Fresh Food: *Food Stores and Grocers*, 186

Boatshed Quality Meats: *Butchers*, 47

Breakfast at Cottesloe Beach: *Gourmet Cafés and Breakfast*, 246

Chez Frederic Gourmet Food To Go: *Food-to-go*, 234

Il Gelato: *Ice Cream and Gelati*, 289

John Street Café: *Gourmet Cafés and Breakfast*, 248

Leaf: *Tea and Coffee*, 335

Ma Cuisine: *Kitchenware*, 299

Moe Sushi: *Food-to-go*, 236

Nature's Harvest: *Organic and Health Food*, 327

Temptations Bakehouse and Patisserie: *Bread*, 41

Van's: *Gourmet Cafés and Breakfast*, 264

DALKEITH

Cimbalino: *Gourmet Cafés and Breakfast*, 250

Finesse Butchery: *Butchers*, 61

DOUBLEVIEW
Peko Peko: *Food-to-go*, 239

DUNCRAIG
Bean There Café: Carine Glades Shopping Centre, 194

Carine Cuisine Gourmet Foods: Carine Glades Shopping Centre, 194

Carine Glades Shopping Centre: *Food Stores and Grocers*, 192

Eufloria: *Florists*, 179

Fresh 'n Crusty: *Bread*, 35

Liquorice Gourmet Foods: *Food Stores and Grocers*, 211

Mr Fresh Growers Market: *Greengrocers*, 277

Splash's Fish House: *Fishmongers*, 172

Torre & Mordini Gourmet Meats: *Butchers*, 88

EAST FREMANTLE
C. LoPresti & Son: *Food Stores and Grocers*, 197

George Street Merchants: *Delicatessens and Cheese Shops*, 143

Hubble's Yard: *Gourmet Cafés and Breakfast*, 253

Lime Flowers: *Florists*, 180

Meat Direct: *Butchers*, 69

Mother India: *Food-to-go*, 237

The Wine Store: *Wine Stores and Courses*, 344

Wine Liaisons: *Books for Cooks*, 28

Wine Liaisons: *Eclectic Shops*, 153

EAST PERTH
City Farm Organic Growers' Market: *Markets*, 307

Heyder & Shears: *Caterers*, 122

Sweet Violets Florist: *Florists*, 181

EAST VICTORIA PARK
Emma's Seafood and Dim Sum Restaurant: *Asian Food*, 13

Flowers and Unique Designs: *Florists*, 180

Kongs Trading: *Asian Food*, 15

Major Cakes: *Cake Decorating Supplies and Services*, 91

Swansea Street Fresh Markets: *Food Stores and Grocers*, 221

EDGEWATER
Kitchen Witch: *Kitchenware*, 296

FLOREAT
For the Coffee Table: *Cakes and Patisserie*, 101

FREMANTLE
Amano – The Gelato Company: *Ice Cream and Gelati*, 284

Annie's Bread Shop: *Bread*, 32

Café 55: *Gourmet Cafés and Breakfast*, 249

Chocolate Factory, see The Chocolate Factory: *Chocolates and Confectionery*, 131

Coffee Connection, see The Coffee Connection, 341

Dolce & Salato: *Cakes and Patisserie*, 99

Frank's Gourmet Meats: *Butchers*, 62

Fremantle Fish Market, see The Fremantle Fish Market: *Fishmongers*, 174

Fremantle Markets: *Markets*, 310

Fremantle Mini Mart: *Asian Food*, 22

herb+spice+teashop, see the herb+spice+teashop: *Tea and Coffee*, 342

LOCALITY INDEX

Home Provedore Baking Essentials, see The Home Provedore Baking Essentials: *Cake Decorating Supplies and Services*, 92

Home Provedore Kitchen Essentials, see The Home Provedore Kitchen Essentials: *Kitchenware*, 303

Il Gelato: *Ice Cream and Gelati*, 289

Kakulas Sister: *Food Stores and Grocers*, 209

Mediterranean Woodfired Ovens: *Caterers*, 125

Mousetrap, see The Mousetrap: *Fremantle Markets*, 311

Mr Organic: *Greengrocers*, 278

New Edition Bookshop: *Books for Cooks*, 28

Oliver's Fine Foods: *Delicatessens and Cheese Shops*, 144

Roasted: *Tea and Coffee*, 337

Scotty's: *Greengrocers*, 281

Sunny Wholefoods: *Organic and Health Food*, 329

The Chocolate Factory, Fremantle: *Chocolates and Confectionery*, 131

The Coffee Connection: *Tea and Coffee*, 341

The Fremantle Fish Market: *Fishmongers*, 174

the herb+spice+teashop: *Tea and Coffee*, 342

The Home Provedore Baking Essentials: *Cake Decorating Supplies and Services*, 92

The Home Provedore Kitchen Essentials: *Kitchenware*, 303

The Mousetrap: Fremantle Markets, 311

X-Wray: *Gourmet Cafés and Breakfast*, 266

GINGIN
Gingin Sunday Market: *Markets*, 312

GOSNELLS
Gosnells Railway Markets: *Markets*, 316

GUILDFORD
Chateau Guildford: *Wine Stores and Courses*, 344

GWELUP
Absolutely Organic WA: *Organic and Health Food*, 319

HAMILTON HILL
Continental Meat Supply: *Butchers*, 53

Forno Wood Fired Ovens: *Caterers*, 120

HENLEY BROOK
Elmar's in the Valley: *Butchers*, 59

HIGHGATE
Beaufort Street Merchant, see The Beaufort Street Merchant: *Food Stores and Grocers*, 222

Daily Supermarket: *Asian Food*, 21

Elmar's Smallgoods: *Butchers*, 58

Pearl of Highgate, see The Pearl of Highgate: *Cakes and Patisserie*, 115

The Beaufort Street Merchant: *Food Stores and Grocers*, 222

The Pearl of Highgate: *Cakes and Patisserie*, 115

HILTON
Hela Continental Smallgoods: *Butchers*, 65

Il Panino Bakery: *Bread*, 36

J. & A. Marchesani: *Butchers*, 66

LOCALITY INDEX

INGLEWOOD
Mondo di Carne: *Butchers*, 71

Mondo di Carne: *Markets*, 317

Mt Lawley Whole Foods: *Organic and Health Food*, 326

INNALOO
Seafresh Innaloo: *Fishmongers*, 168

JANDAKOT
Temptations Bakehouse and Patisserie: *Bread*, 42

Tony Ale & Co.: *Food Stores and Grocers*, 230

JOONDANA
Kong's Oriental Supermart: *Asian Food*, 23

KALAMUNDA
Collodel Ice Cream and Sorbet: *Ice Cream and Gelati*, 286

Kalamunda: *Markets*, 313

Sebastian Butchers: *Butchers*, 82

KARRINYUP
John Walker Chocolatier: *Chocolates and Confectionery*, 129

Wheel & Barrow: *Kitchenware*, 305

LEEDERVILLE
François: *Cakes and Patisserie*, 102

Funky Bunches: *Florists*, 180

Il Gelato: *Ice Cream and Gelati*, 289

Kailis Bros: *Fishmongers*, 160

Manic Botanic: *Florists*, 181

Re Store, Oxford Street, see The Re Store, Oxford Street: *Food Stores and Grocers*, 229

The Re Store, Oxford Street: *Food Stores and Grocers*, 229

Urban Provider, Cooking Passions: *Cooking Schools*, 137

MADELEY
Dubrovnik Butchers: *Butchers*, 57

MALAGA
Festival Fish (wholesale): *Fishmongers*, 157

Malaga Markets: *Markets*, 316

MANDURAH
Kitchen Witch: *Kitchenware*, 296

MELTHAM
Dubrovnik Butchers: *Butchers*, 57

MENORA
Kosher Food Centre, see The Kosher Food Centre: *Food Stores and Grocers*, 225

The Kosher Food Centre: *Food Stores and Grocers*, 225

MIDDLE SWAN
Great Northern Meat Supply: *Butchers*, 63

MIDLAND
Barleyfield Meats: *Butchers*, 46

Fishermen's Basket: *Fishmongers*, 158

Gourmet Deli, see The Gourmet Deli: *Delicatessens and Cheese Shops*, 149

Junction Ice Creamery, see The Junction Ice Creamery: *Ice Cream and Gelati*, 290

Kitchen Store, see The Kitchen Store: *Kitchenware*, 304

Midland Farmers' Market: *Markets*, 316

Midland Junction Food Store: *Food Stores and Grocers*, 214

LOCALITY INDEX

Midland Junction Fresh Markets: *Greengrocers*, 274

Sorelle Deli: *Delicatessens and Cheese Shops*, 146

The Gourmet Deli: *Delicatessens and Cheese Shops*, 149

The Junction Ice Creamery: *Ice Cream and Gelati*, 290

The Kitchen Store: *Kitchenware*, 304

Tony's House of Tender Meats: *Butchers*, 87

MINDARIE QUAY

Temptations Bakehouse and Patisserie: *Bread*, 42

MORLEY

Crimea Growers Market: *Greengrocers*, 272

Crimea Quality Meats: *Butchers*, 55

Dolce & Salato: *Cakes and Patisserie*, 99

John Walker Chocolatier: *Chocolates and Confectionery*, 129

MOSMAN PARK

Absolutely Chez Uchino: *Food-to-go*, 233

Mosman Park Fresh: *Greengrocers*, 276

Pronto Gourmet Butcher: *Butchers*, 78

Simply Beautiful Biscuits: *Cakes and Patisserie*, 112

MT HAWTHORN

Fig Jam: *Delicatessens and Cheese Shops*, 142

Liquorice Gourmet Foods: *Food Stores and Grocers*, 211

New Norcia Bakeries: *Bread*, 39

New Norcia Café: *Gourmet Cafés and Breakfast*, 257

MT LAWLEY

Absolute Flowers: *Florists*, 179

Antonio's Fresh Continental Store: *Food Stores and Grocers*, 184

Coode Street Café: *Gourmet Cafés and Breakfast*, 251

Fresh Provisions: *Food Stores and Grocers*, 204

Globe Coffee House, see The Globe Coffee House: *Gourmet Cafés and Breakfast*, 263

La Vigna: *Wine Stores and Courses*, 344

Lawley's Bakery and Café: *Bread*, 37

Leaf: *Tea and Coffee*, 336

Liquor Barrons Mt Lawley: *Wine Stores and Courses*, 344

Swish 'n' Chips: *Fishmongers*, 173

The Globe Coffee House: *Gourmet Cafés and Breakfast*, 263

MT PLEASANT

Cakes Delight: *Cakes and Patisserie*, 94

Fruit Basket, see The Fruit Basket: *Greengrocers*, 282

The Fruit Basket: *Greengrocers*, 282

MUNSTER

Mad Butcher, see The Mad Butcher: *Butchers*, 84

The Mad Butcher: *Butchers*, 84

MYAREE

Bread Craft: Melville Central, 213

Chan Brothers Oriental Supermarket: Melville Central, 213

Elmar's Smallgoods: *Butchers*, 59

Gourmet Centro: Melville Central, 213

Limes Fresh Fruit & Veg. Co.: *Greengrocers*, 273

LOCALITY INDEX

Melville Central: *Food Stores and Grocers*, 212

Melville Seafoods: *Fishmongers*, 162

Scarfo's Meating Place: *Butchers*, 81

Yee Seng Oriental SuperMarket: *Asian Food*, 25

NEDLANDS

Angry Almond: *Food Stores and Grocers*, 183

Ararat Kebabs: Broadway Fair Shopping Centre, 191

Barrett's Bread: *Bread*, 33

Broadway Fair Health Foods: Broadway Fair Shopping Centre, 191

Broadway Fair Shopping Centre: *Food Stores and Grocers*, 190

Broadway Fresh: *Greengrocers*, 270

Fleurtatious: *Florists*, 180

Grocer, see The Grocer: *Food Stores and Grocers*, 224

Kong's Oriental Supermart: *Asian Food*, 23

Michael's Gourmet: Broadway Fair Shopping Centre, 191

Miss Minnie's Garden: *Florists*, 181

O2H: *Greengrocers*, 279

Partridges: *Fishmongers*, 165

Poppy's Flowers: *Florists*, 181

Pusey's Puffs: *Cakes and Patisserie*, 108

Satay Shop, see The Satay Shop: *Food-to-go*, 242

Spices: *Food-to-go*, 240

Stephen McHenry Wine Merchants: *Wine Stores and Courses*, 344

The Grocer: *Food Stores and Grocers*, 224

The Satay Shop: *Food-to-go*, 242

Weir's Butchers: *Butchers*, 89

NOLLAMARA

Kakulas Sister: *Food Stores and Grocers*, 210

NORTH BEACH

Soda: *Gourmet Cafés and Breakfast*, 262

NORTH FREMANTLE

Old Bridge Cellars: *Wine Stores and Courses*, 344

NORTH PERTH

Festival Fish: *Fishmongers*, 157

Ginger Pig, see The Ginger Pig: *Delicatessens and Cheese Shops*, 147

M. & M. Princi Butchers: *Butchers*, 74

Milkd: *Gourmet Cafés and Breakfast*, 256

Riki Blakes Café: *Gourmet Cafés and Breakfast*, 259

The Ginger Pig: *Delicatessens and Cheese Shops*, 147

NORTHBRIDGE

Atlantic Seafoods: *Asian Food*, 11

Café Mozart: *Asian Food*, 11

Carl Torre and Sons: *Butchers*, 50

Centurion Seafood: *Asian Food*, 12

Corica: *Cakes and Patisserie*, 98

Dat Thanh Butcher: *Asian Food*, 12

Dragon Seafood Chinese Restaurant: *Asian Food*, 12

Dragon Tea House: *Asian Food*, 13

Emma's Seafood Yong Tofu: *Asian Food*, 13

Good Fortune Roast Duck House: *Asian Food*, 14

Icey Ice: *Asian Food*, 14

Il Gelato: *Ice Cream and Gelati*, 289

Kakulas Brothers: *Food Stores and Grocers*, 208

Kongs Trading: *Asian Food*, 15

Little Home Bakery: *Bread*, 38

Lucky Import and Export: *Asian Food*, 15

Mela Indian Sweets & Eats: *Asian Food*, 16

New Life Bakery: *Asian Food*, 16

Prime Products: *Asian Food*, 17

Re Store, Lake Street, see The Re Store, Lake Street: *Food Stores and Grocers*, 228

Red Teapot, see The Red Teapot: *Asian Food*, 17

Roasting Duck, see The Roasting Duck: *Asian Food*, 18

The Re Store, Lake Street: *Food Stores and Grocers*, 228

The Red Teapot: *Asian Food*, 17

The Roasting Duck: *Asian Food*, 18

Tran's Emporium: *Asian Food*, 18

VHT Perth: *Asian Food*, 19

Walson Foods: *Asian Food*, 19

Wandering Wok Tours: *Asian Food*, 20

Wing Hong Butcher: *Asian Food*, 20

O'CONNOR

Azzura Gelati: *Ice Cream and Gelati*, 285

Coral Seafood: *Fishmongers*, 156

Larner's Oyster Supply: *Fishmongers*, 161

Worldwide Seafoods: *Fishmongers*, 176

OAKFORD

Borrello Cheese: *Delicatessens and Cheese Shops*, 140

OSBORNE PARK

Good Mood Food: *Caterers*, 121

Kitchen Warehouse: *Kitchenware*, 295

Lawley's Bakery and Café: *Bread*, 37

Barleyfield Meats: *Butchers*, 46

PERTH

Boffins Bookshop: *Books for Cooks*, 27

Brush Fork + Pencil: *Caterers*, 118

Cut It Out: *Books for Cooks*, 27

Cut It Out: *Kitchenware*, 293

David Jones Food Hall: *Food Stores and Grocers*, 200

Dymocks: *Books for Cooks*, 27

Il Gelato: *Ice Cream and Gelati*, 289

John Walker Chocolatier: *Chocolates and Confectionery*, 129

Leonidas – les Prlines Belge: *Chocolates and Confectionery*, 130

Magnolias of Central Park: *Florists*, 180

No. 44 King Street Pruveyors of Fine Food, Coffee and Wine: *Gourmet Cafés and Breakfast*, 258

Sweets of London: *Eclectic Shops*, 151

Tea for Me – Gourmet Tea: *Tea and Coffee*, 340

ROCKINGHAM

Five Senses Coffee: *Tea and Coffee*, 333

ROSSMOYNE

Rossmoyne Family Meats: *Butchers*, 80

Temptations Bakehouse and Patisserie: *Bread*, 42

SCARBOROUGH

Brighton Meat Supply: *Butchers*, 49

Brighton Road Food Market: *Food Stores and Grocers*, 189

LOCALITY INDEX

Peko Peko (takeaway only): *Food-to-go*, 239

SHENTON PARK

Vintage Cellars Shenton Park: *Wine Stores and Courses*, 344

SOUTH FREMANTLE

Abhi's Bread: *Bread*, 30

Aubergine Gourmet Foods: *Gourmet Cafés and Breakfast*, 244

Manna Wholefoods and Café: *Organic and Health Food*, 324

Patisserie la Vespa: *Cakes and Patisserie*, 105

Peaches Organic: *Organic and Health Food*, 328

Peaches: *Food Stores and Grocers*, 216

Sealanes: *Fishmongers*, 170

SOUTH PERTH

Claytons Quality Meats: *Butchers*, 52

La Galette de France South Perth: *Cakes and Patisserie*, 104

Millpoint Caffe Bookshop: *Books for Cooks*, 28

Scutti – A Taste of Europe: *Food Stores and Grocers*, 219

South Perth Seafoods: *Fishmongers*, 171

SUBIACO

Angry Almond: *Food Stores and Grocers*, 183

Bloom By Design: *Florists*, 179

Boucla Café: *Gourmet Cafés and Breakfast*, 245

Brew-Ha: *Tea and Coffee*, 331

Chez Jean-Claude Patisserie: *Cakes and Patisserie*, 95

Crossways Shopping Centre: *Food Stores and Grocers*, 198

Epicurious: *Books for Cooks*, 28

Epicurious: *Kitchenware*, 294

Flower Guys, see The Flower Guys: Subiaco Station Street Markets, 315

Fresh Yoghurt Place, see The Fresh Yoghurt Place: Subiaco Station Street Markets, 315

Golden Choice, Growers Lane: Subiaco Station Street Markets, 314

Growers Lane: Subiaco Station Street Markets, 314

Il Gelato: *Ice Cream and Gelati*, 288

Kitchen Witch: *Kitchenware*, 296

Lawless Cooking: *Caterers*, 124

Lawless Cooking: *Cooking Schools*, 134

Meat Safe, see The Meat Safe: *Butchers*, 85

Moe Sushi: *Food-to-go*, 236

New Norcia Bakeries: *Bread*, 40

Nippon Fare: *Food-to-go*, 238

Nippon Food Supplies: *Asian Food*, 24

Pressure Cooker Centre: *Kitchenware*, 301

Rochelle Adonis: *Cakes and Patisserie*, 109

Sas's: *Delicatessens and Cheese Shops*, 145

Simon Johnson: *Food Stores and Grocers*, 220

Subi Fresh: Crossways Shopping Centre, 199

Subiaco Station Street Markets: *Markets*, 314

Tea for Me – Gourmet Tea: *Tea and Coffee*, 339

LOCALITY INDEX

The Flower Guys Subiaco: Subiaco Station Street Markets, 315

The Fresh Yoghurt Place: Subiaco Station Street Markets, 315

The Meat Safe: *Butchers*, 85

TR and TR Grower Direct, Growers Lane: Subiaco Station Street Markets, 314

Traditional Gozleme: Subiaco Station Street Markets, 315

Vegetal: *Florists*, 181

Yen's Fruit and Veg, Growers Lane: Subiaco Station Street Markets, 315

SWAN VIEW
Il Paiolo Wood Fired Oven Catering: *Caterers*, 123

SWANBOURNE
Bookcaffe: *Books for Cooks*, 27

Choux: *Cakes and Patisserie*, 97

Jeremy's Exclusive Butchery: *Butchers*, 67

Miss Minnie's Garden: *Florists*, 181

Swanbourne Cellars: *Wine Stores and Courses*, 344

TUART HILL
Meat Lovers' Paradise: *Butchers*, 70

Ruby's Patisserie: *Cakes and Patisserie*, 111

VICTORIA PARK
Good Store, see The Good Store: *Eclectic Shops*, 152

The Good Store: *Eclectic Shops*, 152

WANGARA
Wanneroo Markets: *Markets*, 317

WELSHPOOL
United Bakery: *Bread*, 43

WEMBLEY
Room for Dessert: *Cakes and Patisserie*, 110

WEST LEEDERVILLE
Chez Jean-Claude Patisserie: *Cakes and Patisserie*, 95

International Beer Shop: *Wine Stores and Courses*, 344

WEST PERTH
Fiori: *Tea and Coffee*, 332

The Urban Pantry: *Caterers*, 126

Upper Crust Cooking Classes: *Cooking Schools*, 136

Urban Pantry see, The Urban Pantry: *Caterers*, 126

Whole Food Cooking: *Cooking Schools*, 138

The Wine Education Centre: *Wine Stores and Courses*, 343

WHITE GUM VALLEY
Pansini Seafoods: *Fishmongers*, 164

WILLETTON,
Burrendah Fresh Gourmet: *Greengrocers*, 271

Hadley's: *Butchers*, 64

YANGEBUP
Marco's Fussy Meats: *Butchers*, 68